Losing Place

REFUGEE AND FORCED MIGRATION STUDIES
General Editors: Barbara Harrell-Bond and Roger Zetter

Volume 1
A Tamil Asylum Diaspora. Sri Lankan Migration, Settlement and Politics in Switzerland
Christopher McDowell

Volume 2
Understanding Impoverishment. The Consequences of Development-Induced Displacement
Edited by Christopher McDowell

Volume 3
Losing Place. Refugee Populations and Rural Transformations in East Africa
Johnathan Bascom

Volume 4
The End of the Refugee Cycle
Edited by Richard Black and Khalid Koser

Volume 5
Refugee Policy in Sudan, 1967-1984
Ahmed Karadawi

Volume 6
Engendering Forced Migration. Theory and Practice
Doreen Indra

Volume 7
Arguing and Justifying. Assessing Conventional Refugee Choices of Moment, Motive, and Host Country
Robert Barsky

LOSING PLACE

Refugee Populations and Rural Transformations in East Africa

Johnathan Bascom

Berghahn Books
NEW YORK • OXFORD

First published in 1998 by

Berghahn Books

Editorial offices:
55 John Street, 3rd Floor, New York, NY 10038 USA
3, NewTec Place, Magdalen Road, Oxford, OX4 1RE, UK

© 1998 Johnathan Bascom

All rights reserved.
No part of this publication may be reproduced
in any form or by any means
without the written permission of Berghahn Books.

Library of Congress Cataloging-in-Publication Data
Bascom, Johnathan.
    Losing place : refugee populations and rural transformations in
East Africa / Johnathan Bascom.
        p.   cm. – (Refugee and forced migration studies : v. 3)
    Includes bibliographical references and index.
    ISBN 1-57181-083-8 (alk. paper)
    1. Refugees–East Africa. 2. Eritreans–Sudan. I. Title. II. Series.
HV640.4.S73B37   1998   97-45095
362.87'09624–dc21   CIP

British Library Cataloguing in Publication Data

A catalogue record for this book is available from the British Library.

Printed in the United States on acid-free paper.

Look and see our reproach!
Our inheritance has been turned over to strangers.
Our houses to aliens.
We have become orphans without a father,
Our mothers are like widows.
We have to pay for our drinking water,
Our wood comes to us at a price,
Our pursuers are at our necks;
We are worn out, there is no rest for us.

The Lamentations of Jeremiah 5:1b-5

Contents

List of Maps, Figures, and Tables	x
Preface	xiii
Abbreviations	xix
Acknowledgments	xx
Credits	xxi

***Chapter 1:* Introduction**   1
   The Theoretical Challenge
     Beyond Categorical Reification
     Beyond Conceptual Provincialism
   The Conceptual Framework
   The Tools of Analysis
   Conclusion

***Chapter 2:* Refugees and Rural Transformation**   15
   Introduction
   The Era of Colonial Intrusion and Investment
   The Era of Political Independence
   The Era of Agrarian Change
   The Era of Internal Conflicts
   Conclusion

***Chapter 3:* Migration and Agrarian Change on Border Lands**   37
   Introduction
   History Matters: The Context for Conflict
   No Time to Say Good-by: Patterns of Flight
   Queuing Up: Strategies for Resettlement
   Working Refugees: The Sudanese Political Economy
   Conclusion

viii | *Contents*

Chapter 4: **Integration and the Cultivation of a Hard Life**   67
  Introduction
  The Locality: "A Sweet Place"
  The Reality: A Hard Life
  Breaking Ground: Tractors and Agricultural Intensification
  Sowing Seeds: The State and Capital Formation
  Pulling Weeds: Refugees and Labor Commodification
  Reaping Harvest: Owners and Capital Accumulation
  Conclusion

Chapter 5: **Resettlement and Positions of Poverty**   91
  Introduction
  Not All Refugees Are Alike
  Commodification of Labor and Land
  The Land Tenure Squeeze
  Hunger Rents
  Cash Crop Mortgages
  Merchant Forces
  Dying Fields and Falling Yields
  Conclusion

Chapter 6: **Exile and the Perils of Pastoralism**   111
  Introduction
  The Herd: "One Hundred Head"
  The Flight West
  Feeling the Squeeze: Appropriation of Pasture Land
  Losing the Game: Commodification of Grazing Rights
  Pressing the Odds: Borders and Bandits
  The Market: "Cattle Are Only as Good as the Pasture"
  Winners and Losers
  The Outcome: "Only the Third One Owns Livestock"
  Termination and Transformation
  Conclusion

Chapter 7: **Asylum and the Making of Home Terrain**   129
  Introduction
  Dislocated Households
  Household Configurations
  Patriarchy Rules
  Gendered Space
  Reorganizing Labor Relations
  Redefining Resource Rights
  Age Matters
  Conclusion

Chapter 8: Repatriation and the Search for Home   145
Introduction
Going Home: The Moment and the Myth
Going Home: The Decision-Makers
Going Home: Perceptions and Conditions
   The Political Participation Factor
   The Economic Development Factor
   The Risk Aversion Factor
Going Home: The Expectations for Return
Conclusion

Chapter 9: Concluding Reflections   163
Part I: Primary Findings
Part II: Implications
   The Impress of Context
   The Myth of "Spontaneous Self-Settlement"
   The Importance of Differentiation
   The Lessons for Peasant Economies
Part III: Applications
   The Basic Poverty of Refugee Policy
   Smart Aid in Environments of Decay
Conclusion: Regaining Place

Bibliography   179

Appendices
Census of Wad el Hileau   194
Glossary   195

Index   198

List of Maps, Figures, and Tables

Maps

2.1	Rural Areas with Major Refugee Concentrations in East Africa, 1960–1995	16
2.2	Rural Transformation During Colonialism in East Africa	19
3.1	Distribution of Official Settlements and Unassisted Refugees in Eastern Sudan	50
3.2	Distribution of Mechanized Rainfed Schemes on the Butana Plains During the 1990s	55
4.1	Border Region Surrounding Wad El Hileau	71
4.2	Field Map of Ethnic Wards and Pattern of Settlement at Wad El Hileau	75
5.1	Field Map of the Market and its Merchants in Wad El Hileau	102
6.1	Traditional Grazing Routes in Eritrea	112
6.2	Pastoral Grazing Routes Between Eritrea, Ethiopia, and Sudan	121

Figures

2.1	The Refugee Population in Africa, 1959–1996	24
3.1	Sorghum Production in Sudan, 1960–1990	59
3.2	Sesame Production in Sudan, 1960–1990	61
4.1	Traditional Sudanese Farming Implements	69
5.1	Agricultural Land Availability for Incoming Refugees to Wad El Hileau	98

6.1	Cattle Losses for Refugee Herds, 1967–1993	116
6.2	Monthly Cattle Prices at Gedaref Market	120
8.1	Interest in Repatriation at UN Camp at Wad El Hileau, 1991	150
9.1	Repatriated African Refugees vs. Newly Exiled African Refugees, 1971–1997	164

Tables

4.1	Employment Distribution of Study Population in Eritrea and Sudan, 1988	75
5.1	Class Structure in Unassisted Eritrean Refugee Community	93
5.2	Ownership of Business in Wad el Hileau by Ethnic Group	104
6.1	Occupational Structure for Pastoralists, Before and After Flight	125
7.1	Distribution of Household Sizes and Extra Family Members	133
8.1	Eritrean Lowlanders and Highlanders in Sudanese Refugee Camps, 1991	152

Preface

May 24, 1993 ... That morning the world woke to the news of a brand new nation. The longest war in modern African history was finally over. What began as an isolated skirmish on the arid lowlands of northern Ethiopia in September of 1961 ended with official independence at midnight. Benign rockets splayed light and sound overhead as throngs of people danced through the streets of Asmara, the new capital. The new country is Eritrea ... *but* most of the exiled population has yet to return home. This book is about the experience of these refugees and many other displaced populations living in rural areas throughout the developing world.

Refugee flight, settlement, and repatriation are not static, self-contained, or singular events. Instead, they are three stages of an ongoing process made and mirrored in the lives of real people. For that reason, there is an evident need for historical and longitudinal studies of refugee populations that rise above description and trace the process of social transformation during the "full circle" of flight, resettlement, and the return home.[1] This book will probe the economic forces and social processes responsible for shaping everyday existence for refugees as they move through exile.

The plight of the Indochinese boat refugees brought into stark focus the relationship of refugee populations to global politics. We have witnessed the same in Iraq, Somalia, Haiti, Rwanda, and Bosnia. But refugees are caught in the web of a tightening global economy as well. The circumstances under which refugees flee are certainly not of their own choosing, but neither are the conditions under which they settle. Even rural refugees on the edge of very large countries, as in the specifics of this study, are increasingly being forced to negotiate their livelihoods from the opportunities and constraints posed by the economy into which they move. Hence there is

Notes for this section begin on page xviii.

a greater need than ever to move beyond the bounds of a "refugee-centric" focus that represents displaced migrants as independent beings with little regard for the economic environments that they are moving out of, settling into, and returning home to.[2]

This book required data and evidence that were sufficiently intensive to understand the unfolding dynamics of process and power in rural communities comprised of both refugees and their hosts. This is the principal reason why concentrating on a representative field site was necessary. The bulk of the analysis was completed within a large concentration of refugees living in a border area outside the protection and assistance of the United Nations. Refugees in camps or official settlements are buffered by material assistance and physical location. Unassisted refugees, however, have no choice but to satisfy the conditions of their own subsistence inside the larger processes operating within a host society.

Extensive archival research was completed at documentation centers in the United States, Eritrea, Ethiopia, Sudan, and the United Kingdom. Primary data were gathered during a ten-month-long study in 1987/88 and subsequent research conducted over three weeks in 1992 and three months in 1993. The "lead" objectives for each visit to the field were as follows: to examine the relationship between agrarian transformation and refugee resettlement (1987/88); to assess refugee responses to the opportunity to repatriate back home (1992); and to explore the "terrain" within refugee households and appraise changes during the intervening five years (1993).

My field techniques included survey research with standard questionnaires, open-ended interviews with groups and individuals, oral histories for select households and ethnic groups, and participant observation among unassisted refugees. There is no need here to detail the strengths and weaknesses of these methods, but I would like to highlight a number of factors that contribute to the overall reliability of the study.[3]

I began field work by collecting ethnographic histories from each of seven sheiks (ethnic heads) who outlined the time and circumstances under which his sub-community arrived in Sudan. Each one identified the number of households under his jurisdiction based on a registry for dispersing subsidized sugar quotas from the government. The resulting village census corroborated with another one administered independently by a non-governmental development agency.[4] To ensure representativeness, the number of respondents chosen for each ethnic group was kept proportional to the size of that group compared to others. In addition, interviews were interspersed throughout each residential ward as we moved from home to home.

The final numbers reflect the ratio between farmers and pastoralists among the refugee population.

All interviews were completed during the dry season months of December to June when farmers and pastoralists were in residence. Most interviews were conducted in Arabic. The assistance of university students helped me explore important events and relationships when they emerged during administration of standardized questionnaires.[5] All three research assistants had refugee parents and grew up at the main field location. Two more factors mitigated against refugees dramatizing answers: most respondents had moved beyond the post-flight "crisis" stage and the possibility of securing assistance from a well-endowed relief agency was not at stake.

Data for this study were gathered from four principal sources:

1. *Official reports.*
   Examples include colonial reports at the London School of Economics, Kew Gardens, and the Rhodes House Library in Oxford; documents from various ministries in the capitals of Khartoum and Addis Ababa, as well as from outlying regional headquarters like Gedaref and Showak; and, project reports of various agencies such as the United Nations, World Bank, and European Economic Community.

2. *Refugee documents.*
   Published and unpublished documents were collected from holdings at many documentation centers. Primary examples include the Refugee Studies Programme in the United Kingdom and the offices of the Commissioner for Refugees and the UN High Commissioner for Refugees in Sudan.

3. *Oral histories.*
   Detailed oral histories were obtained from five representative households to illustrate different vocations, ethnic relationships, and social positions among refugees. Extended dialogues with individual members provided a way to trace their social networks, apprehend their points of most vivid identification, and construct a clearer understanding of their "life-world."

4. *Unprinted material.*
   (a) Landsat imagery to evaluate regional land use and environmental degradation.
   (b) A market study to evaluate the scope of entrepreneurial activity occurring at the field site.

(c) Ten representative profiles of production costs, labor requirements, and profit margins for large-scale, mechanized schemes in the hinterland surrounding the field site.

5. *Interviews.*

(a) Focus interviews with groups of leaders from different ethnic backgrounds.

Extended discussions allowed me to probe important issues, clarify the meaning of local terms, and recount critical events in a small group context. They proved ideal to introduce the research project upon arrival at the primary field site, familiarize myself with changes upon subsequent returns, and test tentative conclusions with refugees themselves before leaving.

(b) Interviews with key actors and informants.

Key actors and informants provided an opportunity to investigate important or sensitive topics. Such interviews involved, for example, meetings with the head of the local rural council, the main sheik (*nazir*) of the village, the head of the small farmer association, and operators of large mechanized schemes.

(c) Interviews with members of the institutional hierarchy.

Interviews with civil servants, development officers, and staff members of relief agencies helped place primary data collected from households into the larger context of regional development, agricultural mechanization, and climatic change.

(d) Interviews with survey questionnaires.

The initial field work was completed using a large, standardized questionnaire to interview the male heads of 131 Eritrean, 45 Ethiopian, and 27 Sudanese households, twenty-three percent and ten percent of the households in the refugee and indigenous community.[6] This roster of households became the sampling frame for more interviews in 1992 and 1993. A second questionnaire, built around the topic of repatriation, was administered to a subset of 35 household heads from the original 131 Eritrean households interviewed in 1987/88. Three more questionnaires were used to appraise changes associated with age and gender: one with 15 different women chosen from the subset of 35 households; another with 20 boys and girls between the ages of ten and fifteen selected from the 35 households; a third with a sample of 10 youth between the ages of eighteen and twenty-five. The data collected from these 283 interviews with survey questionnaires formed the basis on which to complete an in-depth and longitudinal study of social transformation in exile.

There are recursive loops of explanation throughout the text because the conceptual framework for this study focuses on junctures between different levels of analysis. But the progression of the book does involve three distinct shifts in the scale of analysis which lend form and structure to the narrative: the region, the locale, and the household.

Chapter 1 maps out the conceptual framework for approaching the process of refugee migration, building on critical themes and tensions in previous studies. Chapter 2 surveys border settings throughout East Africa where refugee populations have settled during the last three decades. It highlights patterns of military conflict, population movement, environmental degradation, and agrarian change. Chapter 3 focuses on the zone where the borders between Sudan, Eritrea and Ethiopia meet. It charts the making of the three economies from the colonial past to set in context what follows when refugees are "catapulted" between different economic settings.

The next part of the book becomes more focused in time, place and theme. It grounds the analysis of refugees and rural transformation to a specific location. Chapter 4 documents the process of agrarian change, prompted by the arrival of refugees and tractors in eastern Sudan. The distinction between two basic sources of livelihood among rural refugees forms the next chapter division. Chapter 5 assesses the integration of refugees who depend primarily on agricultural cultivation to secure a subsistence. Chapter 6 appraises the position of refugees who depend primarily on livestock pastoralism as a way of life. Both chapters explain the different ways in which refugee households are positioned within the local economy and host society.

Chapter 7 moves farther down in scale. It is a study of socioeconomic interaction within refugee homes to provide a clearer understanding of how rural transformation has changed the life experience of individual members, most especially women and children. My primary aim is to focus on the reorganization of gender and age relations among refugees. Chapter 8 examines refugees' motivation and logic for deciding whether to repatriate. As we explore this question through the eyes of exiled Eritreans, the importance of rural transformation resurfaces once again. It plays a prominent role in determining the prospects for repatriation, the process which refugees reach a decision, as well as the success of reintegration in the homeland. Chapter 9 summarizes the principal findings of the study and assesses their meaning from two vantage points – their implications for future studies of refugees, and their applications for refugee policy.

Before setting off, I want to acknowledge my chief limitation. As Wilson aptly notes: "... before we (researchers) can explain and prescribe, we need to understand. That involves us in working with a group, not on them, and it involves an appreciation of their history, culture, lifestyle, and life strategies. In short, it involves grounding our work in the experience of refugee groups ... ."[7] I have sought to ground this work in the experience of a particular group of refugees, following the "footsteps" of many individuals and households living in eastern Sudan. I am not a refugee and therefore I remain a foreigner to the acute realities of disruption, uncertainty, and hardship that refugees endure. I become more aware of this fact each time I return to Africa. And invariably, a displaced person, who is patiently answering questions, will pause to remind me that I can choose to come and when to go, but refugees can do neither.

Notes

1. V. Robinson, "Into the Next Millennium: An Agenda for Refugee Studies. A Report of the 1st Annual Meeting of the International Advisory Panel, January 1990," *Journal of Refugee Studies* 3 (1990): 13.
2. R. Chambers, "Rural Refugees in Africa: What the Eye Does Not See," *Disasters* 3 (1979); Robinson, "Into the Next Millennium."
3. On method, see A. Sayer, *Method in Social Science: A Realist Approach* (London, 1984); B. Harriss, "Analysing the Rural Economy – A Practical Guide," Discussion Paper No. 164 (School of Development Studies, University of East Anglia, 1984); C. Marshall and G. Rossman, *Designing Qualitative Research* (London, 1984); J. Pretty, RRA Notes – Proceedings of RRA Review Workshop, No. 7 (Sussex, 1989); M. Miles, *Qualitative Data Analysis: A Sourcebook of New Methods* (London, 1994).
4. Save the Children, USA completed an unpublished population estimate of 9,597 for early 1987 that agrees with my own estimate of 9,534 late in the same year. See census on page 194.
5. My primary research assistant completed his undergraduate studies in rural sociology at Gezira University between 1986 and 1993. He is an Eritrean refugee from a pastoral family, with whom my wife and I lived for five months. The other two research assistants were also university students. One, the son of a Sudanese merchant and an Eritrean mother, completed his undergraduate degree in education from the University of Khartoum between 1986 and 1993. The other, a refugee and daughter of a prominent civil judge from Eritrea, completed her degree in family and child development at Affad University in 1993.
6. Ten percent of the field site community is from Ethiopia rather than Eritrea. The Ethiopian community is comprised of Amhara, Tigrean, and Wollgeyiet. They are former land owners and their families who fled during a nationalization campaign in 1975 and 1976; young single men who have deserted the army, evaded conscription, or abandoned a refugee camp elsewhere in Sudan; and young single women who are widowed, divorced, or separated. These people are a far more definite minority than their Eritrean counterparts, symbolized by their Coptic faith and by their homes around the market, both of which isolate them from the community at large.
7. Wilson, cited in Robinson, "Into the Next Millennium", 12.

Abbreviations

ABS	Agricultural Bank of Sudan
CERA	Commission for Eritrean Refugee Affairs
COR	Office of the Commissioner for Refugees (Sudanese)
ELF	Eritrean Liberation Front
EPLF	Eritrean Peoples Liberation Front
ICARA	International Conference on Assistance to African Refugees
IMF	International Monetary Fund
MFC	Mechanized Farming Corporation (Sudanese)
OAU	Organization of African Unity
UNHCR	United Nations High Commission for Refugees

Acknowledgments

My appreciation begins with the community, both refugees and Sudanese, in the village of Wad el Hileau. Four persons in particular played important roles in the success of this project: Mecca opened her home to us, while Hamid Ahmed el Amin, Abdul Hakim Ali el Amin, and Kaltoum Idris Totil offered tireless enthusiasm and research assistance. Scholars at the University of Khartoum were a source of indispensable assistance.

I deeply appreciate the advice, counsel, and friendship of numerous professional colleagues, most notably Mike McNulty, Abdi Samatar, Barbara Harrell-Bond, and Leo Zonn. Several institutions provided financial assistance at different stages of the project. The initial fieldwork was completed with a Fulbright-Hays grant from the International Institute for Education and a dissertation support grant from the National Science Foundation. Smaller grants from the American Philosophical Society and East Carolina University supported a second study. Another National Science Foundation grant funded the necessary follow-up field work to complete this book, and a Research Scholar Fulbright-Hays grant provided support for a summer of archival research in Oxford, England. Pat Guyette, Becky Moye, Tim Bascom, Brian Andrews, and Chad Delp gave indispensable reference, administrative, and graphic help. At East Carolina University, I have been privileged to work with a superb group of colleagues in the geography department.

Our friendships with "the group" in Iowa City, the CPC family in Greenville, and the Longwood neighborhood have been a source of welcome delight amid our treks. Some must bear mention by name for time, prayer, gifts, or laughter: the Minges, Bourdeauxs, D'Amatos, Bechtolds, Kimmels, Prices, Carl Brannan, and four generations of Bascoms. Finally, I wish to acknowledge the four persons with whom I am closest: Betsy Page Bascom, my life companion and fellow traveler during three arduous stints of fieldwork; Ethan and Joanna, fountains of great joy for us; and, the One most deserving of praise – the God who *is* really Here.

Credits

The illustrator for this book is Tim Bascom.

The map of the principal field site is adapted from an original rendering by Tom Killion.

All other maps are the work of cartographer, Brian Andrews.

Permissions to use revised material from four venues are gratefully acknowledged. Portions of the following pieces have been reworked and updated after their first publication in view of additional field work that I conducted in Sudan:

"Food, wages and profits: Mechanized schemes and the Sudanese state." *Economic Geography,* Vol. 66, No. 2, pp. 140–55 (April 1990).

"The peasant economy of refugee resettlement in eastern Sudan." *Annals of the Association of American Geographers,* Vol. 83, No. 2, pp. 320–46 (June 1993).

"Border pastoralism in eastern Sudan." *The Geographical Review,* Vol. 80, No. 4, pp. 401–15 (October 1990).

"The dynamics of refugee repatriation: The case of Eritreans in eastern Sudan." In *Population Migration and the World Order,* Gould, B. and Findlay, A. (eds), pp. 225–48, Sussex: John Wiley & Sons (June 1994).

1

Introduction

> As you open this book, consider one enormous fact: something like 1 in every 135 of us on Planet Earth is a displaced person – at least 41 million of us; 17 million refugees outside their own countries, something like another 24 million internally uprooted.
>
> Erskine Childers
> *Refugees: Rationing the Right of Life*

> Although the number of empirical studies on the integration of refugees is increasing rapidly, there is a dearth of theoretical reflection – at least as far as the specific problems of coping with refugee flows in the Third World are concerned.
>
> Tom Kuhlman
> *The Economic Integration of Refugees in Developing Countries*

Africa enjoys an unenviable reputation as the home of poverty, starvation, and displaced populations. Contemporary news stories center on crisis events, so almost inevitably the dominant characterization of the continent's woes telescopes into the grave image of a single, distraught refugee languishing in an isolated region.

A visual image conveys an essence to its viewers, but pictures, shorn as they are of context, are hollow. The same can be true of a written depiction. Attempts to explain problems and processes associated with refugees often dissipate into description, and descriptive studies fall short of providing a coherent and purposeful analysis of the interplay between the forces of change, choice, and context in refugee life experiences – analysis that would help in deriving practical ways to provide relief and assistance.

Conceptual differences are not merely academic. They generate contrasting analyses of the problems that lead to policies and pro-

Notes for this section begin on page 11.

grams that affect people's lives. I have chosen a perspective that relies on recent theoretical developments in social theory, economic geography, and peasant studies. The prime characteristics of my framework are a central concern with the transformation of rural economies grounded in an historical approach. Its chief characteristics include the role of the state, different responses by household units to changes within the relations of production and of exchange, and sensitivity to narrative accounts of events, decisions, and choices by the participants.

In practice, there have been few attempts to identify refugees' structural position within host societies or relate their integration to larger socioeconomic processes at work in agrarian settings.[1] But using a perspective that is more fully cognizant of the transformation of peasant and pastoral economies can strengthen refugee analysis. It provides a basis from which to explain the logic of survival strategies adopted by refugees; explicate the material roots of social tension between refugees and the host community; understand land management practices and labor allocation strategies adopted by refugees; make a more discriminating and considered evaluation of refugees' net impact – contributions and burdens – upon a regional economy; determine more effective policies for resettlement by apprehending mechanisms of impoverishment that impinge on refugees; and predict differential responses by refugees to repatriation opportunities.

This type of approach is particularly appropriate in view of new contextual variables that amplify the complexity of refugee movements in a tightening global economy. Refugee movements are more and more conditioned by identifiable social forces housed at different scales of analysis – global, regional, local, household, and individual. Hence, the basic objective of this study is to place the complexities of everyday life for rural refugees into a larger context, both in time and in social "space." Our basic method will be to explicate the changing dynamics of structure, process, and power that weave rural transformation together with refugee flight, settlement, integration, and repatriation. This emphasis differs from other studies that focus on patterns, typologies, and measurement. The brief review in the next few pages clarifies the components of my conceptual "lens" and specifies basic tools for analysis.

The Theoretical Challenge

A spate of research is rapidly replacing a previous paucity of academic interest in refugees. Anthropologists are challenging the stereotype of refugees as passive and dependent individuals, examining the role of ethnicity in cultural assimilation, and underscoring the "anti-participatory ideologies," which dominate the relationship of many relief agencies to refugees.[2] Psychologists draw our attention to the adaptive process by refugees as a function of individual perception of, and response to, diminished control over their environment.[3] Political scientists are focusing on international refugee institutions, immigration policy surrounding asylum, and the administration of assistance to refugees.[4] Geographers are shifting their concern from spatial patterns of flight and resettlement to a variety of new approaches.[5] Sociologists are exploring acculturation and adaptation in a new society and changing social networks during migration and resettlement.[6]

These studies enhance our understanding of the ways refugee populations move, resettle, and repatriate within a wide array of physical, social, and regional environments. But a fundamental question remains: Are forays from the vantage point of various disciplines sufficient, or, is there a need for additional theory formulation? An ongoing debate continues over the need to pioneer new refugee theory or borrow and utilize theory from the bailiwick of different social sciences.[7]

At least as yet, the distinctiveness of refugees has not been established in a theoretical sense. Perhaps in time it may be proven otherwise, but refugees remain a field of study based on a category of people, for which the defining conditions are more difficult than ever to differentiate. Hence, the present researcher is more optimistic about building a conceptual frame of reference from ideas and findings from the social sciences at large than by pursuing an endogenous theory.[8] The next section begins to clarify the conceptual basis for the present study by citing some deep tensions tugging in opposite directions within the field of refugee studies.

Beyond Categorical Reification

One "tug-of-war" within refugee studies involves definitional distinctions. There is an acute need for more refined bases by which to determine refugee status because it entitles them with valuable forms of legal protection and material assistance.[9] Hence, a growing debate exists over the criteria for determining who is a refugee; what combinations of conditions and motivations are sufficient and necessary grounds on which to make that determination?

The search for more precise criteria is not an academic exercise for it has, quite literally, bearing on matters of life and death.[10] There is, however, a major danger associated with an intense focus on the determinants of refugee status. That danger is the reification of "the refugee" in our analysis. For example, a thorough review of the current geographical literature on refugees reveals that involuntary migration usually is given exceptional status; that is, refugee migration is treated as a separate category from other forms of migration.[11] Although the term "refugee" is critical for purposes of legal distinction and entitlements, researchers are recognizing that the designation itself offers no sustainable analytical coherence.[12] Those who do not realize this fact run the risk of "placing themselves in a conceptual cul de sac, trapped and emasculated by the categorization."[13]

Reversing the logic of this argument is quite plain: for the purposes of analyses, researchers should not box refugees into one category as distinct from other kinds of migrants. Richmond offers a useful alternative. He argues that refugee movements ought to be viewed on a continuum stretching from proactive migrants who seek to maximize net advantage to reactive migrants who face severe constraints in their freedom of choice: "At one end of the continuum is the decision to move after deliberate consideration of all relevant information, rationally calculated to maximize net advantage, including both material and symbolic rewards. At the other extreme, the decision to move is made in a state of panic with few alternatives but to escape from intolerable threats. Between these two extremes, many of the decisions made by both 'economic' and 'political' migrants are a response to diffuse anxiety generated by a failure of the social system to provide for the fundamental needs of the individual, biological, economic, and social."[14]

Richmond's continuum eliminates the problem of exceptional status, thereby opening up the refugee analyses to the insights of a larger literature and theoretical framework. Doing so has encouraged researchers, for example, to examine critically the parallels between the experiences of political refugees and those of other populations who flee natural disasters or development projects.[15] This study brings to bear insights from the wider literature on the dynamics of economic, social, and agrarian change in African peasant societies.

Beyond Conceptual Provincialism

Another tug-of-war involves the appropriate scale for analysis. Clearly, the primary participant, the refugee, should represent a "first circle" of research interest. Whereas refugees were once analyzed using abstract models (likened in Kunz' classic piece to "billiard balls" whose paths were determined by "kinetic forces"), the contemporary literature witnesses a "human face" of involuntary migration.[16] This shift from the search for a "classic" abstract model of refugee flight to a renewed sensitivity to the experience of displaced human beings is a welcome one, but it can pose a problem that is parochial in nature. Robert Chambers has warned of the dangers of a "refugee-centric" approach; one that neglects the wider circles in which refugee experience and behavior occurs.[17] In doing so, he calls researchers into a "second circle" of investigation, one that is sensitive to the relationship between refugees and their hosts and specifically appraises the dynamics that exist between them.

Social theorists call refugee researchers to enter a "third circle" of investigation. Social systems and structures involve a much broader arena of analysis, but they can play a prominent role in shaping refugees' lives. The growing discourse on the nature and meaning of "environmental refugees" is a good illustration. Implicit in that debate are social structures because climatic changes, droughts, degradation, and famines are no longer understood as independent of sociopolitical and economic forces. Many migration studies focus on the micro level (e.g., the psychology of individual decision making)[18] or, alternatively, examine the operation of causal structures (e.g., the manner by which capitalism may create, stymie, or shape flows of labor migrants).[19] So too, refugee studies are apt to split the analysis and, more likely than not, ignore many key structural forces that displace people, shape their flows, or determine the conditions under which they resettle.[20]

The Conceptual Framework

This study attempts to transcend the dualisms of refugee versus non-refugee, of micro level versus macro level, and of structure versus agency. The analysis engages three circles of causality – the immediate sphere of the refugee, the proximate sphere of the recipient society and economy, and the wider sphere posed by systems and structures. To bridge the gap between different levels of explanation, a conceptual framework is needed that is sufficiently reflexive to relate decisions, actions, and normative behaviors made by individuals, households, ethnic groups, or communities to the broader social context. Structuration theory is one means by which to explore causal relations that span different scales of analysis.

A structuration approach moves deductively downward from foundation concepts to historical claims and then to specific conjunctures, but it also moves in an inductive mode upward from actions to reasons, then to rules, and finally to structures.[21] By focusing attention on an ongoing interplay of structure and action with "room" for conflict, opposition, and negotiation, structuration dissolves the common separation of micro level analysis from macro level work.[22]

Structuration is concerned with a basic question: How do individuals respond to constraints and pressures imposed by the structures of the society in which they live? Social structures constrain but they also enable because they open up certain possibilities for action while at the same time restricting or denying others.[23] This is precisely the case for refugees, who formulate survival strategies and secure a livelihood by both negotiating with, and transforming, the set of opportunities and constraints posed by the society and economy into which they move.

Structuration is especially appropriate for refugee studies due to the expanding effect of globalization upon involuntary migrants. Giddens identifies four major subdivisions of the current world system: a global information system; a system of related political institutions (states and international agencies); a world military order; and, a world capitalist economy with related institutions.[24] Refugees are linked to all four. They are associated to the first by an intensifying battle for media coverage, the heightened ability of the media to reach hidden pockets of displaced people, and the growing capacity of displaced populations to relate to other displaced people elsewhere, and then, to emulate their responses. Emigration and labor laws, coercive measures designed to defend national interests, and the widening echelon of relief organizations and administrations connect refugees to many layers of political institutions. And they are linked to the world military order by arms sales and civil conflict. Each theme deserves investigation, but it is the fourth subdivision – the world capitalist economy – that is most central to this study.

We have identified two common dangers associated with conceptual provincialism that lead to less productive analyses. A sensitivity to the reflexive nature of forces acting on refugees, both those that originate outside camps or host communities as well as those that begin within them, is one way to move beyond descriptive generalizations. This study reflects those elements that Zolberg identifies as "the keys to the most stimulating approaches to current migration theories":

> (1) they are generally historical, not in the sense of dealing mostly with the distant past, but rather in paying appropriate attention to the changing specificities of time and space; (2) they are generally structural rather than individualistic, focusing on the social forces that constrain individual action, with special emphasis on the dynamics of capitalism and of the state; (3) they are generally globalist, in that they see national entities as social formations, as interactive units within an encompassing interna-

tional social field, permeable to determination by transnational and international economic and political processes; and (4) they are generally critical, sharing some degree a committment to social science as a process of demystification and rectification, and in particular are concerned with the consequences of international migrations for the countries of origin and destination, as well as the migrants themselves.[25]

These four characteristics constitute the broad theoretical foundation for this book. Structuration provides a more cogent conceptual framework on which to erect the particulars of the study. To begin construction of an in-depth study, we must define in more specific terms some basic tools of analysis required to do the job.

The Tools of Analysis

The fact that all regions are articulated into a global political economy, yet in an uneven manner, has important implications for apprehending the life course of refugees who are forced to move between countries. Refugee movements frequently occur between substantially different social formations. Many refugees leave "production systems" that are relatively cooperative and resettle in economies where a much more competitive system of production conditions their sources of livelihood. For this reason analyzing the social relations of production and of exchange is an appropriate mode of analysis.

Understanding social relations requires careful explication of labor organization, the process of accumulation, and the prevailing dynamics of power at work in a specific locale. When applied to refugee settings this type of analysis relates resettlement, flight, and repatriation to the broader structures of society. Social relations of production and exchange operate at the center of the analysis. On a vertical continuum, they lie at an intermediate point between structures that emanate from above and responses that come from below. On a horizontal plane, they often function as the most significant nexus between households.

Explication of the social relations of production that exist at a specific refugee site can play a critical role in the analysis for a number of reasons: (a) it highlights salient features in the host economy; (b) it clarifies the opportunities and constraints that refugee households and individuals face in securing a livelihood; (c) it examines the appropriation, distribution and utilization of the social product shared between refugees and the host society; and, (d) it differentiates the effect of a refugee influx on different groups. Hence, discussion of the social relations of production plays a lead role in the analysis to follow.

Five other types of conceptual tools used in this study are analyses of economic stratification, mechanisms of immiseration and accumulation, social institutions and normative practices, time-space geographies, and intrahousehold relations. Like the social relations of production and exchange, each provides a meso-level "window" for research into the complex chemistry of refugee migration, resettlement, integration, and repatriation.

Although refugees often are viewed as undifferentiated masses, economic stratification is an normative aspect of refugee settlement.[26] Some refugees become markedly better off during exile while others remain destitute. This study seeks to make sense of social differentiation among refugees. My assumption is that the prevailing social relations of production sort households into meaningful class positions. A clear grasp of the existent stratification is very useful because it provides a basis for understanding how different segments of the population acquire wealth as well as for predicting their fortunes in the future.

What is needed to explain social stratification adequately are analyses that delineate specific mechanisms of immiseration and accumulation. Such mechanisms determine differential access to social, physical, and financial resources among refugees and their hosts and thereby underlie the process of social differentiation. They also rivet together the social relations of production. Generally, the most important mechanisms are those that determine differential access to land, labor, or credit.

Social institutions and normative social practices represent a relatively tangible, enduring, and accessible middle level between structure and agency because they involve critical junctures between choice and constraint. Their decomposition or sedimentation are important signposts of structures at work. Focusing on contrasting institutions among different ethnic groups can provide a significant comparative dimension to the analysis and broaden the texture of a study. Hence, social practices provide researchers with another valuable "keyhole" to explanation.

Another tool of analysis involves the media of time and space. Their use reflects the meeting of agency and structure in a very concrete way.[27] Gender relations, for example, are bound up in contrasting uses of daily activity space among women compared to men. Repetitive use of space and time by workers illustrates the structure of relationships associated with different production systems. In the same fashion, the time-geographies of refugee men, refugee women, refugee children, and refugee workers of many different sorts signify the way in which host societies affect refugees as well as the effects of forced dislocation.

The fifth tool relates to recent debates about the manner in which to conceptualize households. Although the peasant literature is concerned with the relationship of agrarian transformation to household social processes, the refugee literature has paid insufficient attention to changes that occur in the face of rural transformation as well as dislocation itself.[28] This remains the case in spite the fact that forced migration produces crisis conditions which, in turn, loosen and unhinge rules that had governed households before flight. During exile, the process of social "relocation" in a new environment restructures roles and responsibilities as well. Households are arenas that reflect, internalize, and shape conflict and change. Hence, we will pay particular attention to relationships within refugee households and how the larger process of rural transformation affects relations between its members.

The preceding discussion is not to imply that the process of refugee settlement should be read directly from a theoretical framework. Clearly, important and unique contingencies exist in every refugee setting. But the present author is convinced that many critical dynamics of the refugee experience can be grasped by enlarging the sphere of analysis and applying concepts from other research fields. (The addition of longitudinal field data is also important.) The theoretical stance and conceptual tools outlined here will help to explicate the refugee experience as an ongoing process that is lodged within, and shaped by, larger ones operative in agrarian societies.

Conclusion

Theories of refugee resettlement are broadly categorized by their central assumptions as well as by their mode and level of analysis. The classical approach to resettlement operates with a "functionalist orientation" that focuses on cultural assimilation, psychological adaptation, and economic integration as means whereby refugees come to occupy "niches" within a plural society.[29] It contrasts with the "conflict orientation" of this study. This is not an idle distinction. Even in more remote regions of Africa, refugees are moving into social formations that are structured by economies of accumulation that make the locations into which they flee places of contention and conflict. Refugee integration is, indeed, as Harrell-Bond stresses, more apt to involve a situation of unequal access to resources – and one group being exploited by another – than one in which host and refugee communities are able to coexist, sharing the same economic resources.[30] The process of integration between refugees and their hosts is far more of an active scramble than a scenario of either slow cohesion or mutual co-existence. Some refugees struggle to find survival strategies, others maintain a precarious subsistence, and still others build their position by appropriating the labor, capital, and products of those around them.

"Scrambles" may be extremely active, but they are not devoid of logic or structure. Zolberg, Suhrke, and Aguayo underscore that point well in their book. They suggest that "refugee flows ... are patterned by *identifiable social forces* and hence can be viewed as *structured* events that result from broad *historical processes*" [emphasis added].[31] Refugee resettlement, integration, and repatriation will be viewed in the same manner throughout this book; patterned by identifiable social forces, they are structured processes that result from broad historical processes. Conflict between refugees and their hosts may culminate in relatively isolated incidents of naked force and coercion, but many everyday forms of inequity are linked to the asymmetrical distribution of power and wealth within the host economy. Our focus then must include the changing and contended positions that refugees occupy within the host society and new "phases" in the dynamics of process and power that transpire over time.

In summary, I hope to reformulate the idea of refugee integration as an ongoing process of active structuration – between refugees, the host community, and external actors such as the state, relief agencies, and the global economy – that pivots on changing relationships of conflict and inequity. The logic of such relationships played out on the physical and social terrain of East Africa is what I seek to unravel.

Notes

1. R. Black, "Refugees and Displaced Persons: Geographical Perspectives and Research Directions," *Progress in Human Geography* 15 (1991): 281–98; R. Mazur, "The Political Economy of Refugee Creation in Southern Africa: Micro and Macro Issues in Sociological Perspective," *Journal of Refugee Studies* 1 (1989): 441–67.
2. A. Hansen, "Self-settled Rural Refugees in Africa: The Case of Angolans in Zambian Villages," in *Involuntary Migration and Resettlement: The Problems and Responses of Dislocated People*, ed. A. Hansen and A. Oliver-Smith (Boulder, Colo., 1982), 13–36; B. Harrell-Bond, *Imposing Aid: Emergency Assistance to Refugees* (Oxford, 1986); S. Waldron, "Blaming the Refugees," *Refugee Issues* 3 (1987): 1–19; R. Mazur, "The Political Economy of Refugee Creation"; A. Hansen, "African Refugees: Defining and Defending Their Human Rights," in *Human Rights and Governance in Africa*, ed. R. Cohen, G. Hyden, and W. Nagen (Gainesville, Fla., 1993), 226–66.
3. S. Keller, *Uprooting and Social Change: The Role of Refugees in Development* (New Delhi, 1975); G. Duda and H. Schönmier, *Psychological Aspects of the Refugee Situation in the Sudan* (Saarbrucken, 1983); M. Roe, "Central American Refugees in the United States: Psychosocial Adaptation," *Refugee Issues* 3 (1987): 21–30.
4. B. Stein, "Policy Challenges Regarding Repatriation in the 1990s: Is 1992 the Year for Voluntary Repatriation?" Paper commissioned by the Program on International and U.S. Refugee Policy, The Fletcher School of Law and Diplomacy, Tufts University (1992); L. Gordenker, "Refugees in Developing Countries and Transnational Organization," *The Annals of the American Academy of Political and Social Science* 467 (1992): 62–77; R. Gorman, "Private Voluntary Organizations in Refugee Relief," in *Refugees in World Politics*, ed. E. Ferris (New York, 1985), 82–103; G. Loescher and L. Monahan, ed. *Refugees and International Relations* (Oxford, 1989).
5. For examples of a political perspective see N. Kliot, "Borderlands As 'Refugeeland' – Political Geographical Considerations," presentation at the Association of American Geographers (Toronto, 19–22 April 1990) and C. Wood, "Equilibrium and Historical-Structural Perspectives on Migration," *International Migration Review* 16 (1989): 298–319. For examples of a cultural perspective see D. Greenway, "Prospects for the Resettlement of Afghan Refugees in Pakistan: A Cultural-Geographical Assessment," in *Refugees: A Third World Dilemma*, ed. J. Rogge (Totowa, N.J., 1987), 193–99; L. Luciuk, "A Landscape of Despair: Comments on the Geography of the Contemporary Afghan Refugee Experience," presentation at the Association of American Geographers (Toronto, 19–22 April 1990). For examples of a quantitative or spatial approach see K. Conner, "Factors in the Residential Choices of Self-Settled Refugees in Peshawar, Pakistan," *International Migration Review* 23 (1989): 904–32.
6. E. Marx, "The Social World of Refugees: A Conceptual Framework," *Journal of Refugee Studies* 3 (1990): 189–203; J. Berry, "Acculturation and Psychological Adaptation: A Conceptual Overview," in *Ethnic Psychology: Research and Practice with Immigrants, Refugees, Native Peoples, Ethnic Groups and Sojourners* (Amsterdam, 1988), 41–52.
7. V. Robinson, "Into the Next Millennium," 12.
8. For further defense of this assertion see C. Bun, "Refugee Camps as Human Artifacts," a Review of *Vietnamese Refugees in Southeast Asian Camps*, by Hitchcock, L., *Journal of Refugee Studies* 4 (1991): 284.
9. See A. Zolberg, A. Suhrke, and S. Aguayo, *Escape from Violence: Conflict and the Refugee Crisis in the Developing World* (Oxford, 1991); J. Hathaway, "Reconceiving

Refugee Law as Human Rights Protection," *Journal of Refugee Studies* 4 (1991): 113–31.
10. Ibid., 3.
11. Black, "Refugees and Displaced Persons."
12. J. O'Brien, "Understanding the Crisis in Sudan," *Canadian Journal of African Studies* 20 (1987): 275–79; Black, "Refugees and Displaced Persons."
13. R. Bach, cited in Robinson, "Into the Next Millennium," 12.
14. A. Richmond, "Sociological Theories of International Migration: The Case of Refugees," *Current Sociology* 36 (1988): 17.
15. Black, "Refugees and Displaced Persons"; see also C. McDowell, *Understanding Impoverishment: The Consequences of Development-Induced Displacement* (Providence, R.I., 1996).
16. E. Kunz, "The Refugee in Flight: Kinetic Models and Forms of Displacement," *International Migration Review* 7 (1973): 125–46.
17. R. Chambers, "Hidden Losers? The Impact of Rural Refugee Programs on Poorer Hosts," *International Migration Review* 20 (1986): 245–63.
18. M. Todaro, *Internal Migration in Developing Countries: A Review of Theory, Evidence, Methodology and Research Priorities* (Geneva, 1976); A. Richmond, "Reactive Migration: Sociological Perspectives on Refugee Movements," *Journal of Refugee Studies* 6 (1993): 10.
19. M. Castell, "Immigrant Workers and Class Struggles in Advanced Capitalism: The Western European Experience," *Politics and Society* 5 (1975): 33–66; C. Wood, "Equilibrium and Historical Perspectives on Migration," *International Migration Review* 16 (1984): 298–319; G. Standing, "Migration and Modes of Exploitation: Social Origins of Immobility and Mobility," *The Journal of Peasant Studies* 8 (1981): 173–211; R. Bach and L. Schraml, "Migration, Crisis and Theoretical Conflict," *International Migration Review* 16 (1984): 320–41; A. Richmond, "Reactive Migration," 10.
20. Richmond, "Reactive Migration," 10.
21. P. Sarre, D. Phillips, and R. Skellington, *Ethnic Minority Housing: Explanations and Policies*, (Aldershot, U.K., 1989), 50–1; D. Wilson and D. Huff, *Marginalized Places and Populations: A Structurationist Agenda* (Westpoint, Conn., 1994).
22. Given this limitation, I follow Sarre, Phillips, and Skellington, *Ethnic Minority Housing* in taking actors' statements primarily as indications of their practice, and only secondarily to provide some indications of the structures of meaning or signification at work. (For a more complete amplification of modalities see chapter 4 in P. Cloke, C. Philo, and D. Sadler, *Approaching Human Geography: An Introduction to Contemporary Theoretical Debates* (London, 1993).
23. A. Giddens, *The Constitution of Society* (Cambridge, 1985).
24. Giddens cited in Richmond, "International Migration," 17–18.
25. Zolberg, Suhrke, and Aguayo, *Escape from Violence*, 403.
26. T. Kuhlman, "The Economic Integration of Refugees in Developing Countries: A Research Model," *Journal of Refugee Studies* 4 (1991): 1–20.
27. See A. Pred, "Social Reproduction and the Time-Geography of Everyday Life," in *A Search for Common Ground*, ed. P. Gould and G. Olsonn (London, 1982), 157–86. It may be important to comment further on Giddens' theorization of space for geographers. Giddens downplays location in preference for interaction and he downplays place in preference for locale as a dominant arena of interaction that he calls "power containers". See Cloke, Philo, and Sadler, *Approaching Human Geography*, 126, for an expanded discussion.
28. Two notable exceptions are A. Spring, "Women and Men as Refugees: Differential Assimilation of Angolan Refugees in Zambia," in *Involuntary Migration and Resettlement*, ed. A. Hansen and T. Oliver-Smith (Boulder, 1982) 37–47, and S. el Shazali, Eritreans in Kassala (Draft of Final Report), Joint Research Project of the

Development Studies and Research Centre, University of Khartoum and Free University of Amsterdam (Khartoum, 1987).
29. See as an example, A. Hansen, *Refugee Self-sufficiency Versus Settlement of Angolan Refugees (1966-1989) in Zambia*, United Nations Research Institute for Social Development Discussion Paper No. 17 (Geneva, 1990).
30. Harrell-Bond, *Imposing Aid,* 7.
31. Zolberg, Suhrke, and Aguayo, *Escape from Violence.*

In East Africa, grinding grain by hand has largely been replaced by electric-powered grinding mills during the last twenty-five years, thereby reflecting the effect of rural transformation.

2

Refugees and Rural Transformation

> ... it is essential that future studies of population movement ... are clearly related to the social context in which they are set.
>
> C. Pooley and I. Whyte
> *Migrants, Emigrants and Immigrants*

> One's analysis must proceed historically, in order to comprehend the essence and the growth of contemporary rural underdevelopment in Africa.
>
> A. I. Samatar
> *The State and Rural Transformation in Northern Somalia*

Introduction

To where are refugees forced to flee in East Africa? The vast majority resettle in areas adjacent to their homeland along borders of neighboring countries (see Map 2.1). The geography of these mass movements is important in many different respects, but especially so for the participants themselves. They must establish a new livelihood in the country to which they move. Successes and failures hinge on the social and economic formations that exist in the host country, which may be substantially different from their homeland. Many refugees, for example, have left kin-driven "production systems" or "lifeways" and then resettled in an economy where their sources of livelihood are conditioned by a global system of production that is far more competitive and capitalistic.[1] The spatial pattern of development remains highly uneven throughout East Africa where the commodification of the peasant economy may vary widely within a given country as well as on either side of a border between nations.

Notes for this section begin on page 34.

Map 2.1 Rural Areas with Major Refugee Concentrations in East Africa, 1960–1999

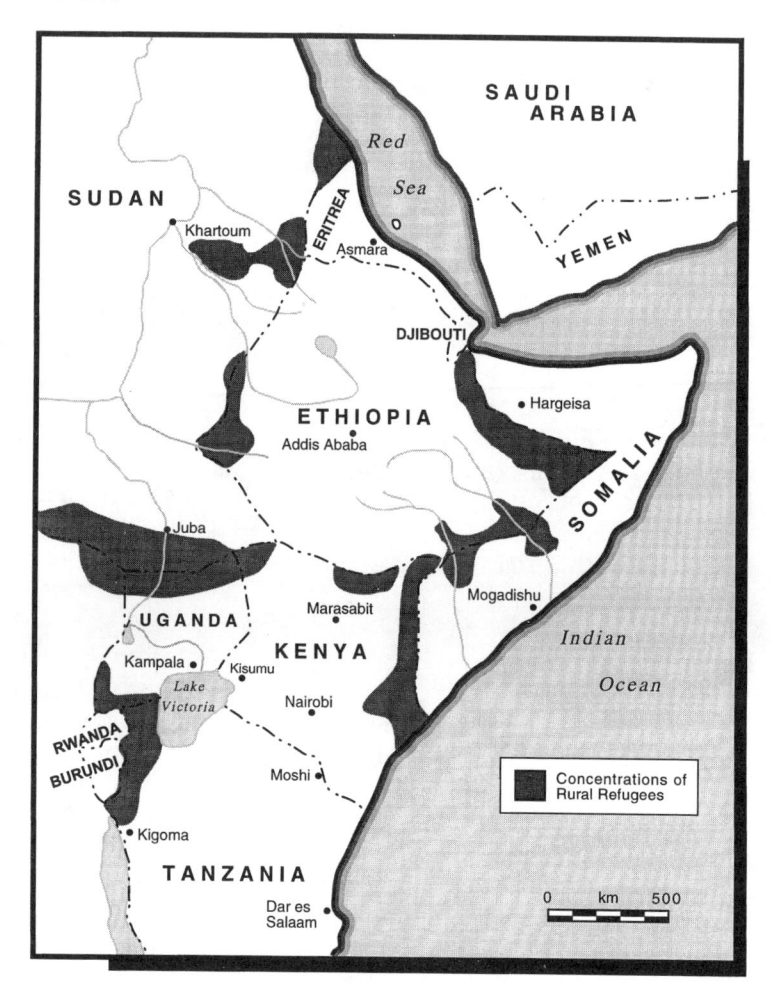

Source: Adapted from the refugee literature on East Africa

The economic landscape that refugees encounter includes peaks of development and valleys of underdevelopment. For these reasons the everyday existence of refugees in East Africa can be understood best by conceptualizing the prevailing character of the social and economic landscape across which they are forced to move.

This chapter surveys the historical process of rural transformation in East Africa with an emphasis on its spatial distribution vis-á-vis the predominant zones of refugee concentration. Establishing a sense of the "bigger" picture may lie beyond the immediate "refugee horizon," but it is fundamental. Analyses fall short if they overlook the larger process of rural transformation and its impact upon refugee migration and resettlement. Hence, the goal of this chapter is to build an historical map of the changing rural landscape, paying special attention to the regions that host large refugee influxes. Because colonialism established the main contours of the contemporary political economy, that era is the logical point in time at which to begin.

The Era of Colonial Intrusion and Investment

The exploration of East Africa by Europeans (Burton and Speke, 1857 to 1859; Speke and Grant, 1862 and 1863; Baker, 1863 and 1864; Stanley, 1874 to 1877; and Von Wissmann, 1880 to 1883) quickly gave way to vigorous competition for colonial spheres of influence. By 1891, the "scramble" for East African territory was virtually over.[2] Ethiopian troops dealt the Italians a resounding defeat at Adowa, but elsewhere European powers prevailed. Protectorates were established in Somaliland (France), Eritrea and southern Somaliland (Italy), Burundi and Rwanda (Germany and Belgium), Tanzania (Germany and Great Britain), and Kenya, Uganda, Sudan and northern Somaliland (Great Britain).

Taxation systems became one of the basic "pillars" of colonial policy in East Africa.[3] In the riverine areas of northern Sudan, for example, British administrators levied direct taxes on land, houses, boats, animals, and date trees. In more outlying areas, they imposed different forms of collective taxes. Taxation measures were heaviest in the Kenyan highlands. The native hut and poll tax was "considerably developed into a more modern form of tax payable only in cash, and it expanded from adult males to include women as well."[4] Elsewhere in East Africa, taxes were comparatively light, but their very introduction played an important role in the transformation of rural, subsistence economies. The basic need to pay taxes represented a new demand for cash that could not be satisfied by the production of subsistence crops or by the exchange of barter goods.

The 1920s saw something of a revival of trade and consequent restoration of revenue and financial stability in East Africa, but the global depression followed in the 1930s. All territories imposed a poll tax on non-natives and renewed their efforts to increase the yield of the direct native tax.[5] Taxes added revenues, but colonial administrators' main goal was to transform the economic orientation of societies so that they would yield and deliver "surplus."[6] The cash requirements to pay taxes forced Africans to cultivate cash crops for sale and encouraged them to enter the money economy further by using extra cash income to purchase imported goods. Products such as groundnuts, gum arabic, livestock, sesame, and sisal are furnished largely by so-called "traditional" producers to this day.

Highly remunerative crops like coffee, tea, cotton, and tobacco were reserved for European settlers and business concessions. The highlands of Kenya represented the dominant locus of European direct investment and settlement. There East Africa experienced the deepest intrusion of colonial imperialism and consequent transformation of society and the economy. More than 16,000 square miles of prime agricultural land were expropriated from Kikuyu, then leased on a long-term basis to Europeans to raise coffee and tea. Under the aegis of the Uganda Company, cotton and coffee gained prominence in the southeastern region of Uganda. Another British company, the Sudan Plantation Syndicate, supervised the expansion of the Gezira cotton scheme – the world's largest "plantation." In Somalia, the colonial administration issued agricultural concessions to Italian citizens or to others of foreign nationality. Large tracts of land along the Shabelle River were appropriated and reallocated for large banana and sugar plantations. These four economic foci played the dominant role in the political economy of East Africa by generating the bulk of the region's export earnings and prompting the formation of a growing agricultural labor force.

The major islands of development in East Africa required large labor forces (see Map 2.2). The imposition of taxes helped to generate the necessary labor power to make these investments profitable. Sir Percy Girouard, Governor of the Protectorate of Kenya, expressed this clearly in the region's principal newspaper, *The East African Standard.* In 1913: "We consider that the only natural and automatic method of securing a constant labour supply is to ensure that there shall be competition among labourers for hire and not among employers for labourers; such competition can be brought about only by a rise in the cost of living for the native, and this rise can be produced only by an increase in the tax."[7]

Map 2.2 Rural Transformation During Colonialism in East Africa

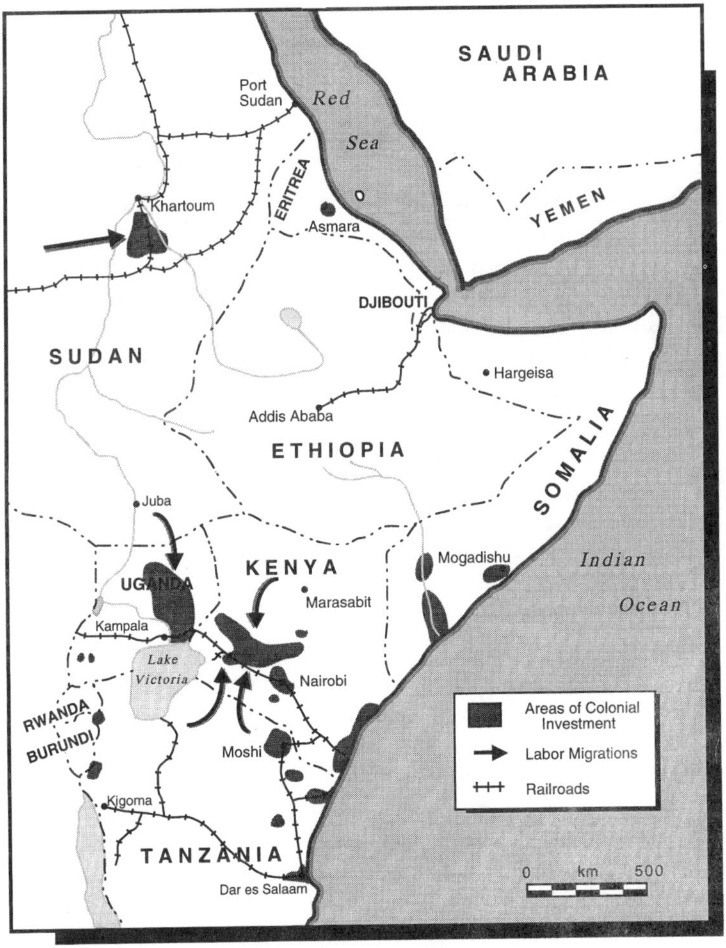

Source: Adapted from W. Hance, *The Geography of Modern Africa*, New York, 1964 and R. Prothero, *Migrants and Malaria*, London, 1965

Other measures, which limited the earnings of African farmers, helped ensure a stable supply of African labor. In Kenya, for example, the Coffee Plantations Ordinance (1918) prevented Africans from growing coffee. Quarantines imposed by the Veterinary Department prohibited African herders from taking their cows to market. Dual pricing systems were applied to many crops whereby Europeans received higher market prices than Africans. This twin system of tax "incentives" and production "disincentives" was very effective; by the late 1950s European-owned farms provided 42 percent of total employment in Kenya and generated 95 percent of Kenya's agricultural exports.[8] Smallholder production remained the norm throughout most of East Africa. However, the Kenyan farms, the two cotton schemes, and fruit plantations on the lower Shabelle River drew labor migrants from many distant regions.

Long-standing patterns of cross-border labor migration have come repeatedly into play during refugee crises. One such example involves the movement of people from southern Sudan to the cotton region of Uganda. Constant migration along that route helped to institutionalize political and social obligations into a network of dependable relatives and kin, especially among Madi and Kakwa, two ethnic groups that live on either side of the border. During Sudan's first civil war (1955 to 1972), many southern Sudanese relied on those established relationships to secure food, shelter, and agricultural land. Hospitality occurred in a reverse fashion starting less than a decade later. When Idi Amin's reign ended in 1979, tens of thousands of northern Ugandans fled to Sudan. Having been well received in their own time of trial earlier, many Sudanese felt a sense of obligation and debt to Ugandans when they came to Sudan in search of refuge.[9] Multivariate analysis of data gathered from Ugandans indicates that those who were Madi fared better than those from other ethnic groups.[10] Several factors underlie this relationship. Upon arrival, Madi procured free food and accommodation among Madi-speaking relatives. They enjoyed greater access to natural resources such as water, wood, and pasture. They also were allowed to participate in local events, attend schools, and become active traders. Similarly, other rural Africans have followed "well-worn paths" from previous labor migration to obtain local assistance during refugee crises. (Such dynamics, for example, characterized the resettlement of Angolan refugees in northwestern Zambia and Rwandan refugees in western Tanzania.)

Recent research, however, suggests that instances of such hospitality is fast becoming the exceptional case.[11] To better understand why ethnic affinity no longer facilitates refugee integration as much as it once did, we must return to colonialism and another important mechanism of rural transformation. The transformation of "traditional" economies depended on two types of commodification. On the "production" side were mechanisms like taxation, cash crop cultivation, and a wage labor market. They served as powerful tools to slowly undermine the traditional hospitality and reciprocal relations that characterize ethnic kinship. But colonial administrators relied on yet another type of mechanism to redirect the predominant "inward-facing," subsistence-based orientation of most societies in East Africa, namely, the market.

Officials knew the importance of altering relationships of exchange. As one civil servant commented with respect to a large Sudanese ethnic group: "They are developing a taste for clothes and luxuries and this makes them tractable and ready to work for money."[12] The need to buy with cash meant the need to sell for cash. One measure to encourage cash purchases was to arrest the growth of domestic industry. Banning the indigenous production of textiles, for example, ensured a market for imported cloth made in Britain. Another measure was to replace African traders with non-Africans. While a Lebanese merchant community came to flourish in West Africa, Indian traders became dominant in East Africa. Often, their economic niche was assured by official ordinances. In the case of Kenya, for example, the Native Produce Ordinance (1935) confined wholesale trade in Kenya to European and Asian merchants. Meanwhile, steady improvements in the transportation network expedited the spread of cheap manufactured goods into rural markets. "Bushshops" were established in outlying areas beyond the transport network. Imported products began replacing domestic utensils – enamel ware for locally produced wooden and pottery food bowls, glass bottles for calabash vessels, tin and aluminum for gourd cups.[13] In his annual report of 1925, a British official underscored the fact that "half the Sudanese population was within the orbit of foreign trade."[14] Drawing East Africans into "the orbit of foreign trade" was important because that meant that "the trading operation was now carried on within a single political economy rather than between two political economies."[15]

In summary, colonialism greatly facilitated the penetration of capitalism into African society. Commodification of land, labor, and consumer goods unraveled the "logic" of subsistence economies and began to restructure the prevailing social relations associated with cash crops and market exchange. Writing in 1950, de Briey concluded that the colonial era had prompted an "economic revolution" in sub-Saharan Africa: "Over the last 60–70 years tropical

Africa has undergone an economic revolution. Its 140 million inhabitants, who for centuries had been producing nothing more than the necessities for subsistence, have now begun living and producing with an eye to the outside world. In other words a market economy has taken the place of the subsistence economy ..."[16]

Significantly, however, the pace at which African societies were articulated into the global economy varied considerably from place to place. The spread of the market economy throughout Africa was uneven in its spatial dispersion, intensity, and social impact, especially in East Africa. Comparatively speaking, West Africa was typified by the most intense development of peasant cash crops (e.g. groundnuts and cotton in French-held areas and palm oil, cocoa, and rubber in British regions). Central Africa was the preferred site of most concession-owning companies. Intensive mining operations dominated in Southern Africa which generated a far-flung labor reserve area as far north as Tanganyika (Tanzania). In East Africa, however, the impact of colonialism was less clear-cut. The experience of rural transformation was greatest where white settlers resided on the highland plateaus of Kenya and Eritrea, but far more restricted elsewhere. In upland Eritrea, for example, the Italian administration removed the heads of ethnic clans, demarcated a formal set of political districts, and then appointed new, salaried chiefs to govern each district. By contrast, however, the lowlands were designated as "tribal areas" rather than districts. Headmen from each ethnic group were retained and given the principal responsibility of collecting "native tribute."[17] The British, who replaced the Italians in the aftermath of World War II, continued the same practice of giving peripheral attention to the lowlands, but they increased their demands on the plateaus. Highlanders were asked to pay school and hospital fees as well as income, property, and municipal taxes.[18] The long history of differential state control allowed peasant farmers and pastoralists in the lowlands to maintain an inward-facing, largely self-contained economy until they were forced to flee their homeland in the mid-1960s.

The prevailing pattern of roads, railways, and ports built during colonialism represented a tangible reflection of the differential effect of rural transformation in East Africa (see Map 2.2). The disparities in rural transformation became evident in another way; they would play a central role in determining the experience of millions of East Africans displaced by wars of independence or civil conflict.

The Era of Political Independence

The first of January 1956 marked the beginning of the end of formal colonialism in sub-Saharan Africa. Sudan became independent on that day, and other colonies followed soon thereafter; Ghana in March of 1957, Guinea in November of 1958. In 1960, the same "wind of change" brought independence to fourteen more African countries. By 1977, European control prevailed in only three remaining countries of Africa – Zimbabwe, Namibia, and South Africa.

Independence came at a distinctly heavier price in some countries than others; that is, refugee populations were created as freedom movements escalated into open wars. In late 1960, conflict in Zaire prompted the United Nations High Commissioner for Refugees (UNHCR) to begin its first relief operation in sub-Saharan Africa. The number of exiled Africans rose slowly but steadily during the immediate, postcolonial period (see Figure 2.1). The slow growth pattern reflected the comparative ease of voluntary repatriation. Liberation wars were once-and-for-all conflicts without serious prospect of the conflict being renewed, and new governments offered sympathetic treatment to what it considered "its" refugee community.[19]

During the postcolonial era rural transformation, including the partiality of its spatial diffusion, played a central role in determining the kind of reception that refugees were given upon arrival in a host country. More than 90 percent of African's refugees originated in rural regions and fled to rural areas.[20] The flight pattern was typically a short hop, en masse, across the closest territorial boundary away from the conflict source. While some entered refugee camps, the majority settled without the assistance and protection of the United Nations. The bands of settlement areas along international borders in Ethiopia, Sudan, Tanzania, and Uganda illustrate well the predominant zones of "self-settling refugees" in East Africa (see Map 2.1).

In 1976, the United Nations estimated that 80 percent of Africa's refugees were unassisted "self-settlers" and that 20 percent were living in organized settlements. The same study concluded that only 5 percent were in urban centers, leaving 75 percent in rural areas.[21] That three quarters of all African refugees were living in rural areas yet outside camps relates to several factors. The pattern of short flight is one. But two more important ones are the general availability of land for incoming refugees given the limited amount of agrarian mechanization in border regions and the nature of the prevailing social and economic relationships in these more remote areas.

Social formations prior to articulation with capitalism, and subsequent transformation, are variously designated in the peasant litera-

Figure 2.1 The Refugee Population in Africa, 1959–1996

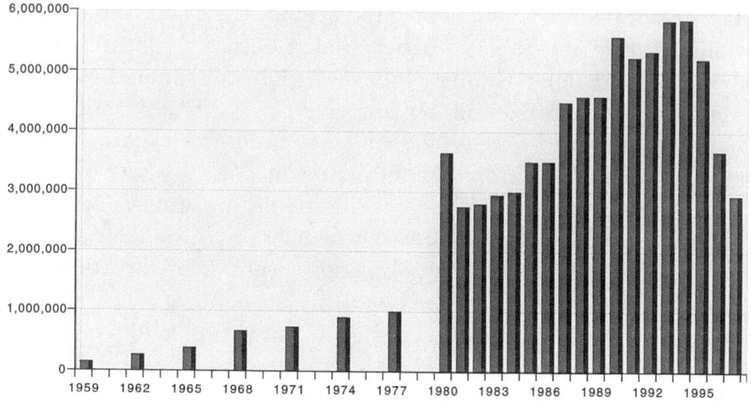

Source: Adapted from UNHCR, *The State of the World's Refugees: The Challenge of Protection*, New York, 1993, with interpolation for 1968–1969, 1971–1973, and 1975, and V. Hamilton (ed), *World Refugee Survey,* Washington, DC, 1993–1997

ture: a moral economy, a domestic economy, a natural economy, a subsistence economy, a non-capitalist economy, or an economy of affection.[22] Agricultural production is not geared to cash sale, exchange, and gain, but toward producers' direct use or to discharge their kinship obligations. Control of land resources is decentralized, local, and familial in extent.[23] Labor relations are governed by an ethic of cooperation, most often as free exchanges of labor in communal work parties to plant, weed, harvest, or construct homes. Hence, communities are interknit by relationships based upon social obligations and reciprocity. These traits differentiate noncapitalist, agrarian societies from capitalist ones driven by an ethic of accumulation, the widespread exchange of monetized commodities, and competitive, class-based social relations of production.

These noncapitalist traits outlined above characterized most border zone societies of East Africa during the 1950s, 1960s, and 1970s; they were largely "peripheral" places where colonial capitalism had least transformed the indigenous economic and social structures. Based largely upon his field experience in East Africa, prominent scholar Goran Hyden (1983) asserted that this social reality was vital for refugee influxes. He argued that the hospitality enjoyed by many self-settled refugees was directly related to the limited degree of economic transformation within host communities. Having defined the same set of culturally defined obligations identified above as the "economy of affection," Hyden argued that "in no other situation has the economy of affection proved itself more important as a mechanism for basic survival than where endless flows of refugees have suddenly overwhelmed a country."[24]

Supporting evidence of "economies of affection" operating on behalf of incoming refugees can be found. Zartman documented Senegalese welcoming refugees from neighboring Guinea-Bissau during the late 1960s. He stressed the fact that Guinea-Bissauans and their Senegalese hosts both "speak the same language, lead a communal life, and sometimes even have shared the same fields which lay across the border. The affinity between the inhabitants and the refugees has proved so strong that, in many cases, the local population has shared everything with the refugees including lodging, tools, seeds, and food stocks."[25] Hansen documented the case of Angolans who fled across the border into northwest Zambia when fighting erupted as early as 1966. Incoming refugees relied on familiar routes and kinship relationships in Zambia to secure food, shelter, and even agricultural land.[26] And Harrell-Bond provides an in-depth illustration of how Ugandan refugees deployed ethnic affinities as a strategic resource upon arrival in southern Sudan during the early 1980s.[27]

Today supportive evidence of "African hospitality" for refugees has become harder to find. One factor is the growth in the sheer size of recent refugee influxes. In the past, lower ratios represented a smaller sociopolitical threat to the indigenous community, less strain on the local infrastructure, and less people with whom to share arable land for agriculture. In the case of northwestern Zambia, for example, a comparatively small population of twenty thousand Angolans sought refugee in a region where population densities were very low to begin with. An estimated 81 percent of the border villages in northwestern Zambia had twenty people or less.[28] A relatively loose configuration of villages left agricultural land available for incoming Angolans. It also served as a built-in mechanism for sorting and spreading incoming refugees; they were self-settled in small pockets that mirrored the loosely-knit spatial pattern of that society. Now, however, population densities are much higher in border zones.

At one time the expression "spontaneous self-settlement" may have typified the ease with which rural refugees moved between non-capitalist economies in the past, relying heavily on social relationships rooted in ethnicity, kinship, labor migration, or an ethic of cooperation.[29] However, researchers are now documenting the diminishing importance of such relationships.[30] Increasingly, unassisted refugees face a debilitating combination of poor access to land, low wages, and costly food. Cultivable land is usually too scarce, too poor in quality, too far away from their home, or some combination of all three. The terms of trade for labor and food generally disadvantage self-settlers as well.

Seeking international assistance is one primary way by which refugees respond to the tightening constraints they face. Not surprisingly, then, the proportion of African refugees who self-settle has dropped dramatically since the mid-1970s. The ratio of unassisted refugees to ones who are assisted by UNHCR has fallen from a 4:1 ratio in 1976 to a 3:2 ratio in 1984, and then, to a 1:1 ratio in 1994.[31]

That this ratio has shifted so dramatically suggests the truth of Lenin's maxim: "Refugees vote with their feet."[32] As recently as twenty years ago, most refugees in East Africa could derive a livelihood from shifting cultivation or pastoralism on sparsely inhabited land at the periphery of host countries. Now, however, they are forced to seek refuge in very different contexts; ones characterized by very competitive social relations of production rather than ones built on reciprocal exchanges of land, labor, and food. Survival strategies are increasingly defined in the social relations of production because the control of land and labor is increasingly passing from refugee control into the hands of the host. As this occurs, class relations are growing in their importance and, in so doing, reducing that of ethnicity and kinship as variables of explanation. Clearly, the transformation of rural economies during the postcolonial period has stretched much further in its geographic reach and much deeper in its social impact. Hence, it is to the aftermath of colonialism and matters of changing tenure relations, labor relationships, and agricultural mechanization that we now turn.

The Era of Agrarian Change

"The end of colonialism was not the end of capitalism."[33] Nor did political independence slow the social and economic transformation underway in rural areas, many of which soon received large refugee influxes. The expression "postcolonial economies" is a convenient way to refer to a specific historical period, but political independence did not mean that national economies no longer retained colonial features.[34] On the contrary, although the locus of political control shifted back to Africans, the shape of the economic systems remained essentially unchanged throughout East Africa. A prime illustration is the continued dependency upon certain export crops (rather than to diversification). In 1987, the share of total export value for the three principal countries in East Africa remained singularly dependent upon the same export crops as thirty years earlier: coffee for Ethiopia (50 percent), coffee and tea for Kenya (46 percent) and cotton and sesame seed for Sudan (48 percent).[35]

Independence did mark a turning point at which agrarian change began accelerating in Africa, both in its spread and its intensity. Racial divisions had seriously hampered the accumulation of wealth by Africans. Now, however, the opportunity opened up rapidly for capital investment, accumulation, and profits. The decades of greatest agricultural growth in twentieth-century Africa (the 1950s and the 1960s) were facilitated by favorable conditions on the world market and government investment in rural areas as undertaken by the new African states.[36] Many governments attempted to generate growth by "modernizing" agricultural production through new crops, seeds, fertilizers, mechanization techniques, management practices, credit schemes, marketing structures, price incentives, and so on.[37] These new input "packages" accelerated agrarian change because they came with several "basic" requirements, namely, the need for more land concentration, more labor, and more capital. The 1960s represented a new and strategic juncture in the ongoing process of transforming social relationships throughout rural areas which in turn would have important implications for the process of refugee resettlement.

The previous section traced the initial phase of a long historical transformation. During colonialism, rural societies began moving away from societies governed by sanction (reciprocity) to ones that were oriented around a system of power (accumulation). During the postcolonial era, agrarian change began to "plow up" societies in new and even deeper ways. This was evidenced by the growth of social differentiation among African peasant farmers living in rural areas. By the 1980s, that process of class differentiation would extend to rural refugee populations in East Africa.

For reasons we shall see, rural transformation was most evident in areas of East Africa where the tractor arrived, bringing with it changes in land tenure and land use as well as prompting considerable land accumulation. The most prominent areas where this scenario occurred are portions of southern Somalia, northwestern Ethiopia, eastern Sudan, southern Uganda, and western Kenya.

Land concentration is considered to be a "fundamental" requirement of agricultural modernization. Neoclassical, populist, or Marxist paradigms all assume that private property rights will prompt the concentration of ownership of productive land.[38] Until the 1930s, colonial administrators had little interest in transforming African communal tenure systems into individual holdings.[39] Many of them actually worked to preserve customary rights to land, allowing chiefs to allocate use rights to land in "their territory." This method, designed to help maintain political control, was clearly in keeping with the philosophy of indirect rule. In so doing, colonial authorities actually played an important role in the creation of African customary tenure. Sara Berry emphasizes such conclusions by eminent anthropologist, Elizabeth Colson. Berry writes,

> The development of customary land laws during the colonial period was the outcome of Europeans projecting their notions of tenure onto African societies. If no individual owner of land could be identified, then ownership was attributed to the political unit residing in the area, whether or not the leaders of these polities actually held such notions or exercised such authority. Colson cogently argues that the official search for the owners of all land encouraged the confusion of sovereignty with proprietary ownership and the creation of systems of communal tenure which came into being with precisely defined rules. These rules now inhibited the development of individual rights in waste land because it was deemed that such rights encroached upon the ancient right of some community, lineage, or 'tribal' polity. The newly created system was described as resting on tradition and presumably derived its legitimacy from immemorial custom. The degree to which it was a reflection of the contemporary situation and the joint creation of colonial officials and African leaders, more especially of those holding political office, was unlikely to be recognized.[40]

Starting in the 1930s, colonial officials began advocating full freehold tenure and registered titles among the indigenous population. This change in philosophy was based on the conviction that "customary tenure" did not provide farmers with the adequate security to prompt them to invest in production, improve their land, or mortgage it to obtain credit.[41] The Buganda and Kikuyu regions were two areas where colonial officials first attempted to encourage the treatment of land as private property. Kitching documents the way in which household heads began to dispose of their land by selling or renting it to tenants outside their own lineage.[42] Colonial administrators referred to this process as the "individualization" of tenure wherein land became a commodity which could be bought or sold. ("Commodification" or "commoditization" is the common term used in the contemporary peasant literature.) Freehold titles were also implemented in some riverine environments for irrigation schemes, but property rights were not ever effectively or completely privatized in most of East Africa.[43] (The disruptive impact of frequent military conflicts is one factor that helps partial privatization remain the norm.)

Today residual rights to land are firmly vested in a village, ethnic group, sheikdom, kin-group, or territory group in very few places of

East Africa. Instead, most land ownership is subject to multiple and interwoven rights. The 1970s was the decade in which many East African states expropriated the rural landscapes. Nationalization of rural lands meant that the "customary tenant" became a "tenant-at-will" of the state, in legal status if not in practice.[44] In Uganda, the Land Reform Decrees of 1975 actually abolished "absolute ownership of the land." (An agreement made in 1900 between the colonial state and Baganda chiefs had established freehold land in that region.) All land was henceforth to be held on a 99-year lease. Land legislation passed in 1975 transferred control of tenure rights of all Somali land from traditional authorities to the Government of Somalia Democratic Republic (GSDR). Land-holders are permitted to register limited amounts of land as state leaseholds or concessions, with usufructory rights for fifty years upon which they may be renewed.[45] Ethiopia experienced a massive land reform program in the late 1970s too. In keeping with agricultural policies adopted by many socialist countries, several hundred thousand acres were appropriated for collective farms.[46]

During the early 1980s, state leasehold tenure based on statutory law became much more widespread in Somalia, particularly in the country's two main river valleys, the Shabelle and the Juba. By 1986, the government had issued 12,561 titles for concessions, covering 256,000 hectares nationwide, roughly 0.5 percent of the total land.[47] In similar fashion, the newly established government of Eritrea has begun allocating large tracts of land in the southwestern region of the country to investors with large capital resources.

It is important to note several very important implications of these efforts to nationalize rural landscapes, including those associated refugee influxes. Land nationalization brought the state into the forefront of agrarian change. Colonial governments were largely administrative bureaucracies that acted on behalf of the motherland and determined policies to that end. With independence, however, the state "emerged" because it could now operate with a new agenda. Soon it represented a condensation of class relations whose interests gave substance and shape to development policies. The new elite in East Africa – civil servants, government officials, and merchants – were able to obtain access to government land because of their knowledge of national laws and their ability to gain influential positions and exert influence on the bureaucracy. In the case of Sudan, for example, the state began leasing land parcels, two kilometers by two kilometers in size, to private Sudanese investors. The shift to leasing land to private investors marked the advent of *mushrooah* or "scheme" farming which has become the hallmark of mechanized agriculture in Sudan's central rainlands. In central Sudan and similar settings in other countries, agricultural change quickly became more contingent upon political influence than the skills of farm managers. As Hoben writes,

> Access to registered land, particularly large tracts of new land believed to have development potential, depends on claimants' ability to mobilize a broad range of political and economic resources, rather than on their ability to generate and reinvest profits from agriculture in additional land. In this sense, land accumulation is thus primarily a political rather than an economic process. The successful individual or agency is one that has contacts in the bureaucracy, knowledge of how to "work the system," clan and personal ties with high government officials, access to government credit and equipment, or is able to obtain support from foreign aid agencies.[48]

The power of civil servants (i.e., the old "native administration") has diminished since the early years of independence. Today the locus of state control rests in the hands of government officials, merchants and military officers. These "modern big men" profit from the ambiguous coexistence of national and local tenure systems.[49] In fact, it is in their interests if tenure relations remain ambiguous. This is the primary reason why tenure relations so frequently remain in a state of transitional flux.

The assertion of state control over land resources also represented an enclosure movement. Writing about northern Uganda (current home to thousands of Sudanese refugees), Mahmood Mamdani notes that the Uganda Land Reform Decrees of 1975 seemed designed to clear the mesh of pre-capitalist, traditional, or communal relations blocking the path of capitalist development in agriculture. Instead, its main effect was to accelerate the tendency to land enclosure, without any transformation in the pattern of land use. The District Land Commission, a body comprising district level state agents and local notables, was empowered to terminate any lease on "underdeveloped" land and grant it to a potential "developer" who was "free to evict any tenant occupying any part of the leasehold granted to him."[50] Thus, argues Mamdani, land reform became a weapon in the hands of bureaucratic capitalists seeking to expand their property and activities in the countryside. Enclosure movements have meant that less range and agricultural land is available to rural refugees, the vast majority of whom are small holders or pastoralists. (Later chapters will offer an in-depth examination of each group.) The impact of state control over land resources was felt in other, less obvious, ways as well.

First, the number of refugees seeking asylum surged in the late 1970s at precisely the same time land control was shifting away from localized purview. The centralization of control allowed host governments to allocate large tracts of land to the United Nations for refugee reception centers, holding camps, agricultural settlements and wage earning settlements. Second, officials soon recognized that well-placed refugee settlements could supply large quantities of agricultural wage labor. Camp refugees, in particular, represented a ready-made cheap, dependent, and abundant source of labor. Hence, it was not happenstance that many refugee settlements are located adjacent to large private or public farming operations (e.g., Sudan's large Qala en Nahal scheme).[51] Official settlements were also a means by which host governments could open up underdeveloped areas. In the case of Tanzania, for example, incoming Burundis became "pioneers and developers of the periphery."[52] More than 12,500 square kilometers of land in the far west of the country was designated for the Ulyankulu, Katumba, and Misamo settlements. Third, the enclosure of large tracts of land set the stage for serious tensions between self-settling refugees and the host communities to which they fled. Often small holders were being displaced at the same time that incoming refugees were requesting more land. Land depletion and delimitation lessened the ability of host communities to provide land for self-settling refugees, created "land squeezes," and accelerated the process of social differentiation among the indigenous population.

The Era of Internal Conflicts

By 1980, observers could no longer hope that political independence would rid Africa of refugees. While the total number had increased from one million in 1975 to more than 3.5 million, only 10 percent of that total were associated with latent colonial activity (i.e., Zimbabwe, Namibia, and the Republic of South Africa).[53] Other causes became key factors in refugee flight: secession (Eritrea, southern Sudan, and northern Somalia), political repression and persecution (Ethiopia and Somalia), and mixes of ideological and ethnic conflict (northern Uganda and Rwanda). Superpower confrontation compounded conflicts further, especially in the case of East Africa. Ethiopia and Uganda were the largest source countries, while Somalia, Sudan, Tanzania, and Kenya played counterpart roles as the principal host nations.

By 1990, the total number of African refugees reached 5.6 million, more than half of whom were exiled in east African nations of Djibouti, Ethiopia, Kenya, Sudan, Somalia, Tanzania, and Uganda

(2.35 million). While growth in the total number of asylum-seekers has abated slightly, there are important new dimensions of the refugee crises.

First, voluntary repatriation is becoming significantly more difficult to begin, and, when it does occur, it is more delayed and incomplete than in the past.[54] Home governments like Eritrea's have been slow to facilitate the return of refugees in order to garner more resources from donors and, in some instances, to get rid of certain segments of the exiled population.[55] Meanwhile, host countries have begun viewing refugees as an important source of economic assistance. As a result, they may not actively encourage refugee populations to return home. Both Sudan and Somalia, for example, have learned to depend on refugees as a means by which to secure food, financial assistance, hard currency, employment opportunities, and used vehicles. As such, refugees have become a source of quiet accumulation for the vested interests of a few, and the financial resources they bring into a country become an important means of political stability and economic relief.

Second, the potential for volatile conflicts between local communities and incoming refugee populations is growing, given the general deterioration of economic conditions. In 1992, GNP per capita in East Africa ranged between 110 U.S. dollars (Ethiopia) and 310 U.S. dollars (Kenya). Export earnings have declined precipitously and governments face debt problems and the specter of bankruptcy. Other serious conditions are coupled with fiscal crises. The most prominent ones include the loss of health and educational services under the aegis of structural adjustment programs, widespread deterioration of the physical infrastructure, declining economies, chronic shortages of inputs and basic consumption goods, the expansion of mechanized agriculture, and agricultural pricing policies that do not favor small farmers. All these factors and many more are exerting strong pressures on the livelihoods of rural Africans. Hence, the burden of large refugee influxes have become very difficult to bear. Such economic stresses are fertile ground for political tension and conflict, and especially so in rural communities inundated by a large refugee influx.

Third, refugees represent an added threat to environmental resources. The burden of population growth, in itself, has taxed the carrying capacity of many areas in East Africa. (Population density for the region doubled between 1962 and 1992 – from 7.2 persons per square kilometer to 15.0.) Coupled with the added load of more people are the semiarid conditions that predominate in many areas of East Africa. Relatively fragile ecosystems are stretched further by continuous cropping, changes in land tenure, and land lost to the expansion of large-scale schemes associated with mechanization and commercialization. The drought, food, and famine crises of the early 1970s and again in the mid-1980s were more disastrous in northeastern Africa than anywhere else. Here refugee influxes pose the most acute expressions of ecological crisis. Camps in Somalia were some of the first to demonstrate the potential scale of environmental strain and degradation associated with holding concentrated refugee populations for long periods of time in relatively fragile ecosystems. Up to eight kilometers around camp areas were totally cleared of trees and small vegetation. Their efforts to secure building supplies and fuel for cooking meant that settlement areas were "slowly transformed into a stony, arid desert."[56] Clearly, the ecological welfare of land surrounding a refugee camp is of extremely low priority to newly arrived refugees.[57] Hence, there is little doubt that the matter of environmental change in refugee-affected areas will remain a key issue in the future, for local populations, refugee communities, host governments, UNHCR, and implementing organizations.

Fourth, internally displaced people are growing in number far beyond that of international refugees. While two million East Africans are refugees in neighboring countries, another 7.5 million have been forced to move elsewhere inside their own country.[58] Legally speaking, internally displaced persons are under the sovereignty of the state in which they still live and thereby beyond the purview of direct international intervention. The United Nations is, however, beginning to break with its past reluctance to violate national sovereignty. Recent interventions have occurred in Lebanon, in Iraq, in Bosnia, and, in Somalia as well. Internally displaced populations are important for many reasons: in most respects their experience – including the impact of rural transformation – parallels that of refugees, and, in many instances they are often in the same areas as exiled or returning refugees.

Conclusion

Ranger stresses that it is essential to link refugee research with the more general study of rural societies.[59] This chapter has presented an overview of the East African context and in so doing attempted to relate the most salient features of rural transformation to the more specific process of refugee migration. This was the first step toward accomplishing our basic goal; that is, to tie the specifics of what is happening to refugee individuals, households, and communities to larger structures and forces that govern the operation of agrarian societies. Future chapters attempt to explicate, in a more specific way, the dynamics of change between rural transformation and refugee resettlement. This requires that we narrow our geographic focus to a particular setting. Hence, we turn to one border region and the largest refugee population in East Africa.

Notes

1. P. Porter, "Wholes and Fragments: Reflections on the Economy of Affection, Capitalism and the Human Cost of Development," *Geografiska Annaler* 69 (1987): 1-14.
2. R. Oliver and M. Gervase, *History of East Africa* (Oxford, 1963): 385.
3. S. el Shazali, "Peripheral Urbanism and the Sudan: Explorations in the Political Economy of the Wage Labor Market in Greater Khartoum, 1900-1984," PhD diss. (University of Hull, U.K., 1985), 100.
4. African Studies Branch, "Problems of Taxation," in *Africa: Continent of Change*, ed. P. Gould (Belmont, 1961): 153-60.
5. African Studies Branch, "Problems of Taxation."
6. S. Samatar, *The State and Rural Transformation in Northern Somalia, 1884-1986* (Madison, 1989), 9.
7. H. Bernstein, "Agrarian Structures and Change: Sub-Saharan Africa," in *Rural Livelihoods: Crises and Responses*, ed. H. Bernstein, B. Crow, and H. Johnson (Oxford, 1992), 67.
8. P. Curtin, S. Feierman, L. Thompson, and J. Vansina, *African History* (Boston, 1978), 504.
9. J. Rogge, *Too Many, Too Long: Sudan's Twenty-Year Refugee Dilemma* (Totowa, 1985), 66.
10. J. Bascom and K. Wilson, "Refugee Settlements in Southern Sudan: Using Multivariate Analysis to Assess Household Well-Being," Manuscript in review.
11. G. Kibreab, "The State of the Art Review of Refugee Studies in Africa," Uppsala Papers in Economic History, Research Report No. 26 (Uppsala, 1991).
12. Official cited in E. Shaaeldin, *The Evolution and Transformation of the Sudanese Economy Up to 1950*, DSRC Monograph Series, No. 20 (Khartoum, 1984), 20.
13. Reining cited in S. el Shazali, *Beyond Underdevelopment: Structural Constraints on the Development of Productive Forces Among the Jok Gor, the Sudan*, African Savannah Studies, Bergen Occasional Papers in Social Anthropology, No. 22 (Bergen, 1980).
14. Official cited in British Administration Report, Annual Administrative Report (Khartoum, 1947), 45.
15. Wallerstein cited in A. Stavrianos, *Global Rift: The Third World Comes of Age* (New York: 1981).
16. P. de Briey, "The Productivity of African Labour," in *Africa: Continent of Change*, ed P. Gould (Belmont, 1961), 138-53.
17. S. Longrigg, *A Short History of Eritrea* (Westport, 1974), 135.

18. G. Trevaskis, Eritrea: *A Colony in Transition: 1941-1952* (London, 1960), 44.
19. H. Hakovirta, "The Global Refugee Problem: A Model and It's Application," *International Political Science Review* (1993): 47.
20. C. Weeks, *Africa's Refugees: The Uprooted and Homeless* (New York, 1978), 3.
21. A. Hansen, "Refugee Dynamics: Angolans in Zambia 1966-72," *International Migration Review* 1 (1981): 177.
22. See J. Scott, *The Moral Economy of the Peasant: Rebellion and Subsistence in Southeast Asia* (New Haven, 1976); C. Meillassoux, "The Economic Bases for Demographic Reproduction: From the Domestic Mode of Production to Wage Earning," *Journal of Peasant Studies* 11 (1983): 51-66; H. Bernstein, "Concepts for the Analysis of Contemporary Peasantries," *Journal of Peasant Studies* 6 (1979): 421-43; A. Samatar, "The State and Rural Transformation in Northern Somalia," Manuscript (1989).
23. Sahlins cited in E. Wolf, *Peasants* (Englewood Cliffs, 1966), 3.
24. G. Hyden, *No Shortcuts to Progress: African Development Management in Perspective* (Berkeley, 1983), 12.
25. I. Zartman, "Portuguese Guinean Refugees in Senegal," *Refugees South of the Sahara: An African Dilemma* (Westport, Conn., 1970), 151.
26. Hansen, "Refugee Dynamics."
27. B. Harrell-Bond, "Humanitarianism in a Straightjacket," *African Affairs* 86 (1985): 3-14.
28. Hansen, "Refugee Dynamics."
29. See L. Holborn, *Refugees: A Problem of Our Time* (Metuchen, 1975); A. Hansen, "Once the Running Stops: Assimilation of Angolan Refugees into Zambian Border Villages," *Disasters* 3 (1979): 369-74; G. Hyden, *Beyond Ujamaa in Tanzania: Underdevelopment and an Uncaptured Peasantry* (Berkeley, 1980); N. Kliot, "Borderlands as 'Refugeeland' – Political Geographical Considerations," presentation at the 1990 meetings of the Association of American Geographers (Toronto, 19-22 April 1990).
30. S. el Shazali, "Eritreans in Kassala," (draft of final report), Joint Research Project of the Development Studies and Research Centre, University of Khartoum and the Free University of Amsterdam, Centre for Development Cooperation Services (Amsterdam, 1987); M. Bulcha, *Flight and Integration: Causes of Mass Exodus from Ethiopia and Problems of Integration in the Sudan* (Uppsala, 1988); J. Bascom, "The Peasant Economy of Refugee Resettlement in Eastern Sudan," *Annals of the Association of American Geographers* 83 (1993): 320-46.
31. Hansen, "Refugee Dynamics"; UN, Declaration and Program of Action of the Second International Conference on Assistance to Refugees in Africa," A/Con. 125/L.1 (Geneva, 1984); J. Drumthra, Telephone conversation, U.S. Committee for Refugees (Washington, D.C., March 1994).
32. Cited in S. Keller, *Uprooting and Social Change: The Role of Refugees in Development* (New Delhi, 1975), 1.
33. B. Crow and M. Thorpe et. al., *Survival and Change in the Third World* (Oxford, 1988).
34. C. Ake, *A Political Economy of Africa* (Essex, 1981), 188.
35. Bernstein, "Agrarian Structures," 75.
36. Ibid., 69.
37. T. Bassett, "Introduction: The Land Question and Agricultural Transformation in Sub-Saharan Africa," in *Land in African Agrarian Systems*, ed. T. Bassett and D. Crummey (Madison, 1993), 3-34.
38. S. Berry, "Concentration Without Privatization? Some Consequences of Changing Patterns of Rural Land Control," in *Land and Society in Contemporary Africa*, ed. E. Downs and S. Reyna (Hanover, 1988), 53-75.
39. Bassett, "The Land Question," 6.

40. Cited in Bassett, "The Land Question," 6.
41. Bassett, "The Land Question," 6.
42. G. Kitching, *Class and Economic Change in Kenya* (New Haven, 1980); Bassett, "The Land Question."
43. J. Berry, "Acculturation and Psychological Adaptation: A Conceptual Overview," in *Ethnic Psychology: Research and Practice With Immigrants, Refugees, Native Peoples, Ethnic Groups and Sojourners*, Select papers from a North American regional conference of the International Association of Cross-Cultural Psychology held in Kingston, Canada (16–21 August 1987), (Amsterdam, 1988), 53.
44. D. Christodoulou, *The Unpromised Land: Agrarian Reform and Conflict Worldwide* (London, 1990).
45. M. Roth, "Somalia Land Policies and Tenure Impacts: The Case of the Lower Shabelle," in *Land in African Agrarian Systems*, ed. T. Bassett and D. Crummey (Madison, 1993), 298–326.
46. M. Wubneh, *Ethiopia: Transition and Development in the Horn of Africa* (Boulder, 1988).
47. M. Roth, "Somalia Land Policies," 298, 304.
48. Hoben cited in R. Downs and S. Reyna, *Land and Society in Contemporary Africa* (Hanover, 1988), 216.
49. Bassett, "The Land Question," 17–18.
50. M. Mamdani, "Class Formation and Rural Livelihoods: A Ugandan Case Study," in *Rural Livelihoods: Crisis and Responses*, ed. H, Bernstein, B. Crow, and H. Johnson (Oxford, 1993), 197.
51. Bulcha, *Flight and Integration.*
52. P. Daley, "From the Kipande to the Kibali: The Incorporation of Labour Migrants and Refugees in Western Tanzania 1900 to 1987," in *Geography and Refugees: Patterns and Processes of Change*, ed. R. Black and V. Robinson (London, 1993), 25.
53. A. Hansen, "African Refugees: Defining and Defending their Human Rights," in *Human Rights and Governance in Africa*, ed. R. Cohen, G. Hyden, and W. Nagen (Gainsville, Fla., 1993), 226–66.
54. B. Stein, "Durable Solutions for Developing Country Refugees," *International Migration Review* 20 (1986): 264–82.
55. J. Bascom, "The Dynamics of Refugee Repatriation: The Case of Eritreans in Eastern Sudan," in *Population Migration and the Changing World Order*, ed. W. Gould and A. Findlay (London, 1994), 225–48.
56. H. Christensen, *Survival Strategies For and By Camp Refugees* (Geneva, 1982): 11.
57. G. le Breton, "Stoves, Trees, and Refugees: The Fuelwood Crisis Consortium in Zimbabwe," *Refugee Participation Network* 18 (1995): 9–12.
58. The United Nation's mandate limits its purview to those involuntary migrants who cross international boundaries due to a well-founded fear of persecution for reasons of race, religion, nationality, membership of a particular social group, or political opinion. This distinction established by the Geneva Convention delimits the "classical" refugee from voluntary migrants, but it ignores another category of forced migrants – "internal" refugees.
59. T. Ranger, "Concluding Reflections on Cross-Mandates," in *In Search of Cool Ground: War, Flight, and Homecoming in Northeast Africa*, ed. T. Allen and H. Morsink (London, 1996), 318–29.

Millions of East Africans have been forced to seek asylum in neighboring countries, including these Eritreans fleeing across the Sudanese border near the city of Kassala.

3

Migration and Agrarian Change on Border Lands

> Normally social transformation of such a degree would take several decades. In the case of these refugee groups the transformation, catapulted through time and space by the circumstances surrounding flight and the needs of survival, took place almost over night.
>
> M. Bulcha
> *Flight and Integration*

> This country [Sudan] is based on the peasant, not on the financier.
>
> Sir Douglas Newbold

Introduction

The border region of eastern Sudan has been home to the longest refugee concentration in East Africa. The Eritrean exodus began on 5 March 1967. Men, women, and children began arriving in Kassala, a Sudanese town bordering Ethiopia's northern province. By June, the number of refugees grew to 25,503, prompting the United Nations to begin providing protection and assistance.[1] By 1990, more than half a million people had sought refuge in Sudan (one in every seven Eritreans). Despite the Eritrean war's end in May 1991 and national independence two years thereafter, 320,000 Eritreans remain in eastern Sudan as of late 1998.

This chapter introduces readers to the Eritrean refugee population, their preflight socioeconomic context, and the changing nature of the Sudanese economy into which they moved. It begins with causes for forced migration. In addition to highlighting the variable

Notes for this section begin on page 62.

conditions under which different portions of the population left Eritrea, this section of the chapter explores the prevailing social and economic relationships in the principal region of origination. Familiarity with their preflight environment enhances our understanding of the changes that refugees have experienced in Sudan. The later portion of the chapter focuses on rural transformation in Sudan, a process that deeply and increasingly defines the everyday existence of refugees during asylum.

History Matters: The Context for Conflict

Reasons for the forced migration of Eritrean refugees date as far back as the late 19th century. The completion of the Suez Canal in 1869 sharply enhanced the strategic importance of the coastlines along the Red Sea and the Gulf of Aden. Several expansionist powers – Italy, Britain, Egypt, France, Russia, and the Ethiopian kingdom of Shewa – vied for control of the western coastline, but the Italians prevailed. While British and Egyptian forces were preoccupied with avenging General Gordon's defeat at Khartoum and overthrowing the Mahdi's state in Sudan, an Italian expeditionary force occupied the little Red Sea port of Massawa in 1885. This began their colonial venture in Eritrea. From Massawa, the Italians pushed steadily inland despite encountering repeated resistance and even defeat at Dogali. By mid-1889, they had taken the critical towns of Keren and Asmara. On 1 January 1890 the king of Italy announced formation of the colony of Eritrea.[2] The Italians claimed the western lowlands, the central highland belt, the eastern coastal plain, and the Danakil lowlands as their territory. This unified Eritrea as a separate political entity and demarcated its present-day boundaries. To the south lay Ethiopia, newly consolidated under King Menelik, and to the west lay the Sudan, recently reunited under a joint British-Egyptian mandate. By 1905, Italian authority was reasonably effective over most of Eritrea, and it was certainly complete by 1929.[3]

Eritrea remained an Italian colony for fifty-one years (1890 to 1941). The expansion of state power and control, however, was markedly uneven within the colony. In the highlands, the Italians removed the heads of active clan groups *(endas)* to minimize security risks, formed a set of new districts *(commissariats),* and appointed new, salaried chiefs *(meslenie)* to govern each district for the colonial administration. In the lowlands, however, the Italians chose another method (see Map 3.1). The lowlands were designated as "tribal areas"; that is, the tribe was made the unit of government recognition instead of the district.[4] Each tribal headman was given a rank, salary, and a set of responsibilities. Moving from east to west, the Danakil and Semhar were included in the eastern coastal region (Bassopiano Orientale); the Saho tribe in the Akkele Guzai region; the Bait Asghedé, Ad Shaikh, and Maria in the Keren region; the Beni Amer, Nara, Kunama, and two enclaves of West Africans (Bargo and Hausa) in the southwestern corner of Eritrea headquartered in Akordat (Bassopiano Occidentale).[5] In these ethnic areas, the state assessed a "native tribute" collected by sheiks and subsheiks and paid in annual installments. Native tribute, the only form of direct taxation on Eritreans, was quite low (an average of three pence per head). This accounted for 15 percent of the colony's revenues.[6] Although Italian law decreed that all lands below 850 m. altitude in the western lowlands were the property of the state, the effect was negligible because the government recognized the right of usufruct by local communities. Thus, colonialism had a far more definitive impact on highlanders than for pastoralists and peasant agriculturalists in the lowlands.

The lowland regions of Eritrea were deemed unsuitable for Europeans. One colonial report described the western lowlands as follows:

> The western lowlands are typical of semi-desert country which forms the northern fringe of tropical Africa. The country in western Eritrea consists of highly eroded rocky hills, with wadis (or flood beds) draining the central highlands into the two main channels of the rivers Barakka and Gash (or Mareb). Between the wadis there is, in come places, more level ground, parts of which can be cultivated during the short rainy season, but most of it is covered with thorn scrub useful only for desert grazing. On the alluvial deposits close to the wadi beds there is some reasonably fertile land to be found and in a few places gardens are maintained by irrigation from wells. The rainy season is from July to October and over most of the area it is uncertain. The present inhabitants grow one crop of dhurra annually ... . For six months of the year the temperature is excessively hot and during the rains the whole area is malarial.[7]

The Italian colonial venture ended in the midst of World War II. In 1935, Italy had invaded Ethiopia from their northern foothold in Eritrea as well as from eastern Somalia. After the fall of France in June 1940, Mussolini aligned Italy with Germany and led Italy into World War II. This alliance put Italian forces in East Africa (300,000 strong) at immediate odds with British ones. After initial success, the tide swung against the Italians. By 1941, British armies had swept Italian forces out of East Africa, returned Ethiopia to Emperor Haile Selassie, and placed Eritrea under a British military government. Functioning as a temporary occupying power, its freedom to enact new policies was severely restricted by international law.

The new administration maintained the same structure and approach as their predecessors. (Many Italians, in fact, were retained for civil service.) Highlanders were required to pay school and hospital fees as well as income, property and municipal taxes. Lowlanders, however, were only required to pay a native tribute of one shilling and three pence, a rate that produced revenues equivalent to those collected before the war.[8] Headmen of ethnic groups served as tax collectors; each one received 10 percent of the total revenues he collected as commission.[9] Security problems necessitated direct interventions, but the lowland population remained peripheral to state control.

The political economy of western Eritrea remained largely localized during the British administration as well as the Ethiopian federation that followed it. Observers emphasized, for example, "the closed circle of tribal and communal life" and that "the bulk of the population have not gone beyond the interests of their families and clans in their appreciation of political and social problems."[10] Tribal chiefs remained responsible for the payment of a token native tribute, but economic interaction was largely governed by social sanction and an ethic of reciprocity. International observers were quick to note the dominance of kinship relations:

> ... Where the Christian plateau dweller's loyalty is due to his 'enda', his village and the group of villages associated with it, *the allegiance* of the negroid *lowlander* extends from the *kinship group*, of which he is a member, to the tribe formed of the several kinship groups related to his own. *The difference between the two forms of society is that the one is based on territorial, and the other on kinship, considerations.* Thus in those negroid communities, the fact that their members live in villages is incidental to the tribal structure, composed as it is of a community claiming descent from a common ancestor, and subdividing on genealogical lines. Traditionally, the affairs of each kinship group are managed by a council of elected elders, while the direction of the tribe is entrusted to a superior form of council composed of elders elected from the lesser Councils. Councils of this kind continue to function informally despite the institution of a system of chieftainship by the Italian government. (emphasis added)[11]

The dominance of kinship relations was reflected in the visit of the Four Power commission charged with determining Eritrea's political future in the aftermath of World War II. Their assessment included hearings with no less than "753 kinship groups and 54 communities" in the western province.[12] That capitalist forces of production were not paramount in western Eritrea was evidenced further by the rural orientation of the population: 23 percent nomadic; 70 percent in villages; and only 7 percent in towns.[13] Writing about merchant activity in the three western districts of Akordat, Barentu, and Tessenei, the British Administrator in Eritrea noted, "In all the townships (and usually in the few villages where there are shops), trade is almost entirely in the hands of non-Eritreans. It is divided among Yemenis and other Arabs, Sudanese, and a few British Indians, who even comprise the majority of market stall-holders and coffee shop proprietors. Only the dregs of trade are left to Eritreans."[14]

In 1945, the administration estimated the total population of Eritrea to be 758,000 people. Eritreans, however, were fragmented along several lines – nomadic people (193,000) and sedentary people (565,000); Coptic Christians (371,000) and Muslims (341,000); Tigrinya-speakers (371,000) and Tigré-speakers (175,000).[15] In the last official census (1952), the total population exceeded one million people comprised of an estimated 510,000 Coptic Christians and 514,000 Muslims. Coptic Christians (most of whom speak Tigrinya) predominated, as they still do, in the central highlands surrounding Asmara, the capital of Eritrea. Muslims predominated, as they still do, in the lowlands that run parallel to the central highland belt both to the west and to the east. Furthermore, Eritrea was subdivided among a number of ethnic groups – Akelli Guzai, Aswa'orta, Beni Amer, Belain, Hamasein, Kunama, Nara, and Serae.

Despite this diverse constellation of nationalities, religions, languages, and ways of life, Eritreans came to terms with the concept of a common nationhood quickly under the British provisional government.[16] In 1942, a British report had described the "political minded" section of the Eritrean community as "very small," composed of "a number of disgruntled ex-government employees, a few leading merchants and a small number of Coptic priests," and considered the vast majority of people to be "exclusively concerned with the none-too-easy problem of how to earn the daily bread."[17] However, an indigenous political movement rapidly emerged for a number of reasons. First, Eritreans faced the fact that their country would not remain under British control indefinitely. Second, Ethiopia declared its intention to annex Eritrea as its "dismembered" territory. Third, Eritrean recruits returned from the war with a strengthened nationalist vision. Moreover, the British provisional government had taken steps to remove racial barriers, place more Eritreans in different administrative posts, and improve access to, and quality of, education – all of which encouraged the emergence of political opinion among Eritreans.[18] Fourth, the temporary administration allowed for a liberal atmosphere in which nationalist ideas could gather momentum.[19]

Opinion within Eritrea was strongly divided. Whereas 71.1 percent of highlanders favored union with Ethiopia, only 14.9 percent of lowlanders concurred.[20] More than 70 percent of the lowland population favored the Moslem League's pressure for independence instead. The secretary-general of the Moslem League of the Western Province of Eritrea insisted, "Federation with Ethiopia as far as this Province is concerned will completely ruin us. It will mean complete destruction of our traditions and history. We being the minority will be forced to collapse, unless the U.N.O. hears our cries. Are we to be driven as cattle, or are we to receive consideration as human beings?"[21] (The comparison with driven cattle prefigured the massive refugee flight in the decades ahead.)

After failing to reach a decision at the Paris peace conference, responsibility for determining Eritrea's status was transferred to a joint commission comprised of the Four Great Powers (1947). Following an investigative mission to Eritrea, the joint commission returned in a deadlock. British and American commissioners favored either annexation under Ethiopia or federation, while the French and Soviet commissioners favored a trusteeship under Italian control. Given the commission's inability to agree upon Eritrea's status, by previous agreement, the matter was transferred to the United Nations. A five-party UN commission, with representatives from South Africa, Norway, Burma, Guatemala, and Pakistan, made its trip to Eritrea in early 1950. It was charged with recommending a course of action based on several considerations: (a) the wishes and welfare of the inhabitants of Eritrea, including the views of the various racial, religious, and political groups of the provinces of the territory and the capacity of the people for self-government; (b) the interests of peace and security in East Africa; and, (c) the rights and claims of Ethiopia based on geographical, historical, ethnic, or economic reasons, including in particular Ethiopia's legitimate need for adequate access to the sea.[22] It returned with another split decision. The majority report recommended federation with Ethiopia or unconditional union, and the minority report (by Guatemala and Pakistan) recommended complete independence.

Significantly, cross-border affiliation with Sudan was a key consideration during negotiations. Although the established international boundary with Sudan demarcated the domination of different powers, important cross-border affinities – historic, religious, and ethnic – remained true then and continue to the present. After liberation of Eritrea from the Italians, British officials considered a plan to annex the western lowland area of Eritrea to the Sudan.[23] Although rescinded, the proposal reflected existing linkages to eastern Sudan that helped to shape a sense of shared Eritrean identity despite five decades of Italian control. The first affinity is the shared experience of Islam, particularly to the Khatmiya sect established by Sayed Mohammed Osman al-Mirghani (1753 to 1853).[24] Mirghani's descendants are found in both Sudan (Kassala) and Eritrea (Keren). During the key period of Sudanese history, the Mahdist state – the Khatmiya sect opposed the Mahdi, thereby distancing itself then and now from other political parties based in central and eastern Sudan. Second, Eritrea and eastern Sudan encompass a large confederation of more than twenty Beni Amer subgroups. The Beni Amer's traditional territory crosses the border. In 1944, for example, sixty thousand Beni Amer were residing in Eritrea while another thirty thousand lived in Sudan.[25] Third, the existence of cross-border trade was strong. Coffee, sugar, and other commodities like liquor, soap, and clothes from Eritrea and Ethiopia were exchanged for sorghum and sesame from Sudan. The same factors and affinities were important during the post war debate over Eritrea's future. The Muslim League, chaired by a descendent of al-Mirghani, led the call for the independence of Eritrea and included parts of eastern Sudan in its territorial objectives.[26]

With contradictory recommendations in hand, the United Nations General Assembly opened debate on Eritrea's future in late 1950. The Soviet bloc took a position favoring complete independence. U.S. Secretary of State John Foster Dulles was characteristically blunt when he stated the United States' position before the Security Council: "From the point of view of justice, the opinions of the Eritrean population must receive consideration. Nevertheless, the strategic interests of the United States in the Red Sea basin and considerations of security and world peace make it necessary that the country has to be linked with our ally, Ethiopia."[27] The U.S. position prevailed.[28] On 2 December 1950 the General Assembly passed resolution 390A by 46 votes to 10 stating that Eritrea should "constitute an autonomous unit federated with Ethiopia under the sovereignty of the Ethiopian crown."[29]

No Time to Say Good-by: Patterns of Flight

Federation was enacted on September 11th, 1952, but it was predictably short-lived. A first Eritrean Assembly was elected, but political ferment intensified on the eve of the second Assembly elections in 1956. The Eritrean Assembly passed resolutions accusing Ethiopia of political and civil rights violations. Next, the elected chief executive and president of the assembly resigned. Emperor Haile Selassie promptly appointed replacements who took strong, pro-

Ethiopian stances. The new chief executive banned all opposition parties and began a campaign to completely absorb Eritrea into Ethiopia. At the same time, the former chief executive left Eritrea to join a fledgling liberation movement in Egypt. The federal arrangement continued to disintegrate until finally, in 1962, a puppet assembly voted unanimously to dissolve the federation and fully incorporate Eritrea into Ethiopia. After this heavily stage-managed decision, guerrilla warfare began almost at once.[30] Initially, the fighters were largely composed of lowland Muslims of the Nara and Beni Amer. Although it would change in the mid-1970s, the freedom movement at first was associated with religious and ethnic factors in Eritrea as well as with the Arab cause generally.

In 1967, Emperor Haile Selassie launched the first of many major military campaigns in Eritrea. Ethiopian forces focused on the home of the resistance movement in the western lowlands. The army devastated the countryside surrounding the towns of Akordat and Barentu by burning villages and crops to the ground, slaughtering livestock, and poisoning well water. The offensive drove twenty-five thousand Eritreans across the border to Sudan. These original refugees were from three main ethnic groups – peasant farmers of Nara descent as well as pastoralists of Beni Amer and Maria descent. Most of them remained in and around the border town of Kassala, but two thousand moved south and resettled in a village named Wad el Hileau, which would become the site of the largest concentration of unassisted refugees in Sudan.

The next large exodus of refugees to eastern Sudan came in the mid-1970s. In 1974, Emperor Haile Selassie was deposed in a coup d'état. After a series of purges among different factions of the military, the Dergue ("committee") took power in Addis Ababa. Almost immediately, its existence was threatened by the Eritrean conflict (as well as five armed insurrections elsewhere in Ethiopia).[31] In a desperate move designed to shore up national morale and curtail the victories of the Eritrean resistance fighters, the Dergue conscripted forty thousand peasants into the army and launched a major Eritrean offensive. The number of Eritreans in Sudan grew from 49,000 in 1974 to 346,000 by 1979.

The year 1976 marked an important transition point as the war began to include wider ethnic and religious representation. More specifically, it marked the emergence of the Eritrean Peoples Liberation Front (EPLF) with its strong highland roots. Three Eritrean fronts reorganized themselves for a protracted war, including a sharp increase in size of their combined military force to thirty-seven thousand fighters.[32] By late 1977, the combined fronts controlled 80 percent of Eritrea. They had driven the Ethiopians out of every major town except Asmara, Assab, Massawa, Barentu, and Adi Qaieh.

Several factors, however, contributed to a downward turn in the late 1978 and thereafter. First, internecine skirmishes broke out between the two principal resistance movements, the EPLF and the ELF. Meanwhile, the Soviet Union began providing the Ethiopian army with massive quantities of weapons such as MIG jets, helicopters, tanks, and armored personnel carriers, and the Ethiopian army began resorting to napalm and, allegedly, nerve gas. The Ethiopian army launched four more major campaigns between 1979 and 1981, the latter three of which were planned and executed with the aid of military advisors from Warsaw Pact countries. In January 1982 the leader of the Dergue, Lt. Colonel Haile Mariam Mengistu, announced Operation Red Star – the Dergue's sixth and largest offensive. He envisioned Operation Red Star as a "multi-purpose revolutionary campaign to wipe out the secessionist bandits."[33] Another one hundred thousand peasants were conscripted to join the nearly forty thousand troops already in Eritrea. Although the Ethiopian army gave maximum concentration to this huge operation, the war continued. The re-escalation of conflict combined with intensive drought and famine drove thousands more Eritreans into Sudan. By June 1987 there were approximately 974,000 refugees in the Sudan, the vast majority from Eritrea.[34]

In March of 1988, the war's momentum began to swing back in favor of the EPLF. After a series of quick victories, many hundreds of refugees returned to Eritrea in April of 1988 to help seal what they hoped would be a final Eritrean victory. Meanwhile, however, Lt. Colonel Mengistu organized another massive conscription campaign in southern Ethiopia, commandeered the national airlines to fly troops to the front, and retaliated with a seventh major offensive in Eritrea. This counter attack blunted the EPLF's success, leaving the conflict deadlocked in a stalemate. From President Mengistu's perspective, the war was necessary "to affirm Ethiopia's historical unity and to safeguard her outlet to the sea and to defend her very existence from being stifled."[35] Meanwhile, Eritreans sought self-determination and insisted they had the right to use any and every means available to wage a struggle against a regime which by its own acts had become "an occupying power."[36] Hence, the longest armed struggle in Africa's modern history continued on into the 1990s.

In 1991, however, after thirty years of conflict, the Eritrean war came to a comparatively sudden end. Twenty-four years of conflict culminated in late May of 1991 when the Ethiopian People's Democratic Revolutionary Front approached the capital of Ethiopia, thereby totally destabilizing Ethiopian forces fighting in Eritrea. The Ethiopian army made a chaotic retreat from Asmara westward to Sudan, where they sought refugee asylum for themselves. A UN-sanctioned referendum for Eritrea's independence was set for May of 1993. An overwhelming "yes" vote (98 percent) opened the way for the creation of the fifty-second state in Africa.[37] Seventy thousand Eritreans repatriated on their own accord during the two years between the war's end and national independence, leaving more than four hundred thousand more in Sudan.[38] Another sixty thousand have returned, mostly with the assistance of a UNHCR-sponsored repatriation program. As of 1998 an estimated 340,000 Eritreans, mostly from the western lowlands, still are in Sudan. Therefore we turn our attention now to Sudan and the status of Eritrean asylum.

Queuing Up: Strategies for Resettlement

Refugee status is granted to Eritreans based on the 1951 UN Refugee Convention, the 1967 UN Refugee Protocol, and the Organization for African Unity's 1969 Protocol. Sudan's refugee policy is outlined in the Regulation of Asylum Act legislated in 1974. The major thrusts of the Sudanese refugee policy expressed in that document include:

1. The granting of asylum by Sudan to refugees is a peaceful and humanitarian act and should not necessarily be seen by the government of the country of origin of refugees as sympathy by Sudan for the cause of refugees. (Although many political analysts argue Sudan has consistently favored the Eritrean position.)
2. The optimum solution to any refugee dilemma is the voluntary repatriation of refugees.
3. In the absence of repatriation or alternative solutions such as third-country resettlement, refugees should be discouraged from spontaneously settling in either rural or urban areas and instead be relocated on government-organized settlement schemes located away from politically sensitive border areas, with the aim of becoming self-sufficient either through agriculture or by selling their labor.
4. The level of support and infrastructure made available to refugees by government agencies and the international community should not be greater than that available to local Sudanese communities; whenever possible, installations on refugee schemes should also be available to local Sudanese.[39]

In early 1968, the Sudanese government established the first refugee settlement for Eritreans at Um Sagata in the Qala en Nahal area. During the first decade of the Eritrean conflict, the presence of refugees in border areas was tolerated as part of Sudan's policy of confrontation with Ethiopia.[40] After 1977, however, this changed when refugees from highland Eritrea began arriving.[41] The highland Eritreans did not share the same cultural, religious, and ethnic affinities with Sudanese as lowlanders. These incompatibilities coupled with the fear that refugees might turn into a political constituency prompted the government to harden its refugee policy. Justified largely on the basis of protecting national security, the Sudanese Ministry of the Interior initiated moves to transfer Eritreans away from the border. Refugees' freedom of movement was curtailed and their dependence on government and international relief aid grew.

At the height of its activities, the Sudanese Office of the Commissioner for Refugees (COR) and UNHCR provided protection and assistance to 153,000 Eritreans and Ethiopians living in twenty-seven settlements throughout eastern Sudan (see Map 3.1).[42] Seventeen settlements remain in existence and house 100,000 refugees.[43] Some agricultural land is available to refugees, but usually only ten *feddans* per household (1 *feddan* equals 1.04 acres). Refugee households without plots must rely even more on other alternatives, e.g. doing agricultural wage labor on commercial schemes (either independently or under the auspices of work parties organized by COR), selling portions of rationed food for cash, or participating in small-scale, income-generating projects within the settlement. The meager prospect of finding sufficient work in official refugee settlements is one reason why many refugees choose to leave camps (and thereby forfeit their food ration quota, housing provision, and access to free health care). Twenty-nine percent of the sampled unassisted refugees currently living in the largest concentration of unassisted refugees in eastern Sudan had lived previously in a refugee camp, but had left either by choice or necessity.

The exact number of unassisted refugees in eastern Sudan is difficult to ascertain. At the height of the war, the Sudanese government estimated that there were nearly two hundred thousand refugees living in urban areas – 45,000 in Khartoum, 35,000 in Gedaref, 50,000 in Kassala, and 60,000 in Port Sudan. Two hundred thousand more resided in rural communities.[44] As Sudan's fiscal crisis has intensified in recent years, refugees have come to be seen as a burden. Sudanese were generally sympathetic to Eritrean refugees during the 1960s and 1970s. During the last decade, however, hyper inflation and the precarious economic situation of the country have taken their toll.

50 | *Losing Place*

Map 3.1 Distribution of Official Settlements and Unassisted Refugees in Eastern Sudan

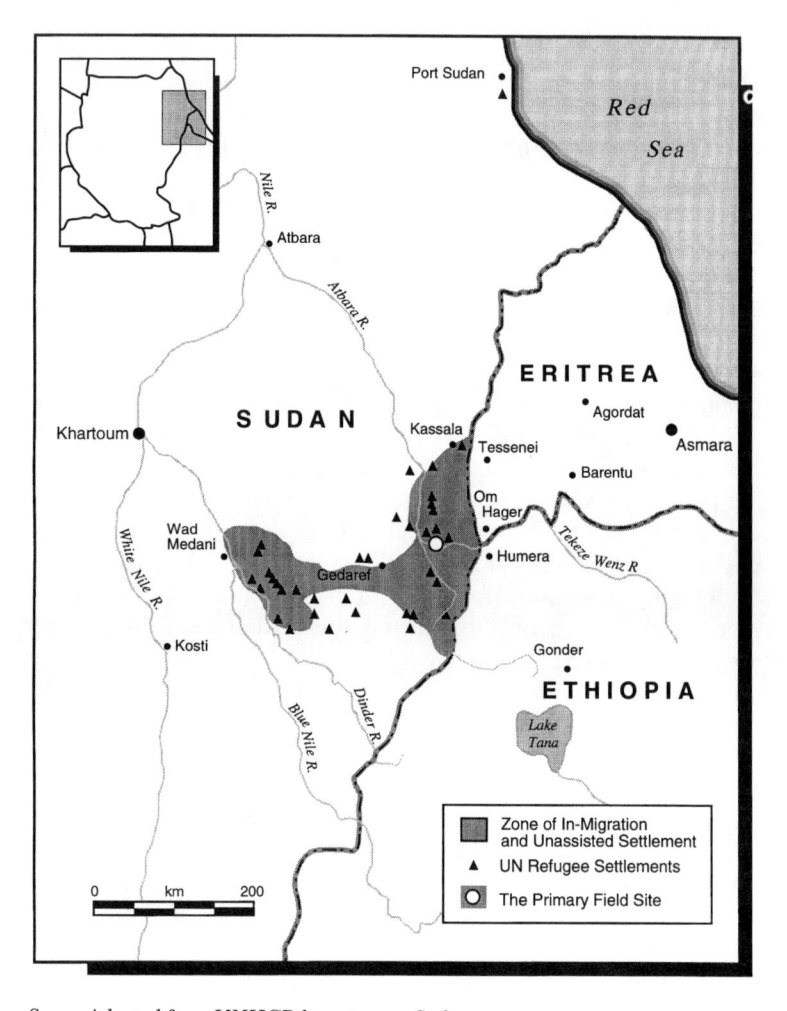

Source: Adapted from UNHCR literature on Sudan

Many Sudanese citizens attribute their sufferings and deprivations to the "intruders," and refugees are the subject of local party elections, debates, announcements, warnings, and directives.[45]

Working Refugees: The Sudanese Political Economy

We have established the basic geographic and historic context for refugee movements across the Eritrean border, but settlement in Sudan requires that we conceptualize the nature of the agrarian-based economy there and establish a clear sense of its ongoing transformation. This section provides a framework for understanding the larger Sudanese political economy, and, how it structures more localized, social relationships of production and exchange within which refugees must secure a livelihood.

Sudan, the largest country in Africa, encompasses nearly one million square miles and a diverse ecology. The Sahara Desert dominates the northernmost third of the country stretching more than four hundred miles from the capital city of Khartoum to the Egyptian border. Shifting southward, the relatively narrow Sahel is an important domain for pastoralists and irrigated agriculture. It extends across Sudan and into Eritrea, ending at the highland escarpment. A dry savanna predominates in the central portion of the county. This climate zone broadens near the Ethiopian uplands that flank Sudan's eastern border. Although the central rainlands have a lengthy dry season, which lasts as long as eight months, there is sufficient precipitation to sustain short grasses, scattered trees, and the country's principal food crops, sorghum, and sesame. Most rainfed cultivation, parceled out as small holdings or extensive farms, occurs in this, the largest climatic region of Sudan. The population density of the eastern portion of this region, and hence that area adjacent to Eritrea and Ethiopia, is comparatively low. Oral traditions and many deserted village sites suggest the existence of a much larger population up to the time of the Mahdi (1880s). The decimation is thought to have been caused by a combination of factors: epidemics of smallpox and cerebrospinal meningitis; years of cattle plague and famine; population displacement during the Mahdi uprising; and the encroachment of the grass plains by Acacia tree forests.[46] Repopulation of the easternmost province of Kassala began in the 1940s and 1950s. By the late 1980s, the population reached 1.36 million Sudanese and as many as 0.5 million refugees. The province had the physical space to absorb not only influxes of Sudanese and refugees, but a massive transformation of agriculture. That the everyday existence of today's refugees is tied to the transformation of agriculture in eastern Sudan brings us back to key elements in Sudan's past. The current fiscal crisis in Sudan is an important contemporary factor, but many refugees' subsistence is rooted in three important initiatives begun during colonialism – taxation, labor recruitment, and mechanization of agriculture.

In Sudan, as it was in every colony, taxation was envisaged as a basic "pillar" of policy. Upon arrival in Khartoum in 1884, General Gordon immediately burned the tax-gatherers' books and thereby cleared the way for a new system of taxation. British officers made that a key objective upon return to Khartoum in the wake of Gordon's death. As one accountant put it, "When the Sudan was reoccupied in 1898 the first and most essential problem which engaged the serious consideration of the newly set-up government was the taxation of the people. Light and simple taxation, adapted to the special conditions of the Sudanese and the mode of life, was gradually introduced."[47] Land tax, date tax, animal tax, *ushur* (tenth or tithe), and tribute were imposed, although assessment figures from 1936 to 1942 suggest a yearly average of only £13,833 for the entire Kassala Province. One sheik in that area recalls asking why he was not asked to collect more taxes or tribute. The colonial official replied, "We do not care so much for money, but the tax is a confession of our control."[48] Official records support his assessment. Direct taxes between 1936 and 1942 produced but 1.4 percent of the Sudan Government's total annual budgetary revenue.[49]

Starting in the 1940s, however, the importance of taxes began to grow. Village sheiks were asked to collect them. During the 1940s and early 1950s tax rates for livestock and sorghum were relatively stable: 7 to 8 Sudanese piasters per sack of sorghum, 7 to 10 piasters per head of goat, 15 to 40 piasters per head of cattle, and 80 piasters per head of camel. Each sheik received a small monthly salary and kept 20 percent of what he collected as a commission.[50] More importantly, taxes represented a new demand for cash that could not be satisfied by the production of subsistence crops or the exchange of barter goods. This hastened the adoption of cash crops for sale in the market. Taxes coupled with the sale of imported goods played an important role in the transformation of a rural, subsistence economy into a commodity-oriented one, moving into the orbit of foreign trade.

Although taxes and tribute helped colonial officials to maintain administrative control, they relied principally upon indirect taxes to underwrite the administration costs. Royalties were levied upon gum, tobacco, palm fruits, timber, charcoal, and firewood. These royalties, however, were completely overshadowed by those collected on cotton. By the turn of the century, the necessity for finding new areas for the purpose of growing cotton had induced capitalists to come to the Sudan in search of "suitable land." Concessions for cotton plantations were given to individuals as well as to several companies during the first decade of the 1900s. In 1910, the British Cotton Growers Association sent inspectors to visit. Three years later the British Parliament approved a loan of £3.0 million (Sudanese) to construct a dam on the Blue Nile and create a series of irrigation canals for a new cotton scheme. World War I forced the project to be suspended temporarily, but construction was completed thereafter and the Gezira Scheme was officially opened in 1925. The scheme grew from 80,000 *feddans* in 1925 to more than 200,000 in the late 1930s and continued expanding in size to one million *feddans* by 1956. The world's "largest farm" has generated the bulk of the country's export earnings during the last sixty years. It consistently produces more than 80 percent of Sudan's cotton and generates more than 50 percent of the country's annual export earnings.[51]

While the Gezira became the dominant source of public revenue and export earnings, it also set in motion the formation of the Sudanese agricultural labor force. The original design of the Gezira's tenancy system was to help insure a stable supply of labor. To encourage tenant residency, each farmer was allowed to devote one quarter of his plot (*hawasha*) to sorghum and animal fodder. But resident tenant farmers could not provide enough labor power, so new recruitment tactics were adopted in the 1930s and 1940s. Village sheiks were contracted to supply a preestablished number of laborers in exchange for a per laborer fee. Rail fares were reduced for passengers who traveled to Gezira stations from western Sudan. Dwelling sites were allocated to migrant West African workers within the scheme and villages were established for them outside the scheme. In the early 1940s, the tax collection time in key labor supply provinces was shifted from the end of the dry season to its beginning (from June to January). Shifting tax collection forward in the year relieved peasants and pastoralists of their cash at the beginning of the cotton-picking season, thereby ensuring more labor migration.[52] Competition within the labor market intensified as West African laborers and seasonal migrants began arriving from western Sudan.[53] The Gezira has played a dominant role in shaping Sudan's economy by generating the bulk of the country's export earnings and prompting the formation of a national agricultural labor force. The Gezira does not rely on refugees for labor, but it fashioned wage labor relations for other cotton schemes and the rainfed grain schemes of the eastern region on which a great number of refugees work.

The first rainfed grain schemes were begun during World War II, when shortages of sorghum threatened the supply of food for British troops stationed in Sudan and forced grain rationing in urban areas. Spurred by shortages, "the unemployed and idlers" in Khartoum, Omdurman, and Gedaref were rounded up to work on a large sorghum scheme near Gedaref. One strategy for dealing with Ethiopian refugees who came to Sudan after the Italian invasion of Ethiopia was to settle them in Gedaref to work as agricultural laborers as well.[54] The government then began trials in mechanized cultivation north of Gedaref. After two years of small-scale experimentation, the British placed twelve thousand *feddans* under cultivation in 1945. Successive seasons produced poor returns (i.e., the costs per ton of sorghum were running twice the market price per ton). Given such poor results, the state ended its direct involvement in mechanized agriculture, but as an alternative, the state began to lease land parcels, two kilometers by two kilometers in size, to private Sudanese investors. The shift to private investors and leasing land marked the advent of *mushrooah* or "scheme" farming that has become the hallmark of mechanized agriculture in eastern Sudan.[55]

Mushrooah farming rapidly expanded on the southern portion of the Butana, vast plains that stretch more than two hundred kilometers between the Blue Nile and the Ethiopian border (see Map 3.2). Eighty-two percent of the entire area is flat plains (i.e., a ground slope average of 2.5 meters per kilometer).[56] Isolated hills and rocky inselberg outcrops pierce the plain at wide intervals. Small seasonal stream beds (*khors* or wadis) radiate away from these inselbergs, but all the rivers in the region – the Atbara, Setit, Rahad, Angreb, and Blue Nile – emanate from Ethiopia. The northern Butana is characterized by immature soils, coarse sand, and gravel, which alternate with patches of clay-filled depressions. Pastoralists like the Shukriya utilize this portion of the plain to move their herds north and south with seasonal rains. The southern Butana, however, has become the homeland of mechanized agriculture.

Neither the colonial nor the successive Sudanese governments have recognized private ownership of land on the Butana. Land registration has never been undertaken. Although rural communities often hold "localized" rights to nearby land – usually subdivided among individual members based on usufruct rights – the plains are government-owned land that is leased in large tracts to *mushrooah* operators. The amount of land devoted to mechanized rainfed agriculture went from five thousand *feddans* in the 1955/56 season to 1.2

Map 3.2 Distribution of Mechanized Rainfed Schemes on the Butana Plains During the 1990s

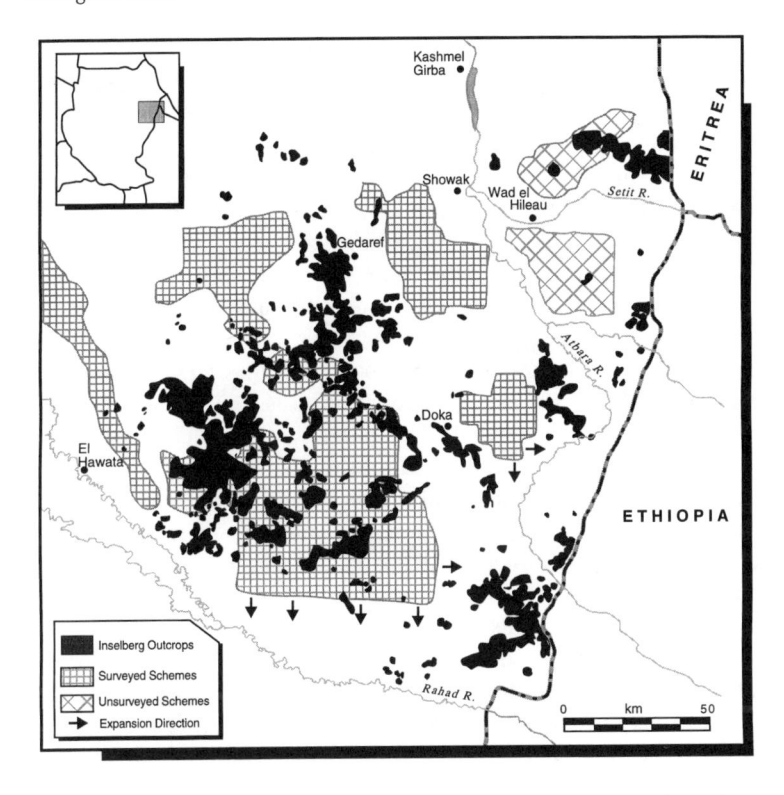

Source: Adapted from Southern Kassala Agricultural Development Project (SKAP), Land Use Survey Report, Masdar (UK) Ltd. and S A Consultants Ltd., February 1992

million *feddans* in the 1959/60 season (27 percent of all farmed land in Sudan at the time) and then leveled off at just under one million *feddans* during the early 1960s.[57] During the first decade of expansion leases were extended to members of the Native Administration and the urban merchant community.

The World Bank helped finance the expansion of irrigated agriculture after independence, but it shifted the locus of its resources and attention to rainfed agriculture in 1967. The Sudanese government established the Mechanized Farming Corporation (MFC) with the Bank's assistance. This corporation was designed to supervise rainfed agriculture and provide supplemental financing. The MFC was charged with several tasks: allocation of land to renters; provision of a land survey for each *mushrooah*; collection of annual lease fees; enforcement of government regulations for *mushrooahs*; estimates of annual production; and guarantees for loans made by the Agricultural Bank of Sudan (ABS) to *mushrooah* farmers.[58] The ABS is the only source of formal credit for private farmers in Sudan. Its mandate, as outlined in section four of the ABS Act (1957), is to provide credit (both in cash and in kind) to farmers for farm machinery, seasonal labor wages, and seeds; to assist in handling, storing, and marketing of crops; and to perform other nonbanking activities such as the importation and sale of machinery, spare parts, tires, and other agricultural inputs. The ABS and the MFC established offices in Gedaref.

The area under rainfed agriculture remained just below one million feddans from the 1959/60 season until the end of the 1965/66 season. Under the auspices of the MFC and the World Bank, however, expansion of rainfed mechanized agriculture began once again. The land under rainfed agriculture rose from less than one million *feddans* in the mid-1960s to more than three million *feddans* during the 1972/73 season, thereby exceeding the number of *feddans* devoted to irrigated agriculture. Slower, steady expansion continued throughout the 1970s. Expansion peaked during the 1981/82 season when the MFC reported more than six million *feddans* under the MFC's supervision.

Meanwhile, illicit, unsurveyed schemes outside of the MFC's auspices developed at virtually the same pace as officially recognized *mushrooahs*. Although they were not entitled to low-interest financing from the MFC, the budding agrarian elite had sufficient capital to finance its own expansion. The total amount of unsurveyed area under mechanized cultivation is the subject of extensive controversy and speculation. A recent evaluation by the World Bank, however, estimated the amount for unsurveyed schemes to be at least two-thirds of that for surveyed schemes (i.e., approximately four million *feddans*).

Unsurveyed *mushrooahs* in the Gedaref area range between five hundred and ten thousand *feddans* in size. *Mushrooah* operators generally plant two crops – a tall-standing, multi-headed sorghum *(dura)* and white-seeded sesame *(sim-sim)*. *Sim-sim* is sown first, followed by *dura*. There are numerous species of sorghum *(sorghum vulgare)*. Consumers favor *safra* (a white grain), but operators plant more *feterita* (a red sorghum) given its lower demand for moisture and superior capacity to withstand drought. To reduce their annual capital expenditures, they prefer to use their own seed rather than purchase new. This practice, however, accelerates the rate of weed infestation, and seed stocks rapidly degenerate thorough cross-pollination with grasses.[59]

A 50/50 percent split between sorghum and sesame and yearly rotation between the two would be ideal if sustainability, rather than profit maximization, dictated the ratio between crops. Sesame not only has far lower soil nutrient demands, but annual rotations would help restrict weed growth. Most operators maintain a 15/85 ratio between sesame and sorghum. This split represents a calculated balance between risk and return. The returns from sesame are higher than those from sorghum, but the risk of crop failure is considerably higher, too. And operators use their net return from sesame, which is harvested first, to hire wage labor for harvesting the sorghum crop that follows. Hence, this ratio minimizes the need for working capital.

The eastern region of Sudan is the most important grain production area in Sudan. Based on an assumed consumption level of 190 kg per person, only 30 percent of the sorghum produced in the central rainlands is eaten within that region.[60] The remaining 70 percent is consumed elsewhere in Sudan or exported out of the country. Trucks with double bed trailers use the country's lone highway to haul sorghum from Gedaref to Port Sudan for international export as well as to population centers along the Blue Nile (principally the Wad Medani–Khartoum corridor). Each of these truck rigs has a hauling capacity of five to six hundred sacks of sorghum. Meanwhile, Gedaref remains the preeminent grain marketing center in the country, symbolized by an enormous grain silo that dominates the town's skyline.[61]

While mechanized schemes have provided high returns on invested capital, a high price has been paid by the environment. The development of mechanized farming both on a large and a small scale has resulted in massive clearance of formerly forested areas. Acacia trees and shrubs once dominated the area; the northern area was dominated by *Acacia mellifera* trees, and *Acacia seyal* was the principal species in the wetter zone to the south of the 600 mm isohyet. Now, however, only 28 percent of the area retains its natural vegetation, mostly on land poorly suited to cultivation.[62] During the last fifty years, the land devoted to farms has expanded from three quarters of a million *feddans* to over six million.[63] The decline in tree cover also contributes to decreased precipitation, reduced humidity, increased soil salinity, and increased rodent infestation.

Clay vertisols are inherently low in organic material, nitrogen, and available phosphate. Moreover, waterlogging minimizes moisture percolation from the surface and nutrient leaching from crops. These factors are basic constraints in the region, but it is use patterns by scheme operators that have led to rapid soil exhaustion and a concomitant decrease in crop yields. Virtually all operators dismiss set fallow periods and sow the entire scheme every year instead. This farming practice reflects the short-term profit logic guiding their farm management decisions. While operators under the MFC's supervision ignore the lease agreement to leave a full one third of their land fallow each year, operators with unsurveyed land are even less likely to remove any land from cultivation. Leaving it fallow is very costly in the short run, particularly in a poor season. Leaving fallow 25 percent of a fifteen-hundred-*feddan mushrooah* means an 85 percent reduction in the total profit during a bad season as compared to 55 percent reduction in the total profit for a good season.[64] This is the logic behind full utilization and continuous cultivation.

Soil fertility drops rapidly under monocropping. *Mushrooah* operators have reported yields in the fifth year that are one half of the yields of their first year in operation.[65] A comparison of yields between 1961 and 1964 with those between 1977 and 1980 suggest that sorghum yields fell at least 20 percent per *feddan* on the Butana Plains in the southern portion of Kassala Province.[66] During the late 1960s and 1970s when land was readily available, it was common for operators to "farm" a *mushrooah* for five to seven years, reap high returns from high yields, desert it, and clear another. An estimated 10 to 15 percent of all *mushrooah* land in the Gedaref region has now been abandoned.[67] In the words of a World Bank consultant, "Great wealth is available to those who can arrange to mine the natural resources of the area. Their motivation seems to be largely short-term, to the detriment of the environment."[68] Recently released data provides dramatic evidence of land fatigue in the eastern rainlands of Sudan. Based on time-series data for thirty years, Figures 3.1 and 3.2 illustrate the substantial fall in yields of both sorghum and sesame, while at the same time the area under cultivation has grown steadily. In summary, declining land productivity has gone hand in hand with the private accumulation of profits.

In addition to environmental noncompliance, capitalist agriculture has depended heavily on capital generated by mercantile activity in

the Eritrean constitution in 1952: "It does not follow that the United Nations would no longer have any right to deal with the question. The United Nations Resolution on Eritrea would remain an international instrument and, if violated, the General Assembly would be apprised of the matter." Davidson, Cliffe, and Selassie (eds.), *Behind the War,* 40. The United Nations did not ever exercise this right to intervene in the conflict, despite being asked to do so when Emperor Haile Selassie preempted the UN agreement in 1962.
29. R. Greenfield, *The OAU and Africa's Refugees: Assistance to Refugees – Alternative Viewpoints* (London, 1980), 31.
30. From many Eritreans' perspective the first bullet of the war was fired on 1 September 1961 in a skirmish between Ethiopian soldiers and a band of rebels led by Hamid Idris Awate.
31. Five other armed insurrections included: the Western Somali Liberation Front in the Ogaden; resistance from the Southern Oromo people in Sidamo and Bale; the Ethiopian Democratic Union (EDU) along the western border; the Afar Liberation Movement on the Danakil plains adjacent to Eritrea; and the Tigray People's Liberation Front (TPLF) in the northern province of Ethiopia, adjacent to Eritrea.
32. Karadawi, "Refugee Policy in the Sudan," 96.
33. C. Legum and J. Firebrace, *Tigray and Eritrea,* Report No. 5 (London, 1983), 11.
34. Bulcha, *Flight and Integration,* 28.
35. Mengistu cited in Legum and Firebrace, *Tigray and Eritrea.* Note as well that the value of exports averaged about 50 percent of the value of imports during the Italian regime. In the mid-1940s, they reached 57 percent when imports were limited and industrial products could find markets abroad; then they dropped back to about the 50 percent average. The difference was realized through transit trade reexporting primary products from Ethiopia to world markets and of petroleum, textiles, and other trade goods back into Ethiopia. Between 1947 and 1949 the annual value of trade moved through the two ports of Assab and Massawa averaged about £3,000,000, or almost as much as the annual value of all imports and nearly twice as much as that of exports during the same period Trevaskis, *Eritrea,* 43. This underscores the critical importance of the two seaports to either Ethiopia or Eritrea.
36. The Eritrean liberation movement was founded on the right of self-determination. Self-determination is linked to a fundamental distinction: All Eritreans consider the Eritrean question as a *colonial* question, not an issue of *secession* or *separatism* from Ethiopia. Legum and Firebrace, *Tigray and Eritrea.* Several reasons were cited: (a) Eritrea was never part of the old Abyssinian empire; (b) Haile Selassie flagrantly broke his United Nations agreement without any attempt by the international body to prevent or rectify it; and (c) successive Ethiopian governments under both Emperor Haile Selassie and Lt. Colonel Mengistu tried to eliminate the Eritrean claim to independence.
37. D. Styan, "Eritrea 1993 – The End of the Beginning," in *In Search of Cool Ground: War, Flight and Homecoming in Northeast Africa,* ed. T. Allen (London, 1996), 80–95.
38. CERA, Repatriation and Reintegration Project (Provisional Government of Eritrea, 1993).
39. Rogge, *Too Many, Too Long,* 56–7.
40. Karadawi, "Refugee Policy in Sudan," 183.
41. Ibid., 31.
42. The Sudanese Office for the Commissioner of Refugees (COR) was established in 1968 as a branch of the Ministry of Interior. During the reorganization of Sadiq el Mahdi's government in mid-1988, COR was reconstituted as an independent the Ministry of Rehabilitation and Relief. This aptly reflects the fact that COR has taken on a life of its own as many institutions do.
43. E. Weisburg, Faxed message from UNHCR, Washington (March 1997).

44. UNHCR, April 1988 Briefing Notes from UNHCR–Khartoum, (Khartoum, 1988).
45. U. Ahmad, *Self-settled Refugees in Gedaref (Eastern Sudan)*, Report for United Nations High Commissioner for Refugees (Khartoum, 1986).
46. J. Tothill, *Agriculture in Sudan* (London, 1948), 729.
47. H. Tunley, 1948, "Revenue from Land and Crops," in *Agriculture in Sudan*, ed. J. Tothill (London, 1948), 198.
48. A. Ajil, Interview with the Sheik of Wad el Hileau, 21 January 1988.
49. Tunley, "Revenue from Land and Crops," 201.
50. el Shazali, *Beyond Underdevelopment: Structural Constraints on the Development of Productive Forces Among the Jok Gor, the Sudan*, African Savannah Studies, (Bergen, Nor., 1980), 35.
51. T. Barnett, *The Gezira Scheme: An Illusion of Development* (London, 1977).
52. J. O'Brien, "The Formation of the Agriculture Labor Force in Sudan," *Review of African Political Economy* 26 (1983): 19.
53. If a farming operation did not meet their satisfaction, field inspectors would have additional work done at double wages and charged against the tenant's account. In essence, tenants' own reproduction has always depended on their ability to hold the wage bill down to an absolute minimum and get maximum output from hired labor. Instead of one 2.1 million *feddan* plantation under a single central management unit negotiating with a labor force of more than one half million, the Gezira scheme, for the purposes of labor relations, is broken down into nearly 100,000 autonomous units, each of which hires a handful of workers and separately negotiates wage rates. Thus, wage rates for seasonal labor have remained low and stable due to the mediating role that tenants play between seasonal labor and scheme management.
54. Karadawi, "Refugee Policy in the Sudan," 125.
55. Although popularly known as "mechanized agriculture," the term is somewhat of a misnomer. Until quite recently when combine harvesters were introduced, the only mechanized portion of the agricultural operation was cultivation with tractors. All weeding operations and the majority of harvesting operations are done manually by hired agricultural wage labor.
56. Southern Kassala Agricultural Development Project (SKAP), Land Use Survey Report, Masdar (UK) Ltd and S A Consultants Ltd. (1992), D2.
57. K. Affan, *Toward an Appraisal of Tractorisation Experience in Rainlands of Sudan*, DSRC Monograph Series, No. 19 (Khartoum, 1984), 23.
58. The Mechanized Farming Corporation was originally a government agency to allocate and supervise the use of land in rainfed mechanized areas. Later, the MFC's mandate was expanded when it became an agency for executing credit for the Sudan government and directly involved in the production of sorghum and sesame on state farms. In 1984, the MFC's role was revised and restricted to extension services, adaptive research, and the provision of some tractor services. D. Shannon, Report of the Institutional Specialist, Pre-Appraisal Mission, South Kassala Agricultural Project, (World Bank, 1988), 5.
59. Many of the weeds are grasses which are members of the sorghum family itself (e.g., sorghum *Aethiopiae* and sorghum *purpurecogericeum*). Use of their own seeds raises the likelihood that weeds will cross-pollinate with sorghum.
60. World Bank, "South Kassala Agriculture Project," Staff Appraisal Report (11 September 1988).
61. This Russian-built silo was reported to be the largest grain silo in Africa at least until the mid-1970s and epitomizes the "breadbasket" optimism in the late 1960s. However, the year the silo was completed (1967) is the only time in which it has been filled to its one hundred ton capacity. E. Zaki, I. Hassan, and A. Settar, *Strategy for Development of Rainfed Agriculture* (Khartoum, 1986).
62. (SKAP), Land Use Survey Report, G3
63. Ibid., I.9

64. Affan, *Tractorisation Experience*, 65.
65. I. Simpson and M. Simpson, Alternative Strategies for Agricultural Development in the Central Rainlands of the Sudan with Special Reference to Damazin Area, Rural Development Studies, No. 3 (Leeds, 1978), 17.
66. World Bank, "South Kassala," 3.
67. H. Abia, *Strategy for Development of Rainfed Agriculture* (Khartoum, 1986), 24.
68. Shannon, Report for the Institutional Specialist, Pre-Appraisal Mission, South Kassala Agricultural Project, by Templeton Shannon Associates for World Bank, 7.
69. Simpson, Alternative Strategies; Affan, *Tractorisation Experience*, Abia, *Development of Rainfed Agriculture*.
70. J. Pendergast, *The Struggle for Sudan's Soul: Political and Agrarian Roots of War and Famine* (Washington, 1990).

Some Eritreans earn income working at a camel-driven mill after the sesame harvest. Sesame oil is Sudan's staple form of cooking oil. Camels do long twelve hour shifts around giant wooden pestle systems.

4

Integration and the Cultivation of a Hard Life

> Men make their own history but not under conditions of their own choosing. They do so under the constraint of relationships and forces that direct their will and their desires.
>
> Karl Marx

> There in our land we had a land to cultivate but here in Sudan we don't.
>
> Eritrean Refugee
> *Interview in Wad el Hileau*

Introduction

In the late 1930s, a group of Sudanese immigrated across the Atbara River and founded a new settlement fifty kilometers from the Ethiopian border.[1] The village name, Wad el Hileau or "Son of the Sweet," was chosen either to honor the place from which they came (Es Sufi) or the "sweet" environment afforded by the waters of the nearby Setit River. This rural village would become home to the largest concentration of unassisted refugees in eastern Sudan. Its sixty-year story provides an ideal window through which to see interwoven dynamics between refugees and rural transformation.

This chapter has several parts. The first half focuses on Wad el Hileau's attractiveness as a site for incoming refugees to settle and for wealthy Sudanese to appropriate large chunks of land (and cheap labor) for rainfed schemes. The latter half of the chapter is concerned with state support for the expansion of rainfed schemes and the com-

Notes for this section begin on page 87.

modification of refugee labor. It gives special attention to wage labor and concomitant opportunities for reaping substantial profits.

The Locality: "A Sweet Place"

World War II first pulled the village of Wad el Hileau into the larger sphere of political and economic activity. British forces recruited wage laborers to help clear a tank trail through the Acacia forest north of the village. Originating in the Sudanese town of Showak, the road helped expedite an attack on an Italian garrison stationed on the border.[2] Soon thereafter, the village sheik was asked to begin collecting taxes. Omda Ali Awad Ajil collected £1500 (Sudanese) in annual taxes, kept roughly £300 (Sudanese) for himself, and delivered the remainder to district officials in Gedaref.[3]

In 1957, a group of ninety new families joined the Sudanese community. Most of them had left Nigeria at the turn of the 20th century when thousands of Hausa left northern Nigeria for Chad, Sudan and Eritrea. In 1956, this group moved from Eritrea across the Sudanese border and resettled at Abu Koto, twenty-five kilometers from Wad el Hileau. Conflicts erupted with nomads in the area who burned their village to the ground, but Omda Ajil provided the Hausa community with a new home and farmland in Wad el Hileau.

Both Sudanese and Hausa practiced shifting cultivation and burning *(harig)*. The size of fields and their yields were constrained by the large amount of labor needed to clear agricultural land, cultivate, weed, and harvest. Cultivation depended on a particularly intensive technique; one person using a poker-type tool with a long handled *(saluka)* to open individual holes while another dropped in seeds and covered them with soil (see Figure 4.1). Weeding, the most labor intensive aspect of production, was – and still is – done by hand with the aid of a small, one-handed digging hoe *(kandunka)*. This implement is made by fixing a blade onto an elbow-shaped branch. Its short hand requires laborers to stoop constantly. There are two main harvesting implements. A double-bladed knife *(sikkin)* is most commonly used to cut sorghum. To cut grass, forage crops, and sesame grain, workers use a short saw-edged blade fitted to a short wooden handle *(mungal)*.

The year 1967 marked a turning point in the history of Wad el Hileau. Two events prompted rapid agricultural change: (a) forty thousand *feddans* of forested land were cleared for the first rainfed schemes; and (b) the first large influx of refugees provided both a new supply of labor as well as an added demand for agricultural land.

Figure 4.1 Traditional Sudanese Farming Implements

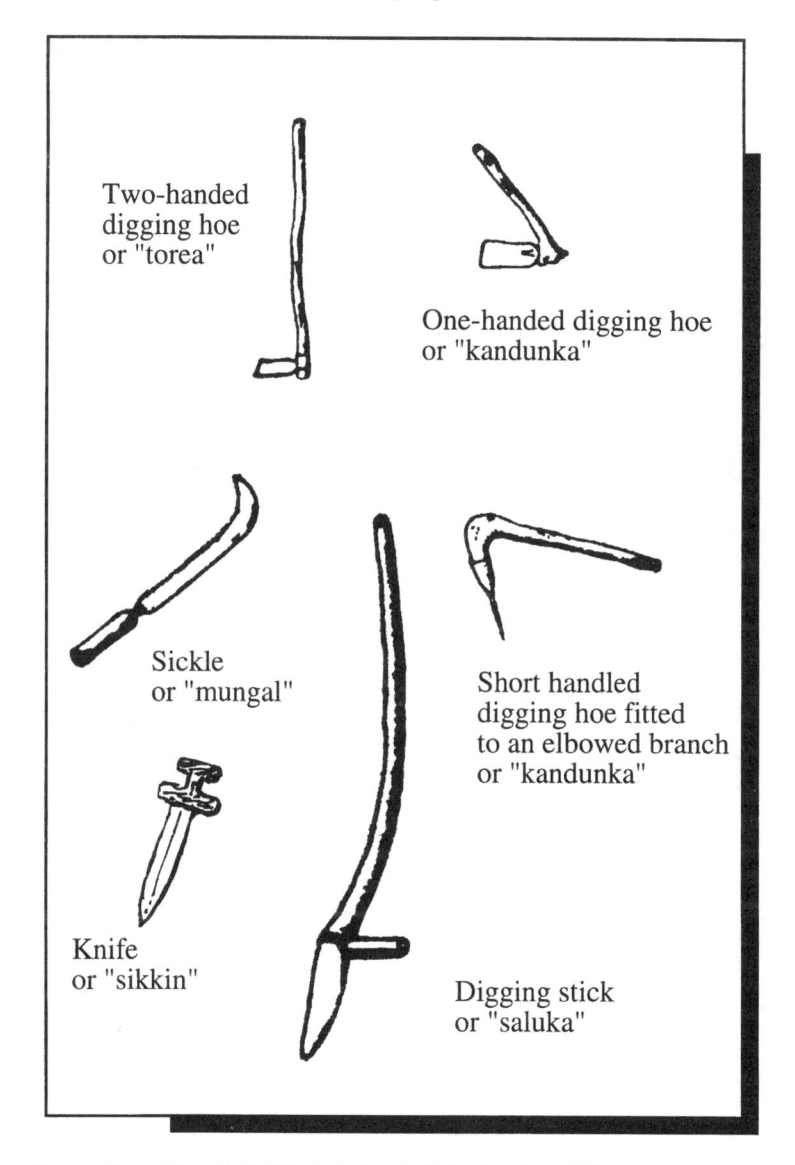

Two-handed digging hoe or "torea"

One-handed digging hoe or "kandunka"

Sickle or "mungal"

Short handled digging hoe fitted to an elbowed branch or "kandunka"

Knife or "sikkin"

Digging stick or "saluka"

Source: Adapted from J. Tothill, *Agriculture in Sudan*, London, 1948

In 1967, one village after another was decimated in the area surrounding Barentu, a town on the Gash river and home to many of the first resistance fighters. Severe fighting forced thousands to flee on foot for Sudan seventy kilometers to the west.[4] One hundred Nara families still live in Wad el Hileau, virtually all of whom left Eritrea during that first year of open conflict. Later in 1967, Ethiopian troops moved northward into Maria and Beni Amer territory. They stole cattle, destroyed property, and burned villages as they went. The majority of the forty-three thousand Maria and eighty thousand Beni Amer living in Eritrea fled to eastern Sudan in mid-1967.[5] A smaller number moved nearer to the Sudanese border, only to flee to Sudan later when the war reintensified in 1975. Most of these pastoral households attempted to bring their cattle herds with them rather than leave them in the care of relatives or a hired herder. Herds were reduced as much as 30 percent, however, due to flight loss and poor acclimatization to Sudan's heat.

When the 1967 refugees arrived in Wad el Hileau, the village sheik, Omda Ajil, remembers "receiving many of them in my own houses and giving them *dura* [sorghum] ... not by my choice, but I was obligated to receive them because they were neighbors and Muslims."[6] Although he and the assistant director of police were summoned to the provincial capital to review security issues posed by incoming refugees, they were allowed to remain in the village.[7]

Another large influx of refugees came to Wad el Hileau when the new government in Addis Ababa mounted new offensives in the mid-1970s. Om Hager and Guluje in the southwest corner of Eritrea were two main origination sites (see Map 4.1). Many of these arrivals were of West African descent (i.e., Hausa and Bargo) who had lived in Eritrea since the turn of the century. Their settlement in Eritrea was associated with rising exploitation of the peasantry in northern Nigeria and religious pilgrimages to Mecca.[8] Conservative estimates suggest that more than thirty thousand West Africans were living in Eritrea when conflict escalated in the mid-1970s.[9] One refugee gave this first-person account of fighting in southwest Eritrea:

In 1975 the Ethiopian Government raided Om-Hager and killed more than 20 civilians and burned more than ten houses. The next day the Government ordered the people to come to an open field and when the people were gathered, the Government opened fire and hundreds of people died. Then I took my family and fled to the Sudan where we can find security. This was the only chance for us because our house was destroyed and all our property was taken by the soldiers. Later on the Ethiopian Government announced that the people could come to Om-Hager and their rights will be secured. We turned back to Om-Hager and

Integration and Cultivation of a Hard Life | 71

Map 4.1 Border Region Surrounding Wad El Hileau

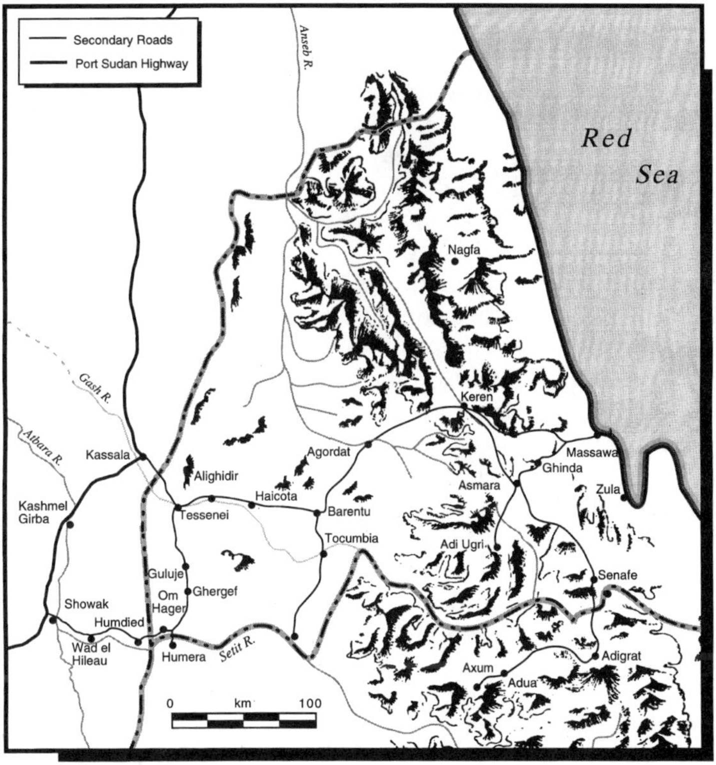

Source: Adapted from S. Longrigg, *A Short History of Eritrea*, Westport, Conn., 1974

built our houses and started to farm. When the harvest was over and the grain collected, the Ethiopian soldiers came from Humera and destroyed the town completely. This happened in 1976. During this time Ethiopian airplanes were also bombarding the town heavily. Thus, our only alternative was to cross the border to the Sudan and we took refuge in Hamzait, a village on the Sudanese border.[10]

As conflict intensified, dead bodies were seen floating down the Setit River at Wad el Hileau.[11] Meanwhile, the leadership in Ethiopia had begun to implement a political ideology of intensive socialization in the agricultural region of Humera adjacent to Eritrea and Sudan (see Map 4.1). Rather than have all their assets nationalized by the Marxist government, commercial farmers in Humera loaded up their belongings, grain, and agricultural implements and left for Sudan. They entered at Humdied and traveled on to Wad el Hileau, considered to be the nearest "safe" area. Thirty-five tractors as well as discs, trailers, water tanks, and grinding mills came with the wealthy landowners from Humera.[12] (This infusion of mechanized implements helped to expedite agricultural transformation in the area.)

All together, more than twenty-five thousand refugees arrived in 1975 and 1976. As he had done in 1967, Omda Ajil received the new refugees warmly. According to an observer at the time, Ajil was "quick to point out these refugees were welcome because they brought prosperity to the area" [e.g., more wage labor and new purchasing power].[13] Meanwhile, however, UNHCR was forced to open a reception center. Wad el Hileau, a small village of fifteen hundred people in 1967, had a total population of more than twenty-three thousand people by 1976.[14]

Most of the new arrivals wanted to remain in Wad el Hileau rather than be transferred to refugee camps. Thirty leaders petitioned the Sudanese government, in writing, to allow them to stay in Wad el Hileau:

> To the authorities responsible for Refugee Affairs in the Sudan and to the United Nations High Commissioner for Refugees. Peace be upon you.
>
> We (the Eritrean refugees of Wad el Hileau) thank you very much and appreciate your help despite the difficulties and distances. We also thank particularly the Sudanese government and the Sudanese people for their warm welcome, providing shelter on their good land, good treatment, and cooperation.
>
> We beg to be allowed to stay in Wad el Hileau. In this we appeal to your mercy and kindness. Our reasons for wishing to stay are that the village is very suitable for us in all respects. It has a very equable climate. It has a sweet water supply. It is not far from our country. We are mentally adjusted to our new situation. Please have mercy on us and permit us to

stay in Wad el Hileau. We repeat our thanks to Sudan Government which exerts great effort for our welfare. In the name of the Eritrean people living as refugees in Wad el Hileau.[15]

Repeated "transfer campaigns" took refugees to UN settlements elsewhere in eastern Sudan, but a large community of unassisted refugees remained in Wad el Hileau. In February of 1979, the Ethiopian army moved twelve kilometers inside Sudan and annexed a Sudanese military post less than thirty-five kilometers from Wad el Hileau. Their advance created considerable tension within the Sudanese army and prompted a renewed call for the evacuation of refugees. Tensions grew between authorities and the refugee community whose vocal leaders demanded that they not be transferred elsewhere. The provincial commissioner insisted, in turn, that he "would not allow refugees to act like a state within the Sudanese state" and ordered the evacuation of all Ethiopians and Eritreans in the area.[16] The reescalation of armed attacks by bandits along the border provided further cause for moving refugees out.[17] Assisted by the Sudanese military, UNHCR managed to close the Wad el Hileau camp by transferring thousands of Eritreans. In 1984, however, a new influx of twenty-nine thousand refugees forced the UN High Commissioner for Refugees to reopen a reception site in Wad el Hileau. Twenty thousand refugees were transferred on to other settlements, but nine thousand were left in a camp on the northeast side of the village that the UNHCR eventually designated a "permanent settlement."

Many factors account for Wad el Hileau's popularity as a settlement location, but proximity to Eritrea is the most important one. The village is fifty-four kilometers from the border on one of three main roads entering Sudan from Eritrea. Interviewees prioritized the following factors in response to a survey question when asked why they chose to settle in Wad el Hileau: staying close to home (43 percent); the opportunity to join relatives (19 percent); familiar environment and available services (17 percent); other reasons (21 percent). That 90 percent of the refugee population came directly from their homeland is further evidence of the importance of proximity. During the first few agricultural seasons after their exodus in 1975, refugees could still return to their fields at Om Hager. Pastoralists also could return to check the well-being of livestock herds left in the care of relatives or hired herders. Other refugees traveled back to Eritrea to visit relatives or attend important social gatherings (i.e., weddings and funerals). By the late 1970s, however, transborder movement was reduced to a minimum due to the occupation of lower Eritrea by Ethiopian troops as well as increased land mines on roads. Nevertheless, refugees still desired to be "near home," a trend noted in other refugee contexts.[18] Wad el Hileau allowed more politically conscious refugees to keep abreast of progress on the front lines. Both the ELF and the EPLF established offices in Wad el Hileau to raise money, morale, and political awareness as well as to provide supplemental food stuffs to soldiers' families.[19] In 1984, the EPLF began paying monthly salaries. Eventually the payroll included more than 160 men or their families.[20]

May of 1991 marked the end of the war and the attainment of freedom (*huria*). But of nearly one thousand unassisted households residing in Wad el Hileau, less than twenty repatriated back to Eritrea during the first two years after the cessation of conflict. Why the removal of pressures that forced them to migrate was insufficient to assure their return is a question that relates in large measure to the various ways in which refugees have been integrated into the host economy and society.

The Reality: A Hard Life

Wad el Hileau remains home to the largest concentration of rural, unassisted refugees in Sudan. Sixty-five percent of Wad el Hileau's total population consists of unassisted refugees (see census on page 194). They are distributed throughout the village in wards under the jurisdiction of different sheiks. The most notable feature of Map 4.2, a sketch map of the field site, is the social organization of sub-communities. The original village was built on the highest ground available; the Sudanese community occupied the western portion of the village and a small West African immigrant community resided on the eastern side leaving the village bounded on the south by the Setit River and on the north by a large wadi that drains off surface water during the rainy season. The current layout reflects the sequence of three major refugee influxes, primarily involving displaced people from six different ethnic communities in western Eritrea.

In 1967, refugees from three different Nara villages in Eritrea established separate wards in the east, west, and north corners of the village. (Sudanese often use the designation of "Baria," a reference that Nara people consider to be a derogatory one.) Refugees from two pastoral communities – Beni Amer and Maria – settled along the southern rim of the village, thereby optimizing access to the river for watering livestock. Twelve hundred current residents are associated with early arrivals. The 1970s influx was comprised primarily of

Map 4.2 Field Map of Ethnic Wards and Pattern of Settlement at Wad El Hileau

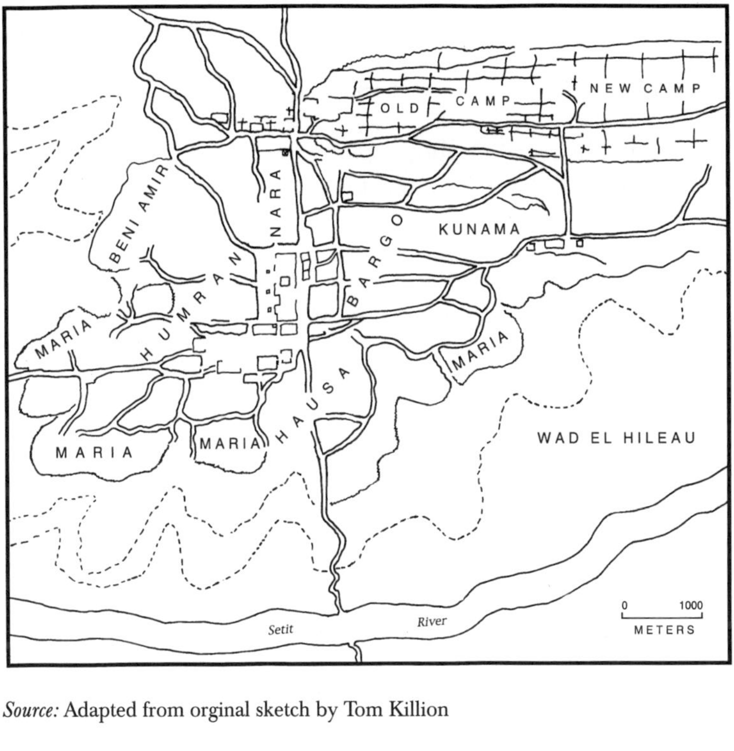

Source: Adapted from orginal sketch by Tom Killion

Hausa and Bargo people. (Under the broader terms adopted by the Organization of African Unity, these people of West African descent were considered refugees because they had been forced to leave their place of "habitual residence.") They settled alongside the original West African community in the northeast portion of the village. Taken together, this influx constitutes twenty-five hundred of the village's ninety-two hundred inhabitants.[21] Refugees from a sixth ethnic group, the Kunama, reside on the least desirable land in Wad el Hileau, adjacent to the refugee camp and at the foot of a large flood plain. (Sudanese often use the designation "Baza," a reference which Kunama consider to be a derogatory one.)

Table 4.1 compares the occupational structure of the unassisted population before flight with that of 1988. It depicts a significant move into agricultural wage labor or non farm employment. The realignment also represents a marked shift from relative well-being to poverty. Refugees are forced to rely on a vast array of "survival occupations." These include agricultural wage labor, in particular; as well as collection and sale of water, wood, and charcoal; alcohol brewing and sales; petty trade of grain, vegetables, charcoal, cigarettes, and chewing tobacco; assorted handicrafts such as making wooden beds or blacksmithing; prostitution; smuggling items such as coffee, tea, soap, and cigarettes; and low-salaried employment as porters, waiters, clothes washers, and sales clerks. At very best, these survival occupations provide a meager income.

Table 4.1 Employment Distribution of Study Population in Eritrea and Sudan, 1988

Occupation	Eritrea (percentage)	Sudan (percentage)
Small-holder cultivation only	44.0	11.0
Small-holder cultivation and agricultural wage labor	3.5	12.0
Small-holder cultivation and nonfarm employment	9.5	25.0
Small-holder cultivation, agricultural wage labor, and nonfarm employment	0.0	11.0
Livestock herding only	35.0	11.0
Livestock herding and agricultural wage labor	0.0	3.0
Livestock herding and nonfarm employment	2.0	9.0
Livestock herding, small-holder cultivation, and nonfarm employment	0.0	5.0
Agricultural wage labor only	0.0	2.0
Agricultural wage labor and nonfarm employment	1.0	7.0
Nonfarm employment only	5.0	4.0
Total	100.0	100.0

Source: Household survey (N = 131) conducted by author in Wad el Hileau, December 1987 through June 1988

Refugee poverty has been measured in several ways, but a "first floor" and "second floor" distinction has been employed in eastern Sudan.[22] Meeting the first floor needs involves the absolute basic needs for existence, that is, food, clothing, shelter, and health. Meeting the second floor involves quality of life concerns, that is, maintaining a living standard with more than the basic needs (both psychological and social). Based upon detailed income data from refugees at six field sites throughout eastern Sudan, Bulcha reported that 64 percent of all respondents earned an income below the first floor, "existence minimum."[23] The same refugees were asked to compare their present standard of living with that of their homeland. Seventy-four percent answered that they had become poorer, 18 percent indicated that they had the same standard of living, and 6 percent considered themselves to be better off.[24] Another research project assessed poverty levels in Wad el Hileau. In early 1984, a team of research assistants compiled income data from a sample of forty-two Eritrean households. Fifty-two percent of the households fell below a predetermined "self-sufficiency threshold" despite the fact that most of them had been in Sudan for more than ten years.[25]

What explains this lack of economic well-being? Why is poverty endemic among rural refugees? And why are refugee households locked into a "minimum existence"? At one level, the answers can be attributed to the fact that involuntary migrants typically arrive without prior preparation, bring very little capital, and face severe employment constraints. But less immediate forces are no less important. The process and pace of agrarian change occurring out in fields is, for example, a key facet of refugee poverty. Hence, the remainder of the chapter places the rapid expansion of mechanized agriculture into a localized and specific context. Particular attention is paid to the process of labor commodification and how the process of agricultural change has precipitated the collapse of reciprocity among refugees.

Breaking Ground: Tractors and Agricultural Intensification

The year 1967 marked a turning point in Wad el Hileau's history and the lives of its inhabitants. In Khartoum, Sudan's capital, the World Bank shifted its attention and support to rainfed agriculture. In Wad el Hileau, forty to sixty thousand *feddans* of forested area were cleared for mechanized schemes during that year alone. Land surveys have not ever been conducted for the area, so acreage is difficult to determine with any exactitude.[26] But the four hundred *mushrooahs* registered with the Mechanized Farming Corporation encompass as much as 450,000 *feddans*.[27] The largest ones north of Wad el Hileau in an area known as Wad Omer for its prominent inselberg, are more than five thousand *feddans* in size. The largest one in the Fashaga, a triangular tract of land to the south of Wad el Hileau bordered by the boundary with Ethiopia (east), the Atbara River (west), and the Setit River (north), is reported to be greater than ten thousand *feddans* in size. The high labor demands associated with scheme expansion precipitated the widespread exchange of labor as a monetized commodity and the wholesale reorganization of the social relationships of production for Wad el Hileau's residents, both Sudanese and refugees.

Two rainfed crops, sorghum *(dura)* and sesame *(sim-sim),* dominate the agriculture of the area. Both are characterized by low inputs and low yields. Since no satisfactory high-yielding sorghum varieties exist in Sudan, it is almost impossible to increase productivity per unit area.[28] To raise financial returns, the only alternative is to expand the area under cultivation by employing tractors and large labor forces. The most labor-intensive stage of the agricultural cycle occurs during a forty-five-day period in late August and the month of September. Work parties cut weeds away from both crops with a short-shafted hand hoe and thin sorghum by hand. Estimates obtained elsewhere in Sudan vary between 2.0 and 2.5 person/days to weed each *feddan.*[29] My scheme management studies suggest an average of 1.92 person/days a *feddan* for schemes in the low moisture area north of Wad el Hileau and as many as 3.5 person/days in a higher moisture regime further south (i.e., 600 mm of rainfall or more).[30] Early rains necessitate spot weeding of low-lying areas of the field, which collect more rainfall. Heavy rains require weeding the entire scheme a second time.

Sesame harvest follows the weeding segment. Sizable labor parties are required to reap sesame in a timely manner. If harvest does not occur within ten days after it ripens, as much as 15 percent of a year's crop can be lost to dehiscence.[31] In late October, wage laborers turn their attention back to sorghum. In Sudan, moving combines have not harvested multi-headed sorghum efficiently so laborers are required to cut and collect the stalks of grain manually and, in many cases, to thresh and winnow it by hand.

The production areas adjacent to Wad el Hileau (314,000 *feddans*) require an estimated 13,500 workers during the peak of the weeding process in July and August, 8,500 during the sesame harvest, and another 3,750 during the sorghum harvest. Resident Sudanese supply only a small portion of the needed labor. Instead, Eritrean refugees and migrants from western and southern Sudan complete the bulk of the weeding and harvest work on *mushrooah* schemes. The importance of mechanized agriculture to refugee resettlement is ascribed, in part, to the fact that rainfed schemes provide the context for a widespread exchange between two types of commodity owners, i.e., those who purchase labor and those who sell it. The success of scheme operators, who own money and have access to the means of production, is largely dependent upon their appropriation of labor from refugees. Competition between Eritreans and Sudanese to become scheme operators does not exist because there are no Eritreans refugees who possess sufficient capital, equipment, or experience to manage a large scheme, and they are barred from leasing land from the government.

The coming of the tractor also prompted the reorganization of labor relationships among small-holders in the area. Before the tractors' arrival, field sizes were measured in the farming hinterlands *(bildats)* with knotted rope. To defray their operating costs, however, scheme operators began renting out their tractors to plow small plots. The initial rate was £1.5–2.0 (Sudanese) for five *feddans*. Both Sudanese and refugee farmers began turning from traditional methods of cultivation to mechanized cultivation. Small farmers welcomed tractors because mechanized plowing eliminated the manual labor necessary for planting; discing turned the soils deeply, thereby reducing weeds and the need for more labor to remove them; and, tractorization opened the door for expanding the size of small-scale farms. By the mid-1970s, tractors had become the primary method of cultivation among farmers based in Wad el Hileau. This was graphically symbolized by the new unit of land measurement – the tractor hour. Small-holders report the size of their fields in five *feddan* increments because so many hire tractors to disc fields; tractors are hired by the hour, and five *feddans* is the area that can be plowed in one hour by a tractor.

Mechanization brought new land into cultivation, which in turn prompted the growth of wage labor. In the past, field size was primarily a function of family size. If additional labor was needed to weed or harvest, a farmer called a cooperative work party (*nafir*). Men, women, and children would congregate to work together on a given day that ended with a shared meal. Wealthier farmers were expected to slaughter a goat or sheep for the occasion. *Nafirs* were noncommodified exchanges of labor built upon relationships of reciprocity among neighbors and kin. But tractors brought two types of wage labor into use on the small-holders' farms – *dahawa*, three hours of work in the morning, and *yoomiiya*, a full work day seven and a half hours in length. Most employers prefer *dahawa* because workers finish by morning breakfast (10:00 am) and employers are not required to provide food. Much of this work was predicated on the close proximity of the village *bildat*, the immediate farming area adjacent to the village, reserved for small-holders.

The combined pressure of scheme expansion, the use of tractors on small farms, and periodic refugee influxes precipitated a land squeeze for the inhabitants of Wad el Hileau. By the mid-1970s, small farmers had expanded their fields to rounded tractor-hour equivalents, merchants had begun a new set of larger farms beyond the village *bildat*, and *mushrooahs* encompassed most of the arable territory beyond these farms. By 1975, more than sixty-five thousand *feddans* had been brought under cultivation.[32] This capped the expansion of the village *bildat*, a fact that became very important when the 1975 influx of Eritreans arrived in Wad el Hileau. A few early arrivals managed to claim land in the interstitial areas throughout the *bildat*, but most could not secure farming land. Only 16 percent of those refugees who arrived after 1975 own land.

Sowing Seeds: The State and Capital Formation

The Sudanese state has consistently favored the expansion of agrarian capitalism in eastern Sudan. It began with the Agrarian Reform Act (1968), which waived investors' debts for failing cotton schemes, thereby facilitating a shift to rainfed *mushrooah* schemes instead.[33] Since then, government policy has consistently placed the services of the state at the disposal of agrarian capital. For the last three decades, *mushrooah* operators have paid leasing fees well below the market value for rented land. Those under the supervision of the Mechanized Farming Corporation (MFC) paid 5 Sudanese piasters per *feddan* during early 1970s, 10 piasters per *feddan* from 1978 to 1983, and £1.0 (Sudanese) or $0.22 US at 1987 exchange rates per *feddan* from 1983 to 1987.[34] Moreover, the MFC has failed to enforce *mushrooah* regulations established by the state. Regulations require that one third of each *mushrooah* be left fallow, another one third be planted in food crops, and the remaining one third be planted in an alternative crop to ensure soil fertility. Instead, *mushrooahs* are consistently mono-cropped, and required shelter belt regulations have been ignored completely as well. A recent land use study based on detailed analysis of imagery concluded that 72 percent of the entire eastern rainlands were farmed.[35] State support underlies the dramatic transformation of the landscape. As summarized in the words of a recent World Bank report, "The Board of Directors [for the MFC] seem largely to represent large farmers' short-term interests."[36] According to the 1972 Land Registration Act, the Sudanese government retains ownership of *mushrooah* lands. There are no "owners" in a tightly defined legal sense, only "operators" who may own capital but must lease land from the government. But operators substitute their annual lease receipts from the regional government as a title. Unsurveyed *mushrooahs* are leased from the district, regional, or provincial government. Typically, those who farm more than one thousand *feddans* rent the first thousand "officially" and then farm the remaining land without payment, or, they lease additional land under another family member's name.

A study by the International Labor Organization (ILO) found that most scheme operators consider themselves to be the owners of the land they cultivated.[37] Although the same study concluded that operators recognized prohibitions on renting and selling their *mushrooahs*, fieldwork for the present study suggests the contrary. Not having a legal title to "their" land does not keep them from buying, selling, renting, and sharecropping their schemes. For example, one merchant in Wad el Hileau produced this January 1986 bill of sale: "I, Sabaah Al Kher, hereby announce that I have given up my share of the *mushrooah* (1000 *feddans*) for £2000 (Sudanese) to Hassan Beshir Abdul Wahab which is situated north of Mohammed Omer, west of Sulieman Abdulrahman, and I received the above mentioned money and this certificate for that amount – Sabaah Al Kher." Another operator rented his *mushrooah* for £3,500 (Sudanese) during the 1986/87 season and sharecropped it with a 15/85 split – 15 percent to the land "owner" and 85 percent to the operator – during the 1987/88 season.[38] This ratio is common throughout the area. In fact, it is not uncommon for a vacant *mushrooah* to be plowed and planted without formal permission from the "owner" based on an informal agreement among operators that "empty" *mushrooahs* can be used if the "owner" receives 15 percent of the yield. The fact that *mushrooahs* are rented, sold, and sharecropped despite prohibitions against such practices is one of several ways in which operators remain virtually unanswerable to the state.

Meanwhile, the Agricultural Bank of Sudan (ABS) issues credit to *mushrooah* operators at very generous interest rates. ABS loans are issued to as many as seven hundred operators in the Gedaref region each year.[39] In 1987, the ABS offered 15 percent interest rates for short-term, seasonal loans and 22 percent rates on two year tractor loans, at a time at which the inflation rate was well above 46.5 percent per annum.[40] In addition to cheap credit, operators are able to repay a substantial portion of their loans in kind, rather than in cash. In the mid-1980s, for example, the ABS Branch in Gedaref received grain for loan repayments equivalent in value to five million Sudanese pounds per year.[41]

The state also plays another supportive role by providing laborers with subsidized food rations of sorghum flour, cooking oil, dried fish, lentils, onions, dried okra, coffee, sugar, and tea. *Mushrooah* operators can purchase a set quota of diesel fuel, engine oil, and foodstuffs at subsidized rates from the state through the Large Farmers' Association. Procurement of subsidized fuel and foodstuffs from the state is the virtual *raison d'etre* of the Large Farmers' Association, whose membership is limited to those cultivating more than five hundred *feddans*. Mushrooah operators with more than one thousand *feddans* usually receive an additional amount of fuel and engine oil as well. Often senior members of the association receive additional subsidized items such as cigarettes, tractor batteries, axle grease, and automobile fuel.

Pulling Weeds: Refugees and Labor Commodification

Once rains stabilize in late June or early July and the first flush of weeds appear, tractors begin cultivating fields.[42] Two or three weeks after sowing, the most labor-intensive stage of the agricultural cycle begins. Sorghum and sesame are both weeded. Workers thin sorghum by uprooting individual sprouts by hand and cut the weeds off at soil level using a short-shafted hand hoe. Two weedings (July 7 to 30 and August 1 to 15) are necessary if rains are unusually early or heavy. Most operators argue that the expense of a second weeding is not justified by the extra crop yields. Hence, *mushrooah* operators opt for a complete weeding during the month of August followed by spot weeding in sections of the field where weeds are particularly dense. If the initial flush of weeds is dense, operators often replow and reseed their land again to minimize weeding costs. In this manner, they work the area's rainfall to their advantage. *Mushrooah* operators for areas south of Wad el Hileau, however, have no alternative but to absorb heavy labor costs.

Day labor for weeding or harvesting is the exception rather than rule on *mushrooahs*. Instead, small work parties are contracted to weed a specific portion of the field. The "contract" or *guwaal* is a verbal agreement between a work party and the manager of a *mushrooah* (*wakeel*) for weeding or harvesting. A typical work party is comprised of three to four members. One member negotiates with the *wakeel* to establish the terms of the *guwaal* (i.e., its size and price). After reaching an agreement the plot is marked with stakes or bushes, and weeding begins. The operator provides food and shelter for as long as it takes the work party to complete the guwaal. The operator or his foreman pays the group a lump sum upon completion of the work, which is then split among its members.

The size of the work party and the size of contracted area are both chosen with care. To fulfill the terms of their verbal contract, the laborers must thoroughly "clean" the negotiated section, regardless of how many days that may take. If laborers contract too large an area, they may finish weeding at one end of the plot only to have new weeds reemerge where they had begun. If a member of the work party becomes sick, the work slows, thereby increasing the likelihood that if there is more rain, weeds will reemerge, and remaining members of the work party will become exhausted or sick. Refugees in Wad el Hileau recounted frequent instances when they became locked into a "perpetual *guwaal*" due to heavy rain, illness, or exhaustion. In such cases, laborers can either leave the *mushrooah* without pay or keep working until the manager gives them a portion of their pay and releases them from their contract.

Laborers generally work from dawn to dusk with breaks for breakfast *(fatuur)* and a mid-day meal *(ghaada)*. Bearing in mind that the weeding segment is generally completed within a thirty-day period, *mushrooahs* require work parties of seventy-five to one hundred laborers apiece at the height of the weeding cycle. Thus, the Wad el Hileau region requires between fifteen and twenty thousand workers during the peak of the weeding season. Resident Sudanese supply only a small portion of the needed labor force. Most migrants from western Sudan do not come this far east. Instead refugees supply the bulk of the labor demand. Hamid Asalah Hangoos is one of those refugees. His field experience typifies that of many others.

> In 1967, despite the onset of conflict in his village of Tucumbia, Hamid remained in Eritrea rather than flee to Sudan as did many members of their community. Using oxen to plow, he and his wife expanded their sorghum and millet field to as many as twenty-five *feddans*. Significantly, they depended on group work parties to complete many agricultural tasks. These nafirs brought ten people together on average. As Hamid puts it: "In Eritrea, people are more cooperative so that the poor do not suffer as much." Occasionally Hamid did wage labor, but that work remained quite secondary in two senses – most wage labor was done during "idle time" (the dry season) and most wages were used for "luxury needs" rather than subsistence needs.
>
> In 1978, Hamid was pressured to join the Eritrean Liberation Front (ELF). Until then, he summarizes his life as one in which "life was going

up." He fought two years but received no salary thus leaving his family completely dependent upon relatives. In 1980, Hamid arrived in Wad el Hileau to visit a sister. Soon thereafter, he received word that fighting was intensifying in Tucumbia so he sent for his family to join him. The family of five settled on the southeastern edge of Wad el Hileau along with many other Kunama refugees. As for most refugees, agricultural wage labor has been, and remains, Hamid's only means of provisioning the family. Hamid summarizes his livelihood in terse fashion: "My only work is *kalla* (i.e., wages earned away from home) .... It is what I have to do."

There are two main variations in his constant cycle of wage work – changes in the type of work and brief rests back in Wad el Hileau. Hamid weeds in June, July, and August. He cuts sesame in October. He harvests sorghum in November, December, January, and, if he is fortunate, on into February. In early March, Hamid begins charcoal work. His 1993 wages follow that sequence: £4,656 (Sudanese) for eighteen days of clearing brush on *mushrooahs* with two other men; £1,656 (Sudanese) from another four days of brush clearing with two others; £3,000 (Sudanese) for charcoal work (100 bags of charcoal at £30 apiece); £400 (Sudanese) for ten days of weeding a *mushrooah* in an unfinished *guaal* contract with another man; £9,000 (Sudanese) as his split from eight days of weeding on *guaal* contract with three other men on the Fashaga; £3,000 (Sudanese) for cutting *sim-sim* (£200 per *hilla*); £13,000 (Sudanese) from forty-five days of cutting *dura* with his family (130 sacks of *dura* at £100 apiece). The total year's earnings of £34,712 (Sudanese) represent the price of eighteen sacks of sorghum; that is, approximately four-fifths of the family's grain needs and nothing more.

Hamid's family supplements his income in several ways. His wife, Amoona, gleaned a half sack of sorghum from a deserted scheme and grew two more by planting two *feddans* on the edge of the *mushrooah*. During the dry season while he is away doing charcoal, she brews sorghum beer for sale to patrons who are willing to visit her home, usually under cover of night. Although illegal, she makes money as long as she is not fined or imprisoned. Subject to frequent harassment by the police, when she was last arrested she successfully argued that "her husband was away and she had to provide for their small children." Meanwhile, Hamid's eldest daughter, eighteen-year-old Afica, earns income selling biscuits during the dry season and then doing *mushrooah* work with other Kunama women. In 1993, she earned £2,500 (Sudanese) from ten days of weeding with five girls and another £2,000 (Sudanese) from five days with four others. Hamid's younger daughter Amoona started weeding at age seven and cutting dura at the age of ten. All this work notwithstanding, at one point during the last year Hamid's family went hungry for days. After four or five days without food, his daughter sold three grams of gold. Survival for this family and many more like them depends on deploying the one major resource they have, exiled as they are from home – their labor.

Reaping Harvest: Owners and Capital Accumulation

Harvesting season begins with sesame, a crop that takes from early July to mid-October to reach maturity. Once ripe, sesame is very susceptible to drying out, whereby seed heads shatter and burst (dehiscence). Fifteen percent of a year's harvest can be lost if the crop is not harvested within ten days. Hence, sesame demands both careful handling and timely harvesting. The first requirement means that it must be harvested completely by hand; the second necessitates another large labor party to complete the task.[44] Because the timing is so critical, managers secure as many workers as possible. For the same reason wage rates for cutting sesame are significantly higher than for any of the other three main forms of agricultural work in eastern Sudan – weeding, harvesting rainfed sorghum, and harvesting cotton on irrigated schemes.

Sorghum harvest usually begins in early November, but timing is less crucial than with sesame. The labor is also less demanding physically. Rather than stooping to cut each stalk at soil level (as with sesame), workers cut sorghum just below the head. Multi-headed sorghum has not been harvested efficiently in Sudan with moving combines, but combines are sometimes used as stationary threshing machines beside piled sorghum. Far more commonly, one sees sorghum being threshed manually, usually by a trio of men beating the heads with sticks or wooden T-shaped flails in a rhythmic sequence on a mud-packed threshing floor (*gelli'itta*). Working in this fashion, three man can winnow approximately two sacks (90.9 kilograms) an hour.[45]

What kind of net profits are *mushrooah* operators able to obtain? Estimates must be qualified as suggestive rather than definitive because time-series data for profitability are not available. Previous studies rely on balance sheets from a single year. One study in the Gedaref region concluded that operators netted profits of 93 percent for sorghum and 113 percent for sesame.[46] Another study estimated a 53.3 percent return on capital for *mushrooahs* in western Sudan.[47] Many factors determine profit margins, but three are most important – yields, cheap labor, and market price. Yield data for individual *mushrooahs* in the Fashaga or Wad Omer region (or elsewhere in Sudan) are not available in a longitudinal time series. Yield data for the Wad el Hileau vicinity and the surrounding region indicate a substantial decrease in fertility associated with continual use (see Chapter 3).[48]

The ability of operators to raise profits depends greatly on their ability to hold grain reserves until the "price is right." After harvest, most operators immediately sell 50 to 70 percent of their crop in order to cover production costs or repay temporary loans. However, market prices are at their lowest point at this time.[49] Storage of the harvested crop for a few months can raise profit margins significantly. The basic means of capital accumulation occurs through the appropriation of cheap wage labor, and, much of that from exiled refugees. Contracting labor on a piecemeal basis is important for reasons beyond its sheer predominance. The *guwaal* labor arrangement is tailor-made for operators. Precipitation works to their advantage in two ways: a) workers are forced to extend their working day to its limits given the constant possibility of rains forcing them to reweed; and b) wage laborers are usually intent on finishing each *guwaal* as soon as possible given the abbreviated periods of time in which their labor is in demand. Except for merchants, everyone in Wad el Hileau must generate the majority of their cash incomes during the brief agricultural season because the dry season offers very few income-generating opportunities. In fact, most households are financially strapped by April, a month that is commonly referred to as "the penniless month." Thus the seasonal nature of agricultural labor raises the amount of labor expended by workers and the amount of profit procured by operators.[50]

Conclusion

Social formations prior to their economic transformation are ones in which most production is geared to producers' use or to discharge kinship obligations.[51] Until the late 1960s, neither land nor labor were widely sold as commodities in the border region of eastern Sudan. Mechanized rainfed schemes, their expansion, and their fundamental requirement for wage labor has precipitated the wholesale reorganization of social relationships of production in a region which is also home to several hundred thousand refugees. The new system of production has created economic relationships of coercion and exploitation with corresponding social relationships of dependence and mastery. Refugee households are engaged in competitive, class-based social relations of production in which many must forfeit much of the value of their labor to members of the classes above them, thereby setting in motion the process of social differentiation. The next chapter specifies the mechanisms and relationships that define the predominant class positions for Eritreans exiled in Wad el Hileau.

Notes

1. Both major groups of ethnic Sudanese in Wad el Hileau – the Humran and Ja'aliin – were forced to live in Eritrea at one time. In 1822, the Ja'aliin killed the Egyptian Pasha's son and were forced to flee to the Humera area of Ethiopia for protection. In the 1880s, the principal Humran sheik during the Mahdi's era aligned himself against the Mahdi and therefore, was forced to flee into Ethiopia as well.
2. The oldest sheik in Wad el Hileau (Ali Awad Ajil) recalls a 1941 occasion when a British officer purchased seventy camels in Wad el Hileau which he then had driven in a close-bunched herd in front of his armored vehicles to detonate land mines hidden on the road to Om Hager (Field Note Entry 8:42).
3. Field Note Entry 8:42.
4. Field Interview 102.
5. Trevaskis, *Eritrea*, 132.
6. Ajil, Interview.
7. M. el Sammani and M. Adam, "Settlement Project for Ethiopian Refugees from Eritrea in East Central Sudan," Preliminary report for UNHCR (London, 1976), Entry 10.1.76.
8. Recent scholarship suggests that this was not "a natural process, free from contradictions, which took place outside of, and unconnected with, the existence of a colonial or neo-colonial society." M. Duffield, "Change Among West African Settlers in Northern Sudan," *Review of African Political Economy* 26 (1983), 46. The introduction of the capitalist relations of production and the colonial state gradually eliminated captive or slave labor from the Fulani Emirs (an estimated one quarter to one half of the population of the Fulani Emirates), thereby expanding the already large, but poor peasantry. At the same time, the peasantry was being reorganized under the imposition of "indirect rule" to produce cash crops for export. Not surprisingly, the poorest sections of the peasantry were the first to leave as reflected by the lack of traders or craftsmen in the ranks of the migrants. Exogenous factors such as drought, famine, and land shortages sped up the process as well. M. Watts, *Silent Violence: Food, Famine, and Peasantry in Northern Nigeria* (Berkeley, 1983).
9. Longrigg, *Short History of Eritrea*.
10. Refugee cited in D. Smock, "Eritrean Refugees in Sudan," *Journal of Modern African Studies* 20 (1982): 454–55.
11. el Sammani and Martin, "Settlement Project."
12. M. el Sammani, Original Field Notes from Consulting Assignment for Huntington Associates, Entry 1, Dated 5.1.76., 9.
13. Karadawi, "Refugee Policy in the Sudan," 115.
14. Translation of letter in el Sammani and Martin, "Settlement Project."
15. Karadawi, "Refugee Policy in the Sudan," 187.
16. In early 1981, *shiftas* attacked the daily bus from Kassala to Wad el Hileau (Field Note Entry 190).
17. Chambers, "Rural Refugees in Africa," 381–92; Hansen, "Refugee Dynamics," 175–94; Harrell-Bond, *Imposing Aid*.
18. T. Johnson, "Eritrean Refugees in Sudan," 418. Note also that the ELF office remained in Wad el Hileau long after its field activity ended in 1981.
19. The local EPLF administrator reported the following enlisters from Wad el Hileau: sixty to seventy Nara, fifty Kunama, fifty Aswa'orta, fifteen to twenty Belain (Field Note Entry, 5:7).
20. Ethiopian refugees are the definite minority in Wad el Hileau (6 percent). They represent four major ethnic groups – the Amhara, Tigrean, Jabarta, and Woll-

geyiet. All but the last are predominately Coptic Christians. (The Jabarta are actually Wollgeyeit by ethnic descent but so named because of their conversion to Islam.) Most of the Ethiopian community in Wad el Hileau own or rent homes around the western portion of the market (*souq*). With the possible exception of the Jabarta, they receive differential treatment compared to Eritrean refugees. They must, for example, obtain travel permits from the local police, and Amharan refugees are often forced to offer bribes to checkpoint officials under the threat of imprisonment even if they carry an official travel permit.

21. M. Bulcha, *Flight and Integration*.
22. Ibid., 171.
23. Ibid.
24. J. Wijbrandi, *Organized and Spontaneous Settlement in Eastern Sudan: Two Case Studies on Integration of Rural Refugees* (Amsterdam, 1986), 93.
25. In 1971, the Regional MFC office began to record "unsurveyed" *mushrooahs* assuming that "it was just a matter of time before these farms were demarcated and regularized." *Mushrooah* operators registered with the MFC on the assumption that doing so would provide a defendable claim to a land lease when, and if, *mushrooahs* in the area were surveyed. H. Abia, *Strategy for Development*, 28.
26. MFC, Mechanized Farming Corporation Report – Gedaref, 1981 and 1989.
27. I. el Bagir et. al., *Labor Markets in the Sudan, A Study Carried Out Within the Framework of the ILO/UNHCR Project on Income-Generating Activities for Refugees in Eastern and Central Sudan*, (Geneva, 1984).
28. Simpson and Simpson, Alternative Strategies, 39; G. Mickels and H. Yousif, The Problems for Mechanization of Agriculture in Refugee Settlement Areas of Eastern Sudan: A Study of Context and Beneficiaries, Report for FINNIDA (1987), 18.
29. J. Bascom, "Food, Wages, and Profits: Mechanized Schemes and the Sudanese State," *Economic Geography* 66 (1990), 147.
30. S. el Medani, "Rainfed Mechanized Farming in Southern Gedaref," *The Agricultural Sector of Sudan: Policy and Systems Studies*, (London, 1986), 207.
31. Field Note Entry 9:A – MFC.
32. F. Babiker, *The Sudanese Bourgeoisie – Vanguard of Development?* (London, 1984), 48.
33. M. Ib Nauf, Interview with the Eastern Region Officer for the Mechanized Farming Corporation, Khartoum, 16 April 1988.
34. (SKAP), Land Use Survey Report, K1.
35. Shannon, Report of the Institutional Specialist, Attachment 3:5.
36. ILO report cited in Mickels and Yousif, Problems for Mechanization, 16.
37. Field Note Entry 3:25.
38. World Bank, South Kassala Agriculture Project.
39. In 1984, then President Nimeri introduced Islamization to Sudan. "Interest rates" per se were officially banned under Islamic law. However, the new "marginal profit" method is still in essence an interest rate. (A. el Awad, Interview with Collection and Loan Officer for the Agricultural Bank of Sudan, Gedaref Office (7 July 1988). Also see el Shazali, "Eritreans in Kassala," III–21.
40. Mickels and Yousif, Problems for Mechanization, 20.
41. The first discing is to control newly germinating weeds and prepare the surface for seeds. *Mushrooahs* are sown during the second discing, either by mounting a seed drill over the top of the discs or hiring two men to ride the disc and cast seeds in front of it as the tractor moves through the field. A tractor generally takes about fourteen days of twenty hours apiece to cultivate and sow a one thousand *feddan mushrooah* (drawing 32 plate disc harrows). Two teams, comprised of a driver (*suwa'ag*) and an assistant, are employed for the peak period of

Integration and Cultivation of a Hard Life | 89

the season. Cultivation of one *mushrooah* may take from thirty to forty-five days, depending on the frequency of rainfall and mechanical breakdowns.
42. Simpson and Simpson, Alternative Strategies, 39; Mickels and Yousif, Problems for Mechanization, 18.
43. Sesame is first cut by hand using a small sickle and bundled into small hand-sized bunches (*ropta*). Bunches of four *ropta* apiece are tied together to make a *tukul*, stacked in piles of four hundred *tukuls* apiece (*hillas*), and left to dry. A simple threshing operation follows a week to ten days later. A large tarp (or sheet) is spread on the ground next to a *hilla* of sesame, a worker takes a *tukul* (or bunch) in each hand, with the heads facing downwards. He then beats the two bundles together shaking the seed out onto the tarp, the harvested seeds are collected and bagged into jute sacks (76.9 kilograms of sesame per sack). Each of the three units – *ropta, tukul, and hilla* – plays a different function in the harvesting process. The *ropta* is the convenient unit to cut at a time (a handful); the *tukul* is the convenient unit for beating together, but must be tied together before drying to minimize shattering; and a *hilla* is a convenient unit to minimize carrying sesame within the field, to pay wage laborers, and from which to bag sesame before moving to another section of the field.
44. The entire harvesting operation was conducted with manual labor until the mid-1970s. Only in poor seasons, when combines are more available and therefore cheaper, do *mushrooah* operators in the Wad el Hileau area hire them. During the very poor 1987/88 season, for example, the price of £3.5 (Sudanese) per sack threshed mechanically compared favorably with the price of £5.0 (Sudanese) per sack for manual threshing.
45. Abia, "Development of Rainfed Agriculture," Annex IV:II.
46. Affan, *Tractorisation Experience*.
47. J. O'Brien, "How Traditional is 'Traditional' Agriculture?" *ESRC Bulletin*, No. 62 (1977); Simpson and Simpson, Alternative Strategies; Affan, *Tractorisation Experience*.
48. el Medani, "Rainfed Mechanized Farming," 208.
49. The extractive nature of *guwaaks* is illustrated by Affan's research on the actual labor invested in a *mushrooah*. Based on detailed data, he found that, on average, an operator contributes 3.4 percent of the work days expended on *mushrooahs* and receives 56.1 percent of its net incomes, while workers contribute 96.6 percent of the expended days of labor for which they receive 43.9 percent of the net income. Affan, *Tractorisation Experience*, 75.
50. Sahlins, cited in Wolf, *Peasants*, 3.

Eritrean refugees have provided a great deal of the agricultural labor in eastern Sudan. Flanked by a vast mushrooah *scheme, a threesome is beating the cut sorghum with sticks to dislodge the grain for the pile waiting nearby.*

5

Resettlement and Positions of Poverty

> ... the position of the rural population is that of a man standing permanently up to the neck in water, so that even a ripple is sufficient to drown him.
>
> R. W. Tawney
> *Land and Labor in China*

> The only communication we have with Sudanese is money.
>
> Eritrean refugee
> *Interview in Wad el Hileau*

Introduction

Changing class relationships among refugees are some of the rural transformation's effect on refugee populations. Using Wad el Hileau as an illustration, this chapter explores the existence of social stratification among rural refugees. The analysis exposes the underlying mechanisms of immiseration and accumulation that create and perpetuate social differentiation. Such mechanisms are influential and powerful. They play a large role in determining the strategies that unassisted refugees adopt to secure household sufficiency. They dictate the proportion of households in different locations within the agrarian class structure, and they have begun to fragment the refugee household as a self-contained unit of production.

The evidence presented in this chapter provides a broader explanation for why poverty is so endemic among refugees. The first section introduces the positions that refugees at Wad el Hileau occupy in the social relationships of agricultural production and market exchange. The next sections examine five mechanisms that create

Notes for this section begin on page 107.

and mediate social differentiation. The last section highlights environmental factors that are likely to accentuate the process of class differentiation even further in the future.

Not All Refugees Are Alike

Refugees are "sorted" into distinct aggregates by the relations of production in eastern Sudan. Table 5.1 represents a theoretically informed set of class positions that are empirically evident among unassisted refugees in Wad el Hileau.[1] Three basic types of criteria are chosen to define the boundary between five classes identified in column 1: property size, wage labor, and surplus production.[2] These components – ownership of the means of production (land), participation in the labor market, and accumulation of surplus – play such critical roles in determining whether a given household can subsist, accumulate, or do neither that they are appropriate criteria for analyzing class relations within an agrarian society.[3]

Land size is important because it is so closely associated with the ability of a given household to subsist. Column 2 in the table illustrates the proportional distribution of land holdings for different segments of the Eritrean refugee population sampled in Wad el Hileau. Sudanese land holdings average forty *feddans* throughout the southern portion of Kassala province (including Wad el Hileau) compared to an average of thirteen *feddans* for refugees.[4] The second criterion is based on the participation of peasant households in the agricultural labor market. Columns 3, 4, and 5 in Table 5.1 illustrate the decreasing proportion of households in each class selling their labor to scheme operators. Columns 7, 8, and 9 relate to subsistent peasants who neither hire out nor hire in, and accumulators who hire labor, the third criterion – surplus accumulation. They represent the average amount of grain sold and retained by households in that class. Columns 7 and 8 indicate the average amount of grain sold increases substantially for refugee households located in the "upper" positions within the agrarian order at Wad el Hileau.

The ability to obtain a subsistence, or to accumulate a surplus, is a critical issue for every refugee household. Simple reproduction involves the creation of labor power (i.e., family) and the creation of the means of production (i.e., farm). Expanded reproduction is associated with the ability to realize surplus. Whether rural cultivators attain simple reproduction or expanded reproduction (leading to capital accumulation) is contingent on where their household is located compared to others in the social relations of production.

Table 5.1 Class Structure in Unassisted Eritrean Refugee Community

(1) Social strata (Total land used per household)	(2) Distribution of households (Percentage)	(3) Laborers in class position (Percentage)	(4) Average work days	(5) Average season's wage per laborer[a]	(6) Persons in household	(7) Annual sale of sorghum[b] (Sacks)	(8) Annual sale of sesame (Sacks)	(9) Average retention of sorghum (Sacks)
Landless (0 *feddans*) $n = 19$[c]	23.75	63.0	58.5	640.0	6.5	—	—	—
Marginalized (2.5 – 17.5 *feddans*) $n = 40$	53.25	43.0	42.8	453.2	6.9	5.1	5.8	8.4
Subsistent (17.5 – 24.5 *feddans*) $n = 5$	6.25	65.0	16.5	293.5	10.8	11.9	15.3	11.3
Accumulating (25.0 – 19.9 *feddans*) $n = 10$	12.50	—	—	—	9.6	18.7	20.4	23.7
Appropriating (50.0 – 250 *feddans*) $n = 4$[d]	5.00	—	—	—	11.3	114.0	90.0	30.0

[a] In £ Sudanese pounds. One U.S. dollar = 4.45 £S as per the official exchange rate in 1988.
[b] Sorghum data are a combined average reported by respondents for the 1986/87 season.
[c] n indicates the number of observations.
[d] Total $n = 78$. It does not include 51 Eritrean refugee households for which pastoralism was their primary livelihood in Eritrea or three more households for which data was unreliable or missing.

Source: Household survey conducted in Wad el Hileau by author December 1987 through June 1988

Five classes have emerged in the face of agrarian change – landless refugees, marginalized refugees, subsistent refugees, accumulating refugees, and an appropriating elite. Each class represents significant differences in the ownership of the means of production, the degree of participation in the labor market, the ability of households to reproduce themselves, and the capacity to accumulate. Understanding how these classes vie for the control of physical, financial, and social resources becomes essential to an analysis of refugee resettlement. Hence, the next task is to specify the mechanisms of impoverishment and accumulation that structure the rural economy in Wad el Hileau and thereby to explain the predominance of refugees in class positions within the social relations of production.

Commodification of Labor and Land

Social interdependence and reciprocity characterized preflight production relations among ethnic groups in the lowlands of Eritrea. Their economies were characterized by the dominance of production for direct use and a relatively homogeneous peasantry.[5] Taxation and trader activity were limited in the lowlands, leaving communities relatively unaffected by social change.[6] Free exchanges of labor were the quintessential expression of the internally defined social relations of production. Farmers organized group work parties to fill short falls in their labor supply during planting, harvesting and weeding. *Nafirs* were sanctioned by an ethic of reciprocity, and the close proximity of small-holder plots to one another expedited the exchange of labor. In short, they were central to the maintenance and reproduction of relatively self-contained economies in Eritrea.

Although Eritreans depended on communal labor parties when they first arrived in Sudan in the late 1960s, soon thereafter "*nafir* died," to use a phrase oft-repeated by refugees. Sharing free labor became the rare exception. Only nine Eritreans from my sample of eighty-one small-holders had participated in a *nafir* during the last ten years. The agricultural wage labor market is the most important reason for the decomposition of this center piece in the preflight economy.[7] Meanwhile, other forms of reciprocity are disappearing or being replaced by monetary exchanges. Refugees report very few instances in which relatives or friends shared labor or beasts of burden with them since they arrived in Sudan. Other social obligations have been monetized in what amounts to fundraising campaigns. In the event of a fire, for example, a list *(cashif)* is circulated among villagers on which they pledge cash donations. Building supplies and labor are then purchased rather than donated as they were in the past. The fact that reciprocity practices have been suspended or depleted demonstrates that unassisted refugees have been unsuccessful in reconstituting their preflight social and economic relationships.[8] As reciprocal relations of production have been replaced by commodified ones a crucial shift has occurred; communal interests have become secondary and subservient to those of the household, and increasingly, to those of the individuals that dwell within them. As one refugee put it: "Now everyone works for himself."

In Sudan, the relationship between producer and consumer has been severed by the widespread exchange of land, labor, agricultural inputs and consumption goods as monetized commodities. Many types of agricultural inputs have been commodified in Sudan: plowing is performed by tractors rather than oxen or camels; lorry trucks are hired to transport crops instead of using beasts of burden; and hemp sacks are purchased to store grain rather than constructing natural storage bins *(sweebas)*. These all have become fixed production costs for refugee farmers. During the 1986/87 season, for example, unassisted refugees paid £5 (Sudanese) to purchase grain sacks and another £5 to transport each sack from the field to Wad el Hileau. The cost of tractor time to cultivate fields has risen substantially: £1.1 (Sudanese) per hour in 1967; £5 in 1975; £25 in 1984; £40 to 45 in 1987, and £80 to 100 in 1988.

When commodity relations take hold, refugee households are increasingly vulnerable to domestic inflation in the prices they pay to purchase foodstuffs and basic necessities as well as farm inputs. Terms of trade are also swinging against small producers; that is, the prices for peasant-produced commodities have deteriorated compared to those for peasant-consumed commodities. Between 1974 and 1981, the producer price index for sesame, the principal cash crop produced and sold by refugee peasants, averaged 62 percent of the consumer price index during the same period.[9] As refugees sell more of their cash crops or labor power in order to meet their basic needs, there are fewer and fewer who produce agricultural commodities for their own consumption, do little or no wage labor, and rarely employ laborers. "Subsistent refugees" are a remnant, or residual, class category reflecting the transformation of agrarian relations (see Table 5.1). Ten percent of all Eritrean refugees who were small cultivators at one time have lost their plots in the market or through outright confiscation. As commodification pressures intensify, more refugees can be expected to move out of the ranks of these relatively autonomous producers. Omer Abdi al Shafir is one such producer who is struggling more than ever to provide a subsistence for his family of eight as well as many other "meal guests" who are poorer and come to tap his food.

Tall, lean, and possessor of a frequent smile, Omer fled to Sudan in 1975. Years before, his father made the pilgrimage to Mecca, but never returned home to Chad. Instead, his family settled in the southwest corner of Eritrea, where Omer was born and raised. Married in 1967, Omer and his wife prospered; they had a field of twenty-five *feddans*, which yielded an annual average of thirty-five sacks of sorghum and ten more of sesame. They also owned a sizable herd of cows and sheep, plus a small river garden that provided onions, tomatoes, and okra. In 1975, however, tensions erupted in nearby Om Hager. In a matter of days, Omer and his family moved as much food, livestock and belongings as possible out of Eritrea and settled in Wad el Hileau. He and others from the same displaced Bargo community were asked to move to UN camps, but they refused and thereby lost any right to refugee rations and other forms of assistance.

Omer sold many assets to purchase twenty-five *feddans* of farmland near Wad el Hileau. While Omer has the same amount of land as he did in Eritrea, his fortunes have fallen. Many agricultural inputs are now commodities that must be purchased reducing his net earnings considerably. During the 1992/93 season, for example, his production costs included the cost of hiring a tractor to cultivate, the purchase price of seed, the cost of hiring extra laborers to weed (hiring a tractor results in higher weeding costs because the work must be done at one time rather than gradually), the cost of hiring extra laborers to thrash the sorghum, the cost of purchasing sacks in which to transport and store crops, the cost of hiring a truck to transport crops in from the field, the cost of hiring men to load and unload the truck (required with the hire of the truck), and the cost of having a tractor haul water to the field site for workers to drink. Omer's production costs for twenty-four sacks of sorghum and thirty-five sacks of sesame included the following.

£5000 (Sudanese) – Tractor hire for cultivation (£1000 per five *feddans* of land)
£3255 (Sudanese) – Hiring labor for weeding
£2800 (Sudanese) – Combined price for both combine and hiring labor to thrash cut sorghum
£1440 (Sudanese) – Purchase price for twenty-four sacks to store grain in (£60 apiece)
£1100 (Sudanese) – Truck hire (a portion of a truck to transport crops in from the field)
£420 (Sudanese) – Hiring labor to load and porter grain
£600 (Sudanese) – Purchase price to haul water to the field site

Omer spent a total of £10,385 (Sudanese) plus the purchase price of seed for planting (i.e., 2.0 kilograms of sorghum and 3.5 kilograms of sesame). Increased production costs like these make it increasingly difficult for a household like Omer's to secure a subsistence from its land. To insure their survival, family members must join the agricultural labor force. As yet, no members of Omer's household do agricultural wage labor, but the time soon may come.

The Land Tenure Squeeze

The combined pressure of scheme expansion and the introduction of tractors to small-scale production has produced an acute land squeeze for unassisted refugees. *Mushrooah* operators had already appropriated more than 65,000 *feddans* of land surrounding Wad el Hileau when the second large refugee influx occurred in 1975. Some of the early arrivals managed to stake a usufruct claim to cultivable land, but Figure 5.1 illustrates the limited access to land for refugees who have resettled in Wad el Hileau more recently. Only 15 percent of those refugees who have arrived since 1975 own land.

The land squeeze is exemplified further by the fact that land became a rental commodity with a monetary value for the first time in the late 1970s. A decade earlier, Sudanese land owners gave many of the first arrivals small portions of their fallow land. By the mid-1970s, however, they began to recognize the fact that more refugees were coming than leaving and that land was acquiring a monetary value. In some instances, Sudanese sought repossession via court hearings, others used brute force. By the late 1970s, free land was no longer available in the immediate hinterland of Wad el Hileau and subsequent arrivals were forced either to rent, borrow, or buy land. The combined average size of all refugee small-holdings in my sample cohort was 57 percent smaller in Sudan than in Eritrea – twelve *feddans* compared to an average size of twenty-eight *feddans*.

Although 95 percent of the refugee community had owned land in Eritrea, only 47.5 percent do so in Wad el Hileau. Unassisted refugees utilize land on the following tenure basis: own (47.5 percent), rent (22.5 percent), and borrow (6.0 percent). Landless refugees constitute the remaining 24.0 percent. Without access to the principal means of production, landless refugees are forced to secure a livelihood by doing field labor during the agricultural season and petty crafts, trades, or marketing during the off-season. Landless interviewees worked an average of 58.5 days on schemes during the 1987/88 season, earning an average income of £640 (Sudanese). Mickels and Yousif (1987) reported an average agricultural wage per day of £8 (Sudanese) during the 1986/87 season. Translated into their equivalent value in grain, these wages were sufficient to purchase 6.5 sacks of sorghum or approximately one half of the grain consumed by an average household during a year.

Refugees sell their labor at prices that are insufficient to maintain and reproduce their households for a number of reasons. In the late 1960s, scheme operators in Wad el Hileau were forced to recruit

Figure 5.1 Agricultural Land Availability for Incoming Refugees to Wad El Hileau

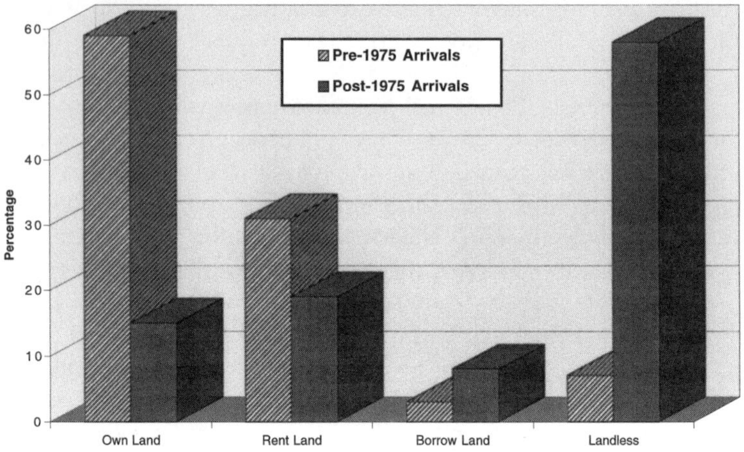

Source: Household surveys conducted in Wad el Hileau by author in December 1987 through June 1988

wage laborers from outside the area and offered short-term loans as an incentive to attract more wage laborers. In the mid-1970s, however, a ready-made labor force, in effect, came to stay and drove down the price of labor. Frequent drought years have driven it even lower. Real wage rates for agricultural labor have not changed appreciably in eastern Sudan during the last two decades.[10] Their rigidity reflects the deep structural imbalances within the Sudanese economy and the fact that agricultural laborers (refugees or not) are explicitly exempted from labor laws in Sudan. Scheme operators are the primary benefactors of extremely low and rigid wage rates. In essence, they are the appropriators atop the agrarian order, although it is important to note that the wealthiest ones are vertically integrated into large-scale trading, grain storage, and export activity as well.

Hunger Rents

Refugee resettlement is occurring in the context of a growing shortage of land causing land rents to rise substantially during the last decade. A typical charge of £5 per hour of tractor time in the late 1970s rose to above £80 by the late 1980s. For refugees who rent land to cultivate, the price can represent as much as half of their total production costs, and refugees frequently pay additional rent in kind. *Mushrooah* operators rent out uncleared land on the edge of their schemes. Before cultivating, renters are forced to clear underbrush first. In essence, this arrangement constitutes a "double rent" – an investment of labor on top of the normal monetary fee. Most land owners limit rent tenures to one year at a time in order to retain maximum control over their land's use and rental price. Sixty-five percent of all renters in my sample farmed a different plot each year. Refugees have an apt colloquialism for these extractive rent relationships; they call them *ta'ackul wa gwoom*, "to eat and to move," in reference to the fact that they have little recourse but to move from one rental plot to another, year by year, paying high rents in order to eat. "Hunger rents" prevail when Eritrean refugees in the 1990s, like Russian peasants in the 1920s, are obliged to pay very high prices to rent small pieces of land in order to feed their families and utilize their households' labor.[11]

In Wad el Hileau, the majority of unassisted refugees have access to land, but only to an amount insufficient to support their families fully. Labor is the only factor of production that marginalized refugees (53 percent) possess in relative abundance so they participate in the prevailing system of seasonal wage labor migration with their landless counterparts (24 percent). Labor expenditures during the growing season are important for all households, but they are especially pivotal for those who occupy a marginalized position. Although the opportunity cost of their labor is almost zero during the slack season, it surges to a peak in July, August, October, and November.

Households at the bottom of the social and economic hierarchy adopt different strategies to offset the limited time period during which wages are available on rainfed schemes. Some do agricultural wage labor first and then attend to the small land holding they rent or own. Often the marginal-value product of labor spent weeding their crop is lower than the ongoing wage labor rate on schemes.[12] In these instances, refugees either reduce the amount of weeding input on their land (particularly if it is poorer land) or hire day laborers. Eighteen percent of the marginalized households in my sample hire wage labor.

As households face increasing economic pressure, refugee women begin to do wage labor. A large survey conducted in settlements throughout eastern Sudan concluded that 12 percent of all refugee women participate in agricultural wage labor.[13] Most commonly they are hired to do day labor on small-holdings. In recent years, however, refugee women have begun working for wages on *mushrooahs*. Despite the general rise of Islamic fundamentalism in Sudan, gender divisions have worn sufficiently thin that some *mushrooah* operators even recruit women. The majority are either Kunama or Nara, two ethnic groups with long histories of subjugation and ingrained poverty. Although these groups referred to themselves as the Nara and Kunama, their more common names, Baza and Baria, mean "slaves"; they were so named by other groups that dominated them in Eritrea and continue to do so in Sudan.

Cash Crop Mortgages

Refugees also face pressure exerted by the social relations of exchange. Some households (17.5 percent) have sufficient land to plant sesame, the cash crop of choice in eastern Sudan. But sesame must be harvested in a timely way, which requires that additional labor be hired. If insufficient cash is on hand, farmers must obtain cash loans to pay wages. They frequently mortgage large portions of their sorghum or sesame crop at prices that are substantially lower than market prices. *Mushrooah* operators appropriate surplus directly from a ready made, cheap labor force comprised largely of refugees, while merchants appropriate surplus indirectly in the form of interest rates concealed in the mortgage terms established with refugees for their cash crops.

Crop mortgages *(sheil)* are widespread throughout Sudan, but their particular impact on rural refugees is significant in several ways. First, crop mortgages are the single most important constraint on the accumulation of capital among the upper portions of the refugee community. Interviewees in Wad el Hileau mortgage nearly two-thirds of their cash crops each year. During 1987 and 1988, the average mortgage price they received was only 59 percent of the market price paid for sesame and sorghum. This price difference translates into "interest fees" of 70 percent paid to merchants. Despite the fact that *sheil* is prohibited by law, most refugees know that it is "better to share the profits than to lose the farm." Second, social relationships from Eritreans' preflight society are coopted for use in mortgage arrangements. Merchants often require a "middleman" *(wusta)* to guarantee their loans. Most often, a sheik is required to be the *wusta* who bears the responsibility of repaying a loan if a borrower fails to do so. Third, crop mortgages provide a synoptic illustration of the prevailing social relations of production and exchange in eastern Sudan. Without adequate land to provide a subsistence for their households, poorer refugees often expend their labor on the farms of fellow refugees or Sudanese in exchange for wages paid at the end of a day's work. Without adequate amounts of cash in-hand to pay these wages, their employers must turn to members of a wealthier class who appropriate sizable portions of their surplus without incurring the cost of management or participating in the production process. Omer is one of many refugees in Wad el Hileau who is intimately familiar with mortgaging cash crops.

Omer mortgages a portion of his yields to a merchant every agricultural season. In 1991, for example, he harvested nine sacks of sesame. He mortgaged off six at £600 (Sudanese) apiece, but sold the other three for £2,000 apiece – a net loss of £8,400. (This is equivalent to the purchase price of nearly six sacks of sorghum.) Omer can be kind and accommodating to a fault; that same year of 1991, he acted as the guarantor for several poorer neighbors and friends who needed cash advances on their crops. Several defaulted, forcing Omer to tap his own crops as settlement on their behalf. After doing *sheil* with the same local merchant for ten years, Omer changed to new money lender in 1992. He obtained 35 sacks of sesame, mortgaged off fifteen at £2,000 (Sudanese), and sold the remaining twenty at £2,500 apiece – thus, a net loss of £7,500. Omer is not given to self-preoccupation or evaluation, but in a rare moment of reflection he summarizes the effect of cash crop mortgages: "I am getting old, but my life is going down." While *sheil* remains a mechanism of impoverishment and social differentiation among those like Omer, it functions as a key means of surplus appropriation for creditors. Omer's new lender came from Sudan's capital city of Khartoum searching for borrowers, thereby reflecting the kind of profit potential available from cash crop mortgages.

Merchant Forces

Trade, and the merchants who control it, constitutes another key factor that structures the economy and class relations that come to bear on incoming refugees. As a refugee who resettled in Wad el Hileau put it, "The only communication we have with Sudanese is money." The circulation of money and goods is the merchant's domain. Profits are made indirectly – by controlling markets – rather than by asserting direct control over the labor process.[14] The greater the control merchants are able to exercise, the higher their rate of profit. In the case of Wad el Hileau, there are nearly four hundred distinct properties (i.e., stores, storage sheds, eateries, repair shops, and others) that together constitute the central market of the village (see Map 5.1). All these sites are owned or rented for trade purposes. A few small shops are scattered throughout the village, and petty traders move about selling peanuts, cigarettes and the like, but the vast majority of cash expenditures in Wad el Hileau take place in the central market.

102 | *Losing Place*

Map 5.1 Field Map of the Market and its Merchants in Wad El Hileau

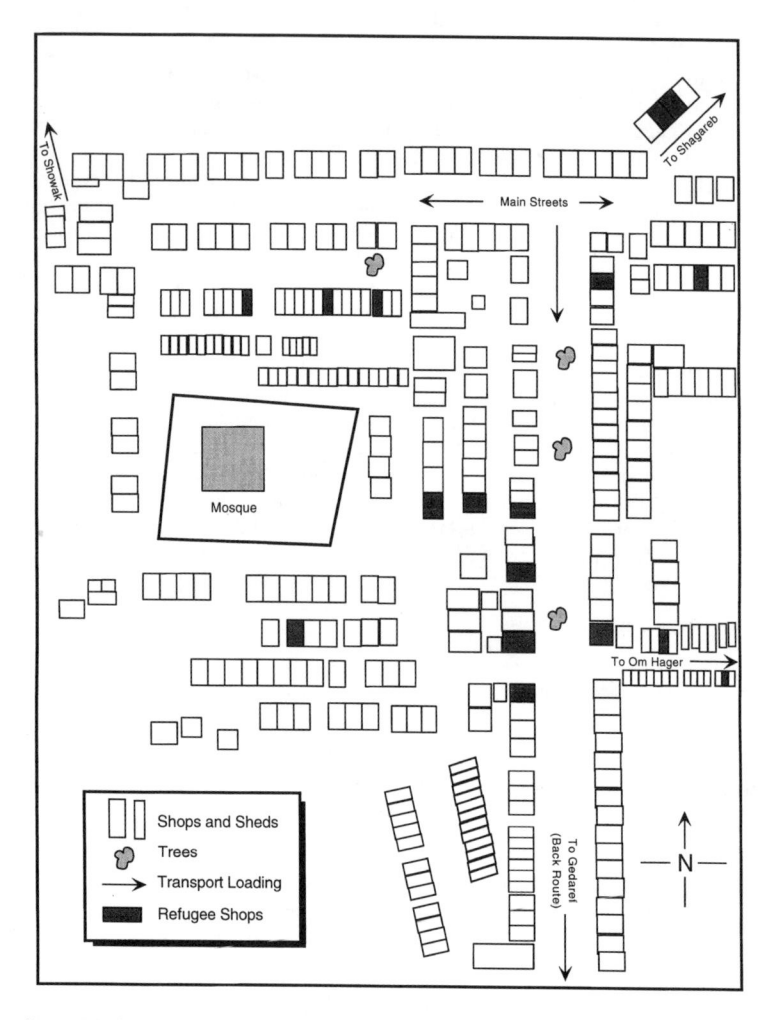

Source: Market survey conducted in Wad el Hileau by Betsy Bascom and Abdul Hakim el Amin in January through May 1988

Although refugees constitute 80 percent of the total population in Wad el Hileau, they own only 6.0 percent of the permanent properties in the central market. A few Eritreans own the small shops, but at the bottom of the market hierarchy are tea shops and laundry operations. The overwhelming majority of the important merchants – wholesale operators who issue substantial amounts of credit by selling goods to smaller retailers – are a particular Sudanese ethnic group. The Jallaba (or *Ja'aliin* as they are known in Wad el Hileau) dispersed out of their home territory in the Nile Valley during the 1930s, 1940s, and 1950s; now they constitute the overwhelming majority of traders and merchants in Sudan.[15] In Wad el Hileau, there are only thirty-five Jallaba households, but they dominate local trade. Jallaba own no less than 53 percent of all permanent buildings in the central market and control almost every highly profitable enterprise in the village (see Table 5.2). Their financial status, ethnic background, and migrant experience all serve to insulate them from members of other Sudanese ethnic groups and isolate them still more from refugees.[16] Interfamilial relationships are key to their continued success. Members of six Jallaba families own nearly 20 percent of all permanent buildings in the central market. These merchants couple their store profits together with credit from relatives elsewhere in Sudan to expand their operations. They are the dominant buyers and transporters of the two main exports, grain and charcoal, that leave the region. In addition to ownership of most rented units in the central market (87 of 154), Jallaba own all eight butcheries in Wad el Hileau, three of the four generator-powered grain mills, three of the four bakeries, and twelve of the sixteen transport lorries. They also have invested in tractors and *mushrooah* schemes.

Two other ethnic groups dominate the "second tier" of merchants in Wad el Hileau (see Table 5.2). Most Humran merchants are direct descendants of the original settlers of Wad el Hileau. Several operate retail stores both for prestige and position, but they engage in other operations as well – *mushrooahs*, large farms *(mezras)*, grain storage, and a milling operation. Their position, largely established by land ownership both in the market as well as the agricultural hinterland, is further augmented by positions of local political influence, e.g., judicial or civil positions. The top echelons of the bureaucratic and mercantile hierarchies in every provincial and district capital form internal alliances, but especially so in border locations like Wad el Hileau. Alliances between traders and officials are mutually profitable facts of life in trade centers like this which remain furthermost from state authority.[17] Hausa merchants are the other strong contingency in this middle tier. Their niche is largely defined by the fact

Table 5.2 Ownership of Business in Wad el Hileau by Ethnic Group

		Jallaba	Hausa	Habish	Fulani	Jabarta	Humran	Beni Amir	Nara	Maria	Bargo	Belain	Other
Grain Storage	(128)	63	20	1	9	5	12	2	2	2	8		12
Small Dry Goods	(61)	15	10	6	6	7	2	3	2	6			6
Tea Shop	(41)		4	21		2		3					1
Restaurant	(20)	5		5	2		1	1	2		0	1	3
Vegetable Stand	(17)	4	1	2	1	4	3	2	2				
Gas & Auto Repair	(14)	8	4		1								1
Cloth Shop	(13)	13											
Large Dry Goods	(13)	8.5				1.5	1.5		0.5	1			
Tailor	(12)	2	4	1	2	1		1		1			1
Butcher	(11)	8					1		1	1			
Single Item Sales	(11)	4		1	1	1		1	1	1	1		
Spice Vendor	(9)		7		2								
Beverage Stand	(8)	2				2						1	3
Household Goods	(8)	3	4			1		2					
Jewelry Sales/Repair	(8)					0	1		4		0		1
Blacksmith	(7)	1	5									1	
Barber	(5)		5						1				
Wood/Grass Furniture	(5)	1	2		1								4
Tobacco Vendor	(5)	1											
Laundry	(5)			5									
Under Construction	(5)	4	1										
Bakery	(4)	3.5					0.5						
Grain Mill	(4)	3					1						
Bike Rental/Repair	(3)		3										
Building Supply	(2)	1			1								
Carpenter	(2)		2										
Office Supply	(2)	2											
Pharmacy	(2)					1	1						
Photo Studio	(1)	1											
Outdoor Theater	(1)			1									1
Total		153	72	43	26	25.5	24	15	13.5	11	9	3	33

Source: Market survey conducted in Wad el Hileau by Betsy Bascom and Abdul Hakim el Amin in January through May 1988

that the Nigerian community frequently relates somewhat exclusively to itself. Hausa merchants tend to focus on service oriented operations like grain storage, tailoring, spice vending, traditional medicine, carpentry, mechanical repairs, and bicycle rentals, rather than capital-intensive shops.

The ethnic character of the "third tier" of traders is far more mixed. Their shops offer the "basics." Often they are indifferent to prospective customers and less inclined to bargain.[18] Given a chronic shortage of capital, these petty traders are almost completely reliant upon the local Jallaba and Humran merchants to provide them with goods and the credit to purchase them. Prayers at the mosque are important because they provide petty traders with opportunities for regular social contact with established merchants on which they must depend for securing goods and credit to finance trading ventures. Eritreans run only twenty-nine shops in the central market. Three of these are sizable enough to be considered in the "second tier," but the rest involve petty trade such as the sale of dry goods and vegetables, food preparation, and jewelry making.

Clearly, incoming refugees remain at a severe disadvantage with respect to merchants. Poorer refugees often make their purchases based on credit and thus are required to sell their grain to the same trader. Traders themselves can constitute an emerging class, but as merchants parlay their function as economic intermediaries into an expanding base of economic and social power, the process of social differentiation is extended even further within a refugee community.[19]

Dying Fields and Falling Yields

Added pressure exerted by the environment is apt to hasten the process of social differentiation among refugees. Because most refugees have an inadequate amount of land to meet their subsistence needs, they have virtually abandoned the practice of leaving land fallow. Less than 5 percent of all landowners in the refugee sample left any portion of their farm fallow during the last ten years. Crop yields are falling because, as Omer simply put it, "the land is tired now." As land becomes exhausted the incidence of *Striga hermonthica*, a parasitic weed that stunts sorghum growth and decimates crop yields, increases dramatically. In 1990, after fifteen years of continuous growth, witch weed invaded Omer's field. The appearance of witch weed is usually regarded as a warning to abandon a particular field, but refugees cannot afford to leave any land fallow. The study sample suggests that 75 percent of the cultivators are replowing their land at least once, and often twice, each year due to increased striga and pest infestation. Thus, refugees are expending more capital and labor time on soils that are becoming poorer and less productive.

A marked drop in precipitation has also contributed to a decline in crop yields. During 1984 and 1985 the area experienced a pronounced drought, and a long-term decline in precipitation culminated in another drought during 1991. In Sudan, 600 millimeters of rainfall per year provides a reasonable degree of crop security.[20] A comparison of recent rainfall data with data from colonial records indicates that the critical 600 mm isohyet has shifted substantially during the last thirty years leaving Wad el Hileau with less than that amount and subject to crop failures in one out of every three years.[21]

The area now receives less than fifty days of rainfall per year. Twenty days account for 75 percent of the annual total.[22] The abbreviated rainy season has heightened competition for tractor services in general, especially at the beginning of the season. More than 90 percent of all refugee small-holders in Wad el Hileau depend on tractor services, but their fields are often plowed last. Tractor drivers are often persuaded to visit Sudanese first, despite previous contractual arrangements with refugees. Informants in Wad el Hileau reported delays that ranged in length from five to twenty days after the promised date for discing. These tractor delays place refugee peasants at a distinct disadvantage relative to Sudanese merchant farmers. Sorghum requires two months of continuous growth after the germinated sorghum breaks the soil. Therefore, planting a month late, as many refugees are forced to do, can result in crop losses of 30 percent to 60 percent.[23]

Refugees expressed the effect of marginalization in their own words during the course of interviews. Several refugees noted that, given minimal precipitation, they could have purchased grain during the last two years for less than it cost to produce it, and others insisted that it was more secure to do wage labor than to work on their own land. The fact that "security" is shifting from the means of production to the commodification of more labor will accelerate the process of social differentiation for those Eritreans who remain in Sudan.

Conclusion

Eritrean refugees occupy class positions in an established regime of capital accumulation that operates largely for the benefit of merchants and *mushrooah* operators. Their positions are tied to mechanisms of impoverishment and appropriation that structure the social relations of production and exchange in eastern Sudan. The commodification of land, labor, and farming inputs has eroded the reciprocal relations of production that characterized preflight economies in Eritrea. Debilitating tenure relations as well as shortfalls in agricultural production and household income are associated with the marginalized position of most Eritreans. Their principal means of survival is to join the ranks of the agricultural labor force, thereby facilitating the rise of a rural elite within the host community. In the absence of any other forms of rural credit, refugees with farming land often are forced to mortgage their cash crops to Sudanese merchants. This places a "lid" on capital accumulation and upward mobility among refugees. Environmental pressures are apt to accelerate social differentiation and refugee impoverishment. In sum, differentiation of refugee populations into class strata denotes the importance of rural transformation for displaced people as well as the importance of a clear understanding of its relationship to the process of flight, settlement, and integration.

Notes

1. Previous efforts have been made – using detailed data bases – to identify very precise criteria for agrarian classes. See U. Patnaik, "Class Differentiation Within the Peasantry: An Approach to the Analysis of Indian Agriculture," *Economic and Political Weekly* 11 (1976): 82–101; A. de Janvry and C. Deere, "A Conceptual Framework for the Empirical Analysis of Peasants," *American Journal of Agribusiness Economics* 61 (1979): 601–11; V. Athreya et. al., "Identification of Agrarian Classes: A Methodological Essay with Empirical Material from South India," *Journal of Peasant Studies* 14 (1987): 148–90; M. Mamdani, "Extreme But Not Exceptional: Toward an Analysis of the Agrarian Question in Uganda," *Journal of Peasant Studies* 14 (1987): 190–222; L. Llambí, "Small Modern Farmers: Neither Peasants or Fully-Fledged Capitalists?" *Journal of Peasant Studies* 15 (1988): 350–72.
2. Rather than conduct a strenuous, methodological exercise in class analysis, the purpose of this section is to illustrate that refugees are in distinct positions within the rural economy. I depend less on quantitative measures of stratification than on qualitative relationships of power that situate households in the social relationships of production and exchange. The emphasis is not on how much income is made, as important as that is, but how it is earned. Households move between classes because of the changing nature of the demands that are placed on them. Basic physiological requirements to reproduce a household vary from year to year. In a drought year, for example, some households move to lower portions of the class structure. In addition to demands associated with the "sur-

vival fund," ceremonial obligations expand or contract over time as do the demands that are imposed on refugee households by the state. E. Wolf, *Peasants*.
3. Class schema have been devised by authors working in different contexts. E. Archetti and K. Stolen, *Explotacion Familiar y Acumulacion de Capital en Camp Argentino* (Buenos Aires, 1975); S. Amin, "Underdevelopment and Dependence in Black Africa," *Journal of Modern African Studies* 10 (1976): 503–24; H. Bernstein, "Notes on States and Peasantry," *Review of African Political Economy* 21 (1977): 44–62; A. de Janvry, *The Agrarian Question* (Berkeley, 1981). This study relies most heavily on de Janvry's book to develop an appropriate schema. Three basic types of criteria are used to define the "boundary" between classes: land size, labor participation, and surplus production. These criteria are associated with the three fundamental components posed in Marxist definitions of class: "... large groups of people differing from each other by the place they occupy in a historically determined system of social production, by their relation (in most cases fixed and formulated in law) to the means of production, by their role in the social organisation of labour, and, consequently, by the dimensions of the share of social wealth of which they dispose and the mode of acquiring it." Lenin cited in Athreya et. al, "Identification of Agrarian Classes," 147. The definition's main components – ownership of the means of production (land), participation in the labor market, and accumulation of surplus – play such critical roles in determining whether a given household can subsist, accumulate, or do neither that they are appropriate criteria for analyzing class relations within an agrarian society. The classical Marxist terms – proletariat and bourgeoisie – are not adopted in this study because rural societies in peripheral capitalist economies are characterized by incipient class differentiation rather than full-fledged polarization. M. Babiker, "Peasantry and the 'Differentiation Question' in 'Peripheral' Capitalist Social Formations: Towards a Resolution of the Debate," Manuscript copy of presentation to the Seminar on Capital, State and Transformation in the Sudan, (University of East Anglia, 16–18 July, 1984). In other words, the process of social transformation has taken sufficient shape to refer to agrarian classes in a meaningful way. However, polarization between classes has not gained sufficient momentum to distinguish proletariat and bourgeoisie.
4. World Bank, "South Kassala Agriculture Project," 13.
5. Scott aptly notes the general tendency to over-romanticize the social arrangements that distinguish a natural economy. He argues that these social arrangements are not so much a product of altruism, of necessity, and that they are often characterized by conflict evidenced by envy, gossip, and paternalism rather than ease and harmony. (J. Scott, *The Moral Economy of the Peasant: Rebellion and Subsistence in Southeast Asia* (New Haven, 1976), 6.
6. Longrigg, *Short History of Eritrea*; T. Johnson and M. Johnson, "Eritrea: The National Question and the Logic of Protracted Struggle," *African Affairs* 80 (1981): 181–95.
7. Two other preconditions for *nafirs* have been stifled during resettlement in Sudan. Legal prohibitions and social values preclude the "public" use of alcohol although many refugees still brew it for home consumption and clandestine sales. In addition, refugee households own fewer small ruminants than they did in Eritrea. The average number of goats and sheep owned by Nara, Kunama, Bargo, and Hausa (2.6 head per household) is nine percent of their ruminant holdings in Eritrea. These two factors make it difficult to satisfy the consumptive demands of *nafirs*.
8. A few newly arrived refugees have retained reciprocal relationships for agricultural production. After living in Wad el Hileau during the dry season thirty-one households farm together from June to November near a Sudanese army post located at the Ethiopian border. They have secured permission from the post

commander to cultivate a piece of land between the post and the Ethiopian border and there, at the edge of Sudan, these unassisted refugees plant, weed, and harvest together in cooperative work parties. The "Lugdi Association" (as they refer to themselves) suggests that refugees may retain reciprocal relations of production. Reciprocity, however, has been reactualized not so much on the basis of tight knit social relations and moral obligations as on the fact that the remoteness of their location has minimized the amount of mechanization and state intervention in the area. The "Lugdi Association" suggests that reciprocal relations of production depend on the absence of capitalist relations of production, not on the presence of an "economy of affection" as Hyden suggests. Hyden, *No Shortcuts to Progress*, 29.

9. World Bank, Sudan Pricing Policies and Structural Balances, Volume III: Agriculture in Sudan, Report No. 4528a-SU (1983), Table II.
10. el Bagir et. al., *Labor Markets in the Sudan*, 12.
11. Scott, *Moral Economy*, 14; A. Chayanov, *The Theory of Peasant Economy* (Madison, 1986); Chambers, "Hidden Losers?"
12. el Bagir et. al., *Labor Markets in the Sudan*.
13. Ninety-eight percent of respondents in that same survey among refugees in eastern Sudan suggested that they considered plowing to be the exclusive task of men, 81 percent consider weeding to be the major task of men, and 72 percent consider harvest as the task of men. M. Bulcha, *Flight and Integration*.
14. Merchant capital cannot directly create or add value to a product apart from the "value-added" by transporting the product to a market. Instead, merchant capital actualizes profits through unequal exchange, that is, by buying commodities below their value and selling them at, or above, their value. In essence, trade commodities are exchanged for labor power and in so doing the "outcome" value is transferred to through unequal exchange. C. Meillassoux, *Maidens, Meal and Money*; A. Zack-Williams, "Merchant Capital and Underdevelopment in Sierra Leone," *Review of African Political Economy* 28 (1982): 74.
15. The domination of the Jallaba is often attributed to the fact that education in the Sudan is concentrated in the central and northern provinces (from which the Jallaba originated).
16. M. Watts, "Survey 11 – Powers of Production – Geographers Among the Peasants," *Environmental Planning D* 5 (1987): 215.
17. P. Doornbos, "Trade in Two Border Towns: Beida and Foro Boranga (Darfur Province)" in *Trade and Traders in the Sudan* (Hanover, 1988), 168.
18. Ibid., 162.
19. J. Barker, *Rural Communities Under Stress: Peasant Farmers and the State in Africa* (Cambridge, 1989), 27.
20. J. Rogge, "When is Self-sufficiency Achieved: The Case of Rural Settlements in Sudan" in *Refugees: A Third World Dilemma* (Totowa, 1987), 91.
21. Mickels and Yousif, Problems for Mechanization.
22. V. Chordi, "South Kassala Agricultural Project – Water Component," Technical Support Service, Mission Report for United Nations High Commission for Refugees, Geneva (1988), 3.
23. J. Koskinies et. al., Mechanization of Agriculture in the Refugee Settlement Areas in Eastern Sudan: Evaluation and Project Perspective, Evaluation/Project Preparation Mission (1987), 6.

Thousands of Eritrean refugee households depend on a nomadic way of life, but many pressures are bringing their cattle herds to the point of extinction.

6

Exile and the Perils of Pastoralism

> Our cattle are eating themselves....
> Refugee pastoralist
> *Interview in Wad el Hileau*

Introduction

An unprecedented number of pastoralists have moved into the eastern region of Sudan having fled the protracted conflict in Eritrea. Most of them attempted to bring their livestock across the border. Their arrival, coupled with the massive expansion of mechanized agriculture in the same region, has accelerated conflict over land resources, particularly along the border. This chapter identifies pressures that are bringing refugee herds to the point of extinction, thereby jeopardizing pastoralism as a way of life for these refugees. We will start by highlighting the logic of production among pastoralists before they left Eritrea.

The Herd: "One Hundred Head"

The Sahel belt is the predominant home for pastoral cattle herds in Africa. This zone straddles the central portion of Sudan, and stretches eastward into Eritrea. The war forced members of two ethnic groups – the Maria and Beni Amer – to leave the western lowlands of Eritrea and shift their grazing areas to eastern Sudan. For more than four centuries, their cattle had ranged back and forth on well-established trek routes, moving east to the Keren foothills in the

Notes for this section begin on page 126.

Map 6.1 Traditional Grazing Routes in Eritrea

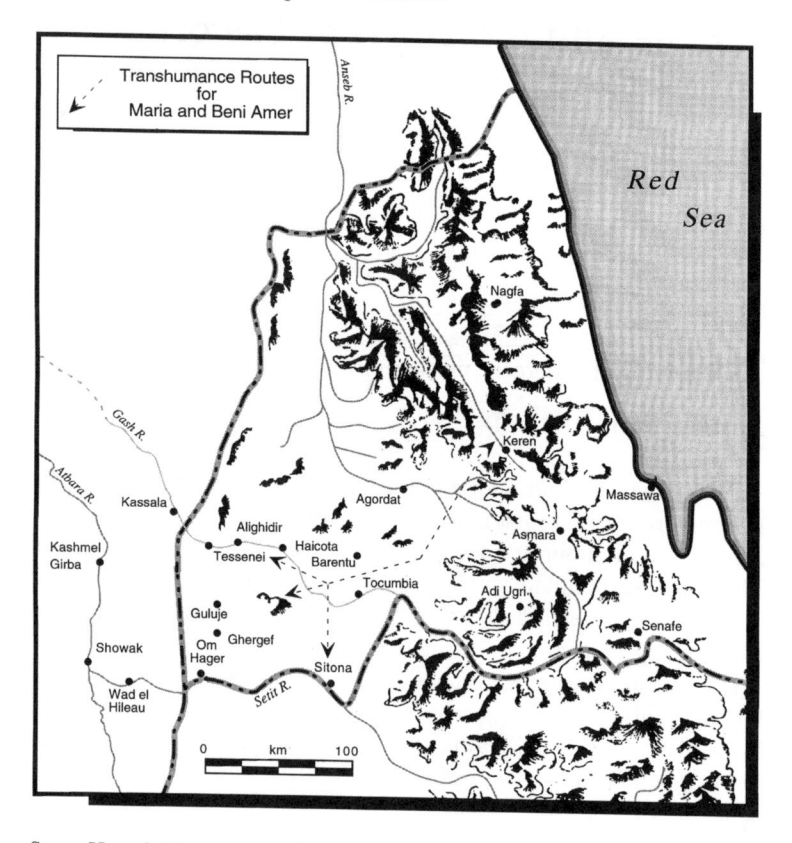

Source: Household surveys conducted in Wad el Hileau by author in December 1987 through June 1988, February 1992, and January through April 1993

late, dry season *(subik)* and then westward out onto the lowlands after the rainy season *(sagim)* (see Map 6.1). The last census before the war (1952) reported eighty thousand Beni Amer and forty-three thousand Maria in the western lowlands.[1]

Cattle were the nucleus of their nomadic society. Milk and its byproducts were central to their diet, and cattle conferred political position, power, and prestige upon their owners. Household heads made it their life objective to develop a "perfect" herd size of one hundred head *(murah)*. Cattle also served as the principal commodity for intrasocietal exchanges. These included, for example, the bride price of seven mature cows, gifts of cattle to the families of prospective brides, and the custom of bequeathing a cow to each son at his naming ceremony and another at his circumcision.

Maria and Beni Amer tribesmen insist that in Eritrea, except at times of crisis, the sale of a single cow was sufficient to meet a household's annual cash needs. Maria sold their cattle in the livestock markets of Agordat, Keren, or Asmara, while Beni Amer sold gelded males to be used as oxen in Kassala.[2] Previous research suggests growth rates of 5 percent per annum for cattle herds in the Sahel. This rate is reflected in preflight herd sizes – an average of eighty-nine head for Maria herds and sixty for Beni Amer.

Nomadic lifestyles tended to favor minimal purchases of commodities, and three factors in particular, limited pastoralists' demand for cash. First, the need for cash was lessened by the cultivation of small plots of land. In Eritrea, pastoral households had plots averaging eleven *feddans*, which, apart from drought years, supplied enough grain for the year. Second, an entrenched caste system supplied cattle owners with indentured help and hired herders were unnecessary. According to tribal mythology, the Qayih Maria ("red") and the Sullim Maria ("black") are descendants of Mereái, the legendary father of the Maria, and his two wives. However, a caste relationship between the two branches intensified during the 1800s – the Sullim Maria providing food, clothing, shelter, and protection for the Qayih, who became, in essence, their indentured herders.[3] In 1952, there were 16,655 Sullim and 8,440 Qayih living in Eritrea.[4] Third, minimal taxes limited the emergence of a cash economy. Taxes were collected from lowland pastoralists during two successive periods of foreign administration, but taxes and tribute remained nominal (as seen in Chapter 2). Hence, colonialism had a far more definitive impact on highlanders than it did on pastoralists in the lowlands; thus Beni Amer and Maria were able to maintain a largely self-sufficient economy and a logic of cattle accumulation rather than cash accumulation until they were profoundly altered by the outbreak of civil war.

The Flight West

In 1967, Ethiopian forces drove twenty-five thousand Eritreans into Sudan, approximately two thousand of whom settled in Wad el Hileau. Idris Fucki Habab was one of the first to arrive.

Born during the dry season of 1950, Idris is the eldest of ten children. His family maintained the centuries-old pattern of seasonal transhumance for twelve years. That pattern changed in 1962, the same year that the fragile federation between Eritrea and Ethiopia broke. Rather than moving continually with their cattle, Idris' family established a permanent residence. Nearly two hundred households settled in Tocumbia (see Map 6.1). When the rains began, men left home and began a four-month trek in the hope of finding good pastures and avoiding confrontations with Ethiopian troops. The Eritrean guerrillas, a small force of several dozen men led by Idris Awate, could not provide herders with protection. But their presence created periodic skirmishes with Ethiopian soldiers and thereby, destabilized the entire region. Maria herders soon came to fear two things – the kidnapping of herds and death. According to Idris, they "carried no guns, lived in fear, and herded by their wits and good fortune." His own worst fears were realized early one morning while herding near Itara, when three armed men suddenly burst into his camp. One of the three attackers held Idris hostage, but released him after the other two men drove six cows away from the herd. Still, despite new dangers, the family's cattle herds prospered. Idris' father achieved the Maria goal, a *murah,* and his own herd numbered nearly eighty head when the exodus to Sudan suddenly became necessary.

Tensions had grown between civilians and Ethiopian troops stationed in the area, although Idris' father, like many other Maria, gave small amounts of money or food to the rebels, who by then were known as the ELF. In 1967, however, confrontation erupted. Early one evening, Ethiopian troops cordoned off Idris' hometown of Tocumbia and then moved from the village outskirts into the central market, shooting anyone who appeared in the streets. Seventy-nine civilians were killed that night. The attack created mass pandemonium in the area and convinced thousands to flee to Sudan. Idris, together with three other men, was given the task of driving the family cattle herds to safety. Traveling on foot at night, then hiding in wadis and dry *khors* during the daylight hours, their journey took four or five days. As he recounted the details of the trek to me, Idris concluded, "They (the Ethiopians) did not want the Eritrean people, they just wanted the land."

Once in Sudan, Idris' clan, comprised of thirty or forty families interknit by marriage, reassembled in Kassala. After a year of waiting to return home to Tocumbia, Idris's father and his peers decided to move the group another ninety kilometers south to Wad el Hileau. (Some men had been there and believed it to be a location better suited for their livestock.) They settled on the southwest fringe of the village, thereby optimizing their access to the Setit River for watering livestock and minimizing the movement of their cattle herds through the village. As the Eritrean conflict became locked in a stalemate, other pastoralists joined them.

According to Idris, life went relatively well at first. Pasture lands were readily available. The size of his cattle herd remained steady, and in 1975 he married. The 1980s, however, brought dramatic changes and rapid impoverishment. Idris' herd steadily diminished in size, and by 1990 he had given up herding his own cattle altogether. By 1993, his 1967 herd of eighty head was reduced to seven.

Today Idris is an amalgam of resilience, fear, frustration, and gentleness. His economic status has plummeted, the range of his geographic movement has shrunk, and his circle of affiliation is growing smaller and smaller as members of his father's generation die. "In Eritrea," he points out, "the poor people were given help by the wealthy. Now life has changed, both those who have and those who have not are suffering ... The high cost of living has made people scatter ... They cannot help each other, not because they do not want to, but only because they are not in a position to do so."

Idris' view of the future is clouded by fear and frustration. While he is encouraged by the war's end in Eritrea, he fears internal conflict, and he recognizes that returning to Eritrea will not bring back his herd. The prospect of added costs to relocate are daunting. Thus, he remains in Sudan, although even after nearly thirty years in Sudan Idris stresses, "I am a guest." His frustration is amplified further by the realization that he is out of step with the next generation of Maria. Looking at his children, Idris remarks, "I was a *kalla* man herding the cattle and they are schoolgoers." ("Kalla" is a Tigré word used in reference to a life of movement herding out on the grass plains.) And unlike generations of Maria men whose primary aspiration was to develop a *murah* of one hundred head, Idris notes that eldest son's aspiration "is to be a merchant."

Idris Fucki Habib's story is by no means unique. Substantial herd losses have occurred during the last twenty years despite an entrenched ethic of cattle accumulation (see Figure 6.1). On average, Maria and Beni Amer herds have dropped from more than seventy head of cattle to an average of just five per household. Losses during flight and poor acclimatization to Sudan's heat reduced some herds by as much as 30 percent in the late 1960s, but cattle have suffered far more during the last two decades in Sudan. The majority of these losses have occurred in livestock markets rather than on the range. The next section details the pressures that force refugee pastoralists to exchange their cattle for cash and thus precipitate depletion of their herds and the impoverishment of their lives.

Feeling the Squeeze: Appropriation of Pasture Land

The first factor is a shift to a more sedentary lifestyle. War forced pastoralists to flee to an unfamiliar environment that, in turn, was a large disincentive against nomadism. Although cattle herds continue

Figure 6.1 Cattle Losses for Refugee Herds, 1967–1993

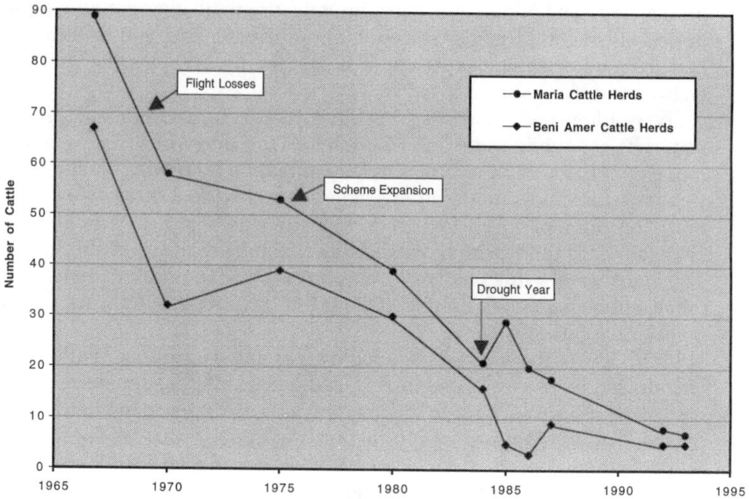

Source: Household surveys conducted in Wad el Hileau by author in December 1987 through June 1988, February 1992, and January through April 1993

to migrate with the changing seasons, households now remain at fixed locations, a pattern that is evident elsewhere in the Sahel.[5] The shift to seminomadism increased the consumption of goods; pastoral households must now purchase daily supplies of water, firewood, and charcoal, as well as more grain to offset the decreasing percentage of dairy products in the diet.

Having abandoned a nomadic existence, families no longer have a constant supply of milk from their herds. Small ruminant herds can be kept year round, but a village cattle herd can be kept near the village for only seven or eight months a year. This home herd, comprising one, two, or perhaps three of the best milk cows owned by each household, grazes in interstitial areas between farms under the care of a hired herder. During the dry season, however, range fodder steadily depreciates, the cost of supplemental fodder increases, and eventually the cows are sent to rejoin the larger "family" herd before it moves across the Ethiopian border. From March to July pastoralists subsist primarily not on milk products but on grain supplemented by goods purchased on credit from local merchants. Another factor in the expansion of grain purchases is that the Beni Amer and Maria refugees have no secured access to cultivable land. In Eritrea, pastoralists relied on small plots to supply their grain, but in Wad el Hileau only 12 percent of the pastoral households cultivate fields, and those that do generally must rent the land. Meanwhile, vast tracts have been transformed from open grazing land to *mushrooahs*, thereby minimizing the availability of rangeland and constricting corridors for migrating herds. Whereas before mechanization farm lands occupied less than 10 percent of southern Kassala province, now they cover more than 70 percent.[6] Cattle herds far exceed the acceptable stocking rate of 25 head per square kilometer in the low rainfall savanna of southern Kassala Province.[7] Overgrazing is particularly intense within pastoral corridors, some of which are fallow strips of land while others line roads or follow dry wadis. As grazing areas have become poorer, calving rates have declined; the calving rate for refugee herds along the eastern border of Sudan is 50 percent, compared with an average of 65 percent for herds in western Sudan.[8]

Tensions between peasants and herders are intensifying along pastoral routes. Cattle must graze within twenty kilometers of their water source and crops are frequently damaged as they move back and forth to the Atbara and Setit Rivers for water. Damages usually occur during the cool night hours when cattle are most active and herders are apt to fall asleep. In 1987, 73 percent of all herds based in Wad el Hileau damaged crops. Although guards are hired to protect crops, the state has been forced to intervene on behalf of smallholders. Livestock holding pens (*zaribahs*) have been installed by the Wad el Hileau Rural Council in seventeen villages. These pens hold livestock until a village committee assesses crop damage and the owner receives compensation for his loss. During 1987, cattle owners in Wad el Hileau paid an average of £475 (Sudanese) per household for damages incurred by their herds during the course of the year. Tensions between refugee pastoralists and Sudanese peasants have not reached crisis proportions for two basic reasons: refugees pastoralists are not as assertive as their Sudanese counterparts, such as the Rashaida, the Lahawien, and the Hadendowa, for whom confrontations with security officials do not pose the same level of threat. The other and more important reason is that grazing rights have become firmly commodified, and hence transformed into an expensive economic good.

Losing the Game: Commodification of Grazing Rights

Idris' interpretation as to why Maria cattle herds had become so small is this: "Before, there was free grazing land. Now all that land has come under cultivation, and the limited land left for cattle to feed on is overgrazed ... Before the price for grass was low, but now it has become very expensive." In the late 1960s and early 1970s, refugee herds grazed freely on the natural fodder left standing on schemes after harvest. In the mid-1970s, however, scheme operators began to charge pastoralists. In some areas, the process of commodification was slowed by in-kind exchanges of cattle milk for fodder, but by the late 1970s all pastoralists were forced to pay cash in exchange for the right to graze their cattle on *mushrooahs*.

After negotiating a price, a herder sends a request for money to the herd owner. If money is not forthcoming, then herders have the prerogative to sell several head in order to pay for the right to enter a scheme. A consolidated group of family herds (e.g., six hundred cattle) can graze an entire *mushrooah* in fifteen to thirty days, therefore, it requires access to as many as five *mushrooahs* during the first three months of the year. The access price has risen steadily during the 1980s from as little as £50 (Sudanese) per *mushrooah* in 1981 to as much as £15,000 in 1988. In 1988, the average lease price for land was £5,710 (Sudanese) or $1,270 (US). This amount was more than ten times the amount of money that operators were required to pay the Sudanese government in order to rent one thousand *feddans*, the typical scheme size. And the price of entering *mushrooahs* continues to increase, forcing refugees to sell more cattle to pay for access privileges. The effect of commodification is summarized in their own, simple, succinct adage: "Our cattle are eating themselves."

Pressing the Odds: Borders and Bandits

Given the massive expansion of schemes in Sudan coupled with the commodification of access rights, herders have been forced to seek new grazing areas. By 1977, 85 percent of all herds were making an annual trek into Ethiopia. Cattle herds now follow a route that is nearly triple the length of their previous one in Eritrea (see Map 6.2).

As the dry season begins in January or February, herds leave the Wad el Hileau area and follow the Atbara River southward. During late February and early March they reach the Wad Kowli vicinity at the confluence of the Atbara and the Bar el Salaam rivers. During the peak of the dry season (April to July) herds move across the Ethiopian border and follow the river valleys of the Angreb and the Bar el Salaam into western Ethiopia. After grazing on a new flush of grass at the beginning of the rainy season, herds reenter Sudan in July and begin to retrace their dry season route northward along the Atbara. By mid-October they reach Wad el Hileau and continue northward along the Kashmel Girba reservoir. In December, they start the same trek again.

Better pastures are located farther inside Ethiopia, but use of these carries the likelihood of attacks by bandits, or *shiftas*.[9] Herders use several tactics to minimize the risk of attack. They hire extra herders for the journey into Ethiopia, camp together in groups of six to eight, scout for one another, slaughter male calves to minimize the difficulty of sending the herd back to the border if bandits are spotted in the area, and divide the herd into two parts: older cattle and those with calves remain nearer the border, while younger, stronger cattle advance further in. If herders see bandits, they break camp immediately and drive each of their herds away from the camp *(cowad)* in a different direction. Then they move the herd back to the border as quickly as possible.

The life of a herder is lonely and dangerous, particularly inside Ethiopia. A herder usually sleeps in the open air during the day and tends the livestock during the cool nocturnal hours when animals in search of forage are most apt to damage crops. Nighttime vigilance is especially important during the months of October, November, and December when crops are approaching maturity. In an arrangement common in the Sahel, the eldest male in the household is generally regarded as the "owner" of a family herd.[10] However, many owners prefer to hire herders rather than perform the labor themselves because herding has become such a "hard and severe" way of life. Some 55 percent of all herd owners hire herders to care for their livestock the entire year; 26 percent more employ herders for a portion of the year (i.e., the months in Ethiopia); only 19 percent handle their own herds or use relatives.[11] Herders used to be paid in cows, but now herders are paid almost exclusively in money. In 1987, the salary for a hired herder averaged £100 (Sudanese) or $22 (U.S.) per month plus *woluuf*, a packet of coffee, tea, and sugar supplied by herd owners.

Access to grazing land in Ethiopia requires another monetary outlay. On entering Ethiopia, each herder is expected to pay the local militia a fee *(werko)* to protect the herd from bandits. The amount of this fee depends on the size of the herd. In 1987, a herd comprised of thirty to fifty head paid £400 (Sudanese), and larger ones paid a minimum of £600. Despite this form of hired protection, "incidents" (as pastoralists refer to them) occur every year. By 1988, 66 percent of all refugee pastoralists had had cattle stolen or herders kidnapped at least once in Ethiopia. In 1977 and 1978, when bandit activity was at its peak, eight herders were killed. This prompted the Eritrean Lib-

Figure 6.2 Monthly Cattle Prices at Gedaref Market

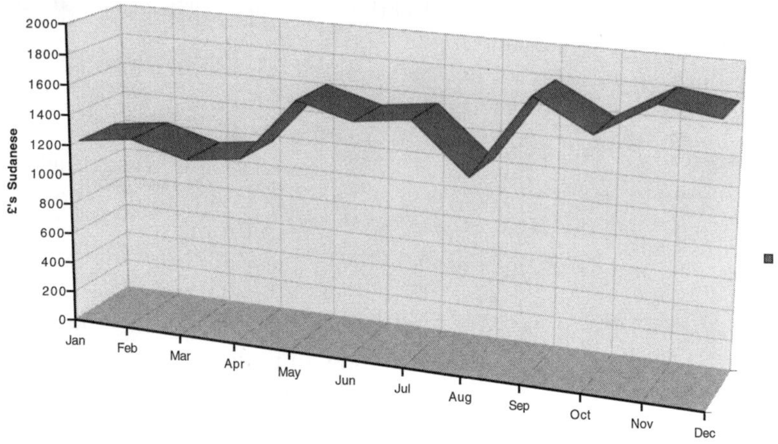

Source: Adapted from Agricultural Commodity Prices, 1987 Summary, Marketing Section, Department of Agricultural Economics, Ministry of Agriculture and Natural Resources, Khartoum, Sudan, February 1988

eration Front (ELF) and the Tigray People's Liberation Front (TPLF) to begin providing armed protection for herders. Although tensions have eased, bandits still capture herds every year. Despite the high risk of such incidents, four out of every five refugee herds based in Wad el Hileau return each year to Ethiopia. One refugee stated the dilemma this way: "You can either go into Ethiopia and risk losing your cattle, or stay here [Sudan] and let your cattle eat your money."

The Market: "Cattle Are Only as Good as the Pasture"

The Beni Amer and the Maria prefer to sell their cattle in August, September, or October, when cattle are in peak condition and prices are high (see Figure 6.2). Selling cattle during these three months requires that market herders drive cattle to Gedaref, the chief urban center of the eastern region. The market herders select designated stock from several herds, form a small market herd, and drive it from Wad Kowli to Gedaref, a four- to -five-day trek, depending on the condition of the cattle. In 1987, these herders were paid £30 per trip (Sudanese) by each of the owners for whom they drove cattle to Gedaref.

Owners incur other marketing costs too. Before 1982, livestock taxes were levied at rates of £3 (Sudanese) per camel, £2 per cow,

Map 6.2 Pastoral Grazing Routes Between Eritrea, Ethiopia, and Sudan

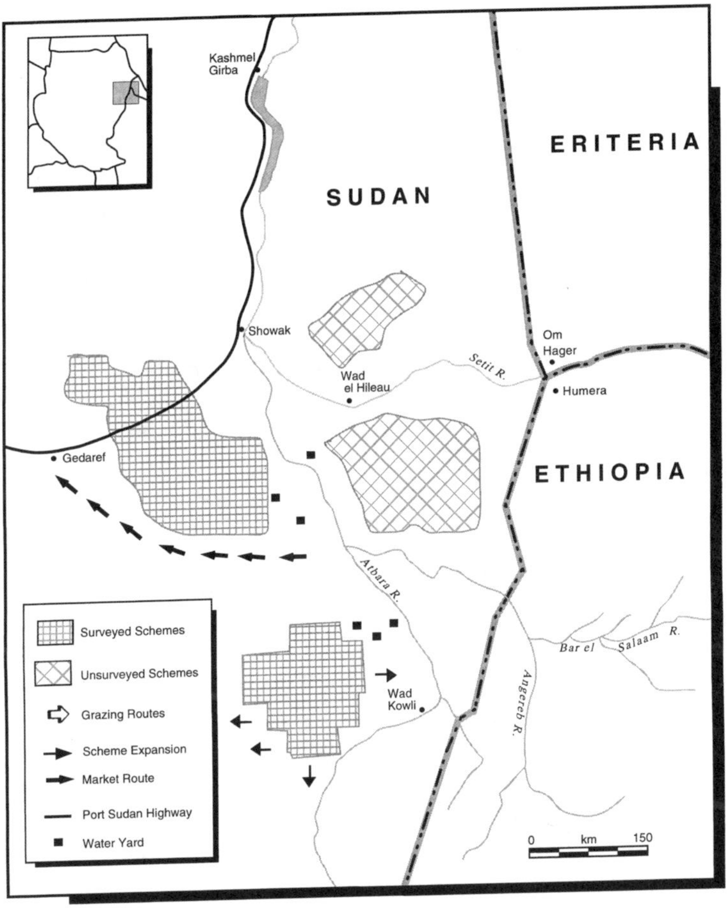

Source: Household surveys conducted in Wad el Hileau by author in December 1987 through June 1988, February 1992, and January through April 1993

£1 per sheep, £0.5 per donkey, and £0.25 per goat. However, since 1982 fees have been collected at livestock markets by a supervisor who, in essence, operates the livestock market for the government. Sealed bids are collected each July. The highest bidder wins the right to collect livestock fees for that year on a designated schedule. He pays the government in installments throughout the year and retains whatever comes in above his bid. In 1986, the winning bidder in Wad el Hileau paid £5,530 (Sudanese) to operate the livestock market and earned an additional £1,470 during the year.

The operator of the livestock market splits the combined buyer and seller fees with two other parties, a *damin* and a *dalal*. The *damin* (usually a sheik) is paid a portion of the livestock fee to guarantee the sale; that is, he guarantees that a seller actually owns the animal he is selling. If, in fact, the *damin* mistakenly allows a stolen animal to be purchased, he must reimburse the true owner for the animal. Meanwhile, the *dalal* is paid for another intermediary role as a broker between buyer and seller to expedite the negotiating process.

The livestock market in Gedaref dominates the border region of eastern Sudan because it offers a large concentration of beef purchasing power. The strength of the Gedaref market vis-à-vis the Wad el Hileau market is similar to other parts of the Sahel, where the demand for beef is as much as six times higher in urban areas than in rural ones.[12] Although the veterinary department in Gedaref reported an average of 11,490 slaughtered cattle per year in Gedaref between 1977 and 1986, a large number were slaughtered in Gedaref, but outside the purview of official control.[13] Additionally, a substantial portion of the cattle sold in Gedaref went to other urban centers within Sudan or was exported from the country. Officials in Gedaref estimate that 50 percent of all the cattle transported from Gedaref go to other Sudanese cities and that the remaining 50 percent go to Port Sudan for export.[14] Government records indicate that an average of 371 cattle (equivalent to 8 percent of all cattle) purchased in Gedaref were shipped to other urban centers in Sudan or to foreign markets. The percentages from these two sources differ because many cattle sold in Gedaref are smuggled from the city to avoid the mandatory tax and vaccination fee for each animal that leaves through official channels.

Winners and Losers

Table 6.1 summarizes the combined effect of the pressures detailed in the previous sections at three different levels of production. Families with smaller herds receive lower prices for their animals because they generally sell animals of poorer quality. At the same time, however, the cost of hiring a herder, accessing *mushrooahs*, and paying *werko* is significantly higher per head for smaller herds. Hence, production costs increase with the constriction of the herd.

In recent years, drought conditions have exacerbated pressures on refugee pastoralists. Poor rains in 1983 gave way to even poorer ones the next year.[15] Emaciated cattle flooded livestock markets and the terms of trade swung completely against cattle producers. The ratio of the price of a single cow to that of one sack of sorghum had been as high as 18:1 in the early 1980s; in 1984, the single cow could be purchased for less than the price of one sack of grain. In Wad el Hileau, cattle prices fell as low as £100 (Sudanese) per head, while sorghum prices climbed as high as £200 per sack.[16]

Table 6.1 Occupational Structure for Pastoralists, Before and After Flight

	Eritrea in 1967 (percentage)	Sudan in 1988 (percentage)
Pastoralism	100	87
Agricultural Wage Labor	0	13
Nonfarm, Non-Herd Income	5	44

Source: Household survey (N = 51) conducted in Wad el Hileau by author in December 1987 through June 1988.

The drought of 1984 led to livestock losses among refugee pastoralists in two ways: the physical death of weak stock, and the loss of cattle under radically altered terms of trade for livestock. The Sudanese government reported livestock deaths to be 30 percent for cattle and 10 percent for sheep, goats and camels in the eastern region, but pastoralists asserted that rates were higher.[17] For Wad el Hileau, cattle herders contended that the average loss was 38 percent, a figure that combined both range and market losses. Losses were far greater in the market (75 percent) than on the range (25 percent) because herders attempted to sell weak stock before they died, and given the altered price differential between grain and livestock, pastoralists were forced to sell more cattle than usual to supply their own grain needs, which increased due to the shortfall in milk production. Pastoralists had to sell still more cattle to purchase fodder and grain for the surviving herd. Although the drought added to pressures on pastoralists, the crisis developed from conditions and forces created by the prior appropriation of rangelands and the commodification of grazing rights.[18]

The Outcome: "Only the Third One Owns Livestock"

Fewer and fewer refugees now own cattle, even those who do are increasingly dependent on other sources of income. As one man remarked, "In the past, all Beni Amer were pastoralists, but now there are three kinds of Beni Amer men – one is an agricultural wage laborer, another is a petty merchant, and only the third owns livestock."[19] The proportion of former pastoralists who now do some agricultural wage labor has grown to more than 15 percent, but the proportion turning to other forms of employment has risen even more. The experience of Amir Mohommed Ali, a Beni Amer refugee in Wad el Hileau, is a case in point.

In 1954, Amir was born into a wealthy and prominent Eritrean family based in Haicota. At age eight, he began to work with the family herds, comprised of one hundred cows, more than three hundred goats and sheep, and fifty camels. Soon, his father insisted that he return home to begin Koranic training. Early in 1967, Ethiopian forces began to target people of high privilege in the lowlands. The death of seven people in Haicota prompted Amir's family to flee the village. Using camels and horses, they went to the border town of Tessenei and spent the night. The next day they traveled southward to Om Hager, encountered more fighting, and decided to leave Eritrea altogether.

They chose to settle at Wad el Hileau because it was "a good place for grazing" and Omda Ajil welcomed them warmly. Most of the camel herd remained in Eritrea. Although their cattle adjusted to the new environment reasonably well, the entire flock of goats and sheep died. In 1976, at the age of twenty-two, Amir took charge of the family herd. That same year he married. He gave his wife the traditional wedding gift of seven cows, and his father gave her seven more. In 1982, Amir still had a sizable herd of seventy cows, but the drought of 1984 decimated his herd. Amir estimates that as many as fifteen cows died during the drought; he had to sell as many as five more per month to weather the famine. The herd never recovered. In 1991, he sold four cows to pay for his father's funeral and another five died during an epidemic. By 1992, Amir's family owned just twelve cows and six sheep.

Tall, handsome, and independent, Amir began seeking other sources of income in the wake of the 1984 drought. He found work at Wad el Hileau's animal market as a livestock trader, or *sababi*. Like other *sababis*, Amir's success depends on buying when prices are low (e.g., on days other than Saturday, the main market day, when other *sababis* are away herding or farming). But competition is becoming fierce as other herders turn to *sababi* work to offset the depletion of their herds. In 1990, Amir tried his hand at farming. He spent £800 (Sudanese) to rent twenty-five *feddans*, but his yield was zero.

Termination and Transformation

The viability of pastoralism among refugees in eastern Sudan is threatened by the rapid depletion of herds. Livestock losses have been exacerbated by the rapid appropriation of rangeland, but this dwindling land use base does not completely explain the demise of cattle herds. Although pressures operate in the market and on the range, structural factors are also at work. Two main social groups compete for pastoral resources in the border region of eastern Sudan, and as pastoralists fast become net losers in the politics of land use, *mushrooah* operators are the net winners. In essence, the retreat of pastoralism among refugees can be attributed to the expansion of agrarian capitalism, which is undermining traditional pastoralism by expropriating rangeland and by raising costs of production.

The demise of pastoralism is being slowed by remittances from migrant workers in Persian Gulf states like Yemen, Saudi Arabia, and the United Arab Emirates to refugees in eastern Sudan. This flow of money is crucial in maintaining the households that receive it. Although this imported capital may sustain pastoral households over the short term, it cannot do so for the long term. Refugees insist that there is no escape from mounting costs. Some herds have already become too depleted to support the next generation of the family, and that circumstance has forced young men to seek new occupations. Intergenerational shifts from pastoralism are an important facet of the ongoing process of pastoral marginalization as well as of the fragmentation of the household, the primary unit of production.

Meanwhile, merchants and *mushrooah* operators have begun to establish large cattle herds and to use their own schemes as dry season grazing areas rather than selling the sorghum fodder to transient pastoralists. This should not be surprising, because pastoralism is not reserved for traditional pastoralists alone but is a method of livestock production that can be employed under a variety of social conditions.[20] Pastoral restructuring is occurring elsewhere in East Africa under similar conditions. In northern Kenya, northern Somalia, and eastern Sudan pastoral restructuring is a predictable offshoot of commodified grazing rights and the rising demand for beef.[21] The degree to which pastoralism becomes the domain of absentee owners who are merchants and *mushrooah* operators will depend heavily upon the future demand for beef. Cattle exports from Sudan have been quite limited, but the domestic market appears to hold promise. The World Bank reports substantial increases in constant meat prices and forecasts increasing demand for beef in major urban centers like Khartoum and Wad Medani.[22] If domestic meat prices continue to rise, the likelihood of pastoralism being dominated by merchants and *mushrooah* operators will increase.

Conclusion

The marks of social communalism are still clear in Maria and Beni Amer society. However, resettlement in Sudan has forced pastoral households to be integrated into a cash economy that increasingly threatens the viability of their productive system. During the 1980s and early 1990s many young men had to postpone marriage because family herds had become too small to meet the traditional bride price of seven cows. During the last five years, however, the payment of cattle has buckled under the pressures of a cash economy; the bride price is now paid in cash rather than cattle and thereby, symbolizes the twilight of pastoralism as a distinct way of life.

We have now witnessed the impact of rural transformation on refugees in a variety of locations by "traveling" out on the range, into the field, and through the market. The next chapter shifts to a different location to assess the crises that rural transformation produces within the refugee home.

Notes

1. Trevaskis, *Eritrea*, 132.
2. W. Shack, "The Central Ethiopians: Amhara, Tigrinia, and Related Peoples," *Ethnographic Survey of Africa*, Part IV – Northeastern Africa, ed. D. Forde (London, 1974), 15.
3. The vestiges of this master/serf relationship still remain today. Qayih are the cattle-poor portion of the Maria ethnic group and comprise virtually the entire corp of hired herders.
4. Shack, "The Central Ethiopians," 71.
5. T. Bassett, "The Political Ecology of Peasant-Herder Conflicts in the Northern Ivory Coast," *Annals of the Association of American Geographers* 78 (1988): 453-72.
6. (SKAP), Land Use Survey Reports, J3.
7. Ibid.
8. A. Mustafa, "Livestock Farming Systems," in *The Agricultural Sector of Sudan: Policy and Systems Studies* ed. A. Zahlan (London, 1986), 220.
9. Although it is a hotly contested issue between Maria and Beni Amer herders, Maria herds usually go further into Ethiopia, which is evidenced by the fact that their stock are generally superior in quality to that of the Beni Amer.

10. Bassett, "Peasant-Herder Conflicts."
11. Despite the somewhat paternal relation between owners and herders, the latter are always referred to by name because designating someone as "my herder" is regarded as a social insult.
12. Bassett, "Peasant-Herder Conflicts," 467.
13. K. Abdulrahim, Interview at Gedaref veterinary office, 10 July 1988.
14. Ibid.
15. H. Ati, "The Process of Famine: Causes and Consequences in Sudan," *Development and Change* 19 (1988): 267–300.
16. Hendrikson Associierte Consultant (HAC), Refugees in the Eastern Region of Sudan, Consulting Report, 1984.
17. el Shazali, *Eritreans in Kassala*, III–26.
18. D. Rahmato, Famine and Survival Strategy: A Case Study from Northeast Ethiopia, Food and Famine Monograph Series, No. 1 Institute of Development Research (Addis Ababa, 1987), 6.
19. Field Note Entry, 10:16.
20. A. Samatar, *The State and Rural Transformation*.
21. P. Little, "Absentee Herd Owners and Part-Time Pastoralists: The Political Economy of Resource Use in Northern Kenya," *Human Ecology* 13 (1985); S. Samatar, L. Salisbury, and J. Bascom, "The Political Economy of Livestock Marketing in Somalia," *African Economic History* 17 (1988): 81–97.
22. World Bank, "South Kassala Agriculture Project."

In Sudan, a woman's place is considered to be around the hearth and in the home. Here an Eritrean woman prepares the staple food, a sorghum-based pancake.

7

Asylum and the Making of Home Terrain

As there is no donkey with horns, so there is no woman with brains.

Eritrean Proverb

Those currently exploring the possibilities for post-conflict development in the Horn of Africa are paying very little attention to gender division in their societies ...

Amina Mama
Beyond Conflict in the Horn

Introduction

This chapter moves down in scale to the "terrain" within refugee homes. It focuses on changes in the constitution of refugee households and the life experiences of exiles, many of which are amplified or accelerated by the process of rural transformation at the resettlement site. In so doing, this chapter is largely concerned with age and gender relationships. Refugee women and children are often overlooked, despite the fact that they constitute 80 percent of the world's uprooted people. Our understanding is weakest for those who reside outside official camps or settlements.[1] Unassisted women and children, however, are the focus of the analysis to follow. Forty such individuals living in Wad el Hileau provide the primary data for this chapter. (The sub-sample was comprised of fifteen married women, five single women and five single men between eighteen and twenty-five years of age, and fifteen children between the ages of ten and seventeen.)[2] These refugee women and children supplied important

Notes for this section begin on page 142.

narrative statements as well as more discrete kinds of data related to sources of income, financial expenditures, time allocation and travel patterns.[3] Their experiences, core relationships and narrative explanations are keys to a clearer understanding of the dynamics within refugee households.

Dislocated Households

The last two chapters outlined the decomposition of reciprocal relationships among refugee households and the concomitant emergence of social differentiation. This chapter shifts from interhousehold relations to those within refugee homes, i.e., intrahousehold dynamics. Becoming a refugee, by definition, involves geographic displacement, but refugees undergo social dislocation as well. As seen in previous chapters, there have been dramatic changes in the amount of time that men are absent from their homes. Among pastoralists, very few household heads herd their cattle throughout the dry season, and therefore they are no longer absent for months at a time. The opposite is true for heads of households that have farming backgrounds. The need to search for wage labor forces them to be away from home much more than was true in Eritrea. Clearly refugee displacement goes beyond a change in geographic locale. Sudden flight may result in the disintegration of the household unit. But even when refugee households remain intact, changes in human relationships almost always accompany the movement of people from one geographic location to another.[4] Important questions emerge from this corollary: How does refugee migration and resettlement affect age and gender relations? Does displacement strengthen or weaken premigration patriarchal social relations? And what are the effects of displacement on the division of labor in the refugee household?

Theories influence the way we see the details of situations. The "lens" of a more classical approach to household economic behavior is based on a central assumption of cooperation; that the household is a single economic unit in which members pool their resources and operate to maximize their joint utility. This model minimizes evidence of conflicting goals, independent decision makers, and divided assets and incomes.[5] However, newer models use a "conflict" orientation, which is better attuned to the dynamics within the household. Rather than minimize or avoid the issues of internal conflict, negotiation, and divisions of power and responsibility, they search for them.

Despite a large body of literature outside refugee studies that questions how households are defined and researched, the refugee "household" is usually envisaged as the essential unit of analysis and, for that matter, of relief.[6] The reconfiguration of interhousehold relations was abundantly clear during my original fieldwork. Surely the same pressures that decomposed reciprocal relationships between households were apt to affect the nature of relations within them as well. Or so I thought. Hence, upon return to the field site, I determined to examine the social "terrain" within households, especially the core relationships of gender and age, and to avoid collapsing individual interests into a single entity.[7]

Household Configurations

Like most villages in East Africa, Wad el Hileau is subdivided into a patchwork of courtyards. Thorn hedges delimit boundaries between a whole gambit of spatial units, interwoven and nested within one another. Large courtyards comprised of multiple dwellings and households that share a central activity space are at one end of the continuum.[8] Smaller house yards that surround an individual home are at the other. Regardless of their size, much of the daily regime transpires in these activity areas as people prepare food, eat, sleep, tend animals, process food, bathe, wash clothes, and relate to one another.

Courtyards both symbolize and define the character of a community. On one hand, the physical design of courtyards gives tangible expression to existing social, political, economic, ethnic and kinship relations.[9] But the manner in which they are used also conditions and composes relationships, thereby blending the "spatial" and the "social" together.[10] In eastern Sudan, meals are often prepared and eaten among households with the same central courtyard, thereby reinforcing communal relationships. In the case of Wad el Hileau, this arrangement is especially true for two ethnic communities, the Bargo and Hausa. Two underlying reasons are large family sizes and multiple wives, but other contributing factors, associated with their collective experience as refugees, exist as well. Having fled *en masse* to Wad el Hileau, these two groups managed to reconstitute their preflight social relations more successfully than did refugees from other ethnic groups who arrived in a more piecemeal fashion. Moreover, the Sudanese sheik allocated large, designated areas to Bargo and Hausa refugees for agriculture. This allocation allowed households not only to farm, but to share adjacent fields, which in turn, expedited their availability to assist one another. Functional cooperation in the field stretches back to the home. It finds expression in the shared preparation and consumption of food among Bargo and Hausa.

By contrast, shared courtyards do not exist among the Maria and Beni Amer. Although women may rotate cooking duties among neighboring families, single family courtyards predominate among refugee pastoralists.[11] The configuration of homes is even more diffuse among Kunama refugees. In fact, the Kunama ward on the outskirts of Wad el Hileau features a lack of spatial definition; dwellings are often physically removed from one another, some with unfinished thorn hedges, others with none. Several factors contribute to this lack of spatial definition. Kunama refugees originate from many areas in Eritrea, and they came to Wad el Hileau in sporadic fashion rather than *en masse*. They are the most recent arrivals and remain the most impoverished, and they do a disproportionate share of the agricultural wage labor in the region. Men, women, and families come and go, often to fields, for days or weeks at a time. Their mobility actively discourages wide domestic units and communal living.

Household space among refugees is also affected by the presence of individuals who are not immediate family members. Table 7.1 illustrates the distribution of household sizes and extra family members – both extended family members and long-term houseguests – for refugee households in Wad el Hileau. They constitute 15 percent of the total refugee population.[12] Thus, unassisted households have a higher proportion than is true of the Sudanese host community as well as of nearby refugee camps, where the proportion of extended family members is 10 percent.[13]

Sex ratios are often assumed to be strongly disproportionate in refugee populations, but that assertion has been found to be inaccurate throughout the Horn of Africa.[14] In the case of Tanzania, for example, women head 25 percent of all rural households. But in a household sample drawn from refugee settlements in Tanzania, Daley found female heads in only 5 percent of all households, and these were either widowed or divorced. She attributes the lower percentage to their migratory pattern (whole communities fleeing together), the presence of lineage members exerting social and familial pressure against abandonment, and state restrictions on refugees' mobility.[15] To assume that women head a large proportion of unassisted households is particularly erroneous in instances where the short-term exigencies of flight have worn off. The vast majority of Eritreans have been in Sudan at least fifteen years. Although some single women do filter into UN camps, most unassisted refugee women do not remain single very long.

Table 7.1 Distribution of Household Sizes and Extra Family Members

Household Size	No Extra Members	One Added Member	Two Added Members	Three Added Members	Four Added Members	Total Households
1–2	0	8	–	–	–	8
3–4	5	15	3	2	–	25
5–6	18	13	–	–	–	31
7–8	12	7	1	–	–	21
9–10	13	4	2	1	–	20
11–12	11	1	1	2	2	20
13–14	3	0	1	–	–	4
15–16	3	0	1	2	1	4
17+	2	1	–	–	–	3
Total	67	53	8	6	3	135

Source: Household survey conducted by author November 1987 through June 1988

Patriarchy Rules

Gender relations are rooted in the cultural, religious, and economic influences governing a society; all three define the social position of refugee women living in Sudan. The roots of female subordination are deeply embedded in agrarian cultures throughout Africa, but especially so in those regions like Sudan in which Islamic religious structures intensify the level of control men can assume over women. Religious custom sharply curtails women's physical mobility and thereby precludes or restricts their economic activity, both in terms of type and amount. As a result, Islamic countries have the lowest rates of women's participation in the wage labor force in the world. In Sudan, women constitute less than 25 percent of the country's labor force. Another cultural tradition, female circumcision, is an almost universal practice. The social significance of circumcision is that it ensures male control of female sexuality, or that of senior women over younger women. This practice also functions as part of the system of male monopolies of property and inheritance whereby women have very little access to, or substantive control over, the most fundamental resources of production – land and livestock. Patriarchy also plays a central role in differentiating the sexual divisions of labor. The workload connected with those domestic activities which maintain or "reproduce" daily life are mainly allocated to women, while men control the more extroverted and distant income-generating activities.[16]

Gender-based subordination is deeply ingrained in the consciousness of both men and women. The clear awareness of male dominance was a recurrent theme in discussions and interviews. Most women conveyed their perception of gender relations in a more oblique fashion, but the youngest married woman that I interviewed underscored the matter in a blunt, straightforward manner: "Women are never unattached .... [They are attached] either to a father or husband from here to the grave."

Gendered Space

The geographic constructs of mobility and scale are useful ways to illustrate gender relations.[17] The practice of secluding women known as purdah is a fact of life that all women in eastern Sudan face, especially given the recent growth of more militant Islamic fundamentalism in Sudan. Its predominance reflects the dominant influence of Islam fused with a patriarchal ideology. The fact that non-Islamic women, most of whom are refugees from the highlands of Eritrea and Ethiopia, are subject to the same constraints of purdah as those from Islamic households shows the power of the combined influences.

The practice of purdah also has very overt spatial aspects. Be she a refugee or not, the activity space for most women in eastern Sudan is largely confined her own house yard and those directly adjacent. I found that to be especially true among refugee women who belong to the Beni Amer, Maria, and Nara. Their strong commitment to Islam discourages women's freedom. Take, for example, Kaltoum, one woman with whom I conducted an in depth interview. Since Kalthoum's arrival in 1967, her entire life sphere, except for three brief trips away from Wad el Hileau, has been the twenty courtyards that make up her neighborhood.[18] Although she and other women could freely visit the market in Eritrea, Kaltoum had never been to the market in Sudan. Another interviewee, Asha, spent the first five years of married life with the freedom to move between the courtyards of only six adjacent households. Yet men enjoy much greater freedom of movement. As Fatna M. put it rhetorically: "Haven't you seen my husband? He is always out!"

Refugee women are even more aware of how infrequently they leave the village. Many of them have relatives in Eritrea as well as scattered throughout eastern Sudan. Yet those with relatives elsewhere have made on average of just two trips outside of Wad el Hileau during their adult life, and these were generally associated with illness or death. The fact that women are usually "crisis travelers" either to attend a funeral or to seek medical attention is a significant departure from the past. In Eritrea, women made visits outside their home villages more frequently and often for a joyful occasion, e.g., a wedding or a child's naming ceremony. When asked to identify the primary reasons why life was better for women in Eritrea compared to Sudan, an interviewee named Miriam pointed out that "men do it [travel] in both places" but that "only in Eritrea could women make visits on lots of occasions." As will be seen later, there are some refugee women who do leave Wad el Hileau in search of economic opportunities, but they represent the marked exception rather than the rule.

Older refugee women sometimes stretch their social and spatial boundaries by entering the market area. But women remain on the "margins" of the market in at least three different ways. The first of those involves physical access to the central portion of the market. Those women who operate out of fixed stalls, principally small tea shops, or who launder clothes, occupy the perimeter of the market, whereas men who offer an identical product and service operate in far more central locations, which afford them a much larger clientele. Some older women, often widows, do enter the central market to sell processed food like roasted peanuts, peanut butter, or sorghum flat bread, the staple foodstuff. However, they have no stalls. Instead, they operate in the open air, generally at the corner of a shop or at a junction point within the market. Women are also marginalized by economics; refugee or not, no female owns a shop in Wad el Hileau. Clearly when petty trade or other forms of petty commodity production become profitable, they tend to become the preserve of men.[19] Only those very small operations directly associated with food processing remain solely in the domain of women.

Reorganizing Labor Relations

The economic transformation of societies is another source of change beyond that of cultural and religious pressure. Chapters 2 and 3 provided an understanding of the contrasting nature of the rural economies on either side of the Sudanese-Eritrean border. By seeking asylum in Sudan, Eritreans were forced to resettle in a substantially different economic formation where their sources of livelihood were conditioned by a dramatic increase in commodification. When asked to compare life in Eritrea with that of Sudan, Fatna K. expressed the contrast between the two in the following way. In Sudan, she pointed out, "If you don't have money you can't eat," but "in Eritrea, you get your food from the farm land."

Changes in the rural production systems, within which refugees live, have a direct impact on the division of labor accorded to women.

In her landmark study, Esther Boserup maintains that the gendered division of agricultural labor becomes more dichotomized as rural production systems become wage economies because women remain locked in an untransformed sector while men work in a sector of enhanced productivity.[20] Although derived from West Africa, her scenario also applies to refugee households in eastern Sudan. In Eritrea, there were many women – mainly Nara, Bargo, Kunama and Hausa – who worked alongside their husbands on the household plot. In fact, some women managed a portion as their "own" fields. Much has changed, however, during exile in Sudan. A great deal of male labor now "seeps" out of the subsistence sector and into agricultural wage work on *mushrooah* schemes. Cash and subsistence demands upon refugee households have also grown substantially. To offset the loss of labor on household plots as well as increasing demand for income, women from those refugee households who have access to land must work harder.[21] As one refugee woman, Khajija A., put it: "Women do more agricultural work here [Sudan]" because "men are tired here."

Refugee women from one Eritrean ethnic group, in particular, regularly compete with men for agricultural wages earned on *mushrooah* schemes. Unlike the other communities from the western lowlands of Eritrea, the Kunama have retained many animistic religious elements rather than convert to Islam, and line of descent is derived maternally. Kunama women share a history of independent decisionmaking, gender autonomy, and familiarity with agriculture. With this background, they have challenged the traditional gender segregation that exists in the Sudanese agricultural labor market. The experience of Baraka, an interviewee who left Eritrea in 1980, is not uncommon among Kunama women. She began working for agricultural wages just ten days after she arrived in Sudan, despite having no previous history of wage work. Kunama women like her supply a significant proportion of the day labor on Sudanese farms, weeding and harvesting sorghum, the region's staple food crop. Because sesame harvest is more profitable than any other type of agricultural wage work, it remains the principal domain of men. In recent years, however, Kunama women have sought higher pay by seeking out work on *mushrooah* schemes. They must travel further from home and stay away longer, but Kunama women prefer working on *mushrooahs* for the simple reason that they can earn higher wages, and earn them faster, by doing wage labor on the basis of a piecemeal contract *(guwaals)* rather than daily rates *(yoomiya)*. For example, another interviewee, Arafa and two other Kunama women completed a *guwaal* contract in 1992 worth £2,500 (Sudanese).

Having completed the work in nine days, each woman made an average £92.5 (Sudanese) per day as compared to the going day wage of £65 (Sudanese).

Higher wages are important to Kunama women like Arafa because they offset the shortfalls in agricultural wages earned by Kunama men, most of whom arrived more recently than other refugees and do not own land. Finally, it is important to note two recent developments. First, scheme managers have begun to come into Wad el Hileau in order to hire Kunama women rather than wait for them to appear on a *mushrooah*. As an incentive to work on their *mushrooahs* for days, weeks, or longer, foremen offer women a cash advance or a credit line for family members to purchase goods in their absence. Typically, the scheme foreman will come to recruit women and immediately transport them to his scheme aboard a tractor and trailer. (Often a woman's children go with her as well.) Second, as Kunama women move deeper into the agricultural labor market, their counterparts from other ethnic groups "move in" behind them. Arafa drew the comparison herself by stressing that all Kunama women work a lot, that all Nara women now do a little work in fields as wage labor, and that only Bargo girls work in fields as wage labor.

Redefining Resource Rights

The experience of exile can reshape women's access to resources in three basic ways. The first and most obvious is the types of disenfranchisement associated with the process of flight itself: the disruption of war impacts productive activity before flight; refugees' inability to take most of their assets with them; losses incurred by sudden flight; and the necessity of selling assets upon arrival in the host country in order to reestablish oneself. Second, displacement can uproot the social guarantee provided by kinship structure. As a general rule, women have less access to productive resources than their male counterparts. However, their position in a kinship structure often serves to guarantee women greater access to, and secure ownership of, property. Typically, this is most common in bride wealth societies where the accumulation of wealth occurs in a repetitive manner from one generation to another. At least in the past, among Eritrean pastoralists, seven female cows were given to a woman as her dowry by her husband. Hence, women in pastoral households were able to control a productive resource with a significant return – the offspring calves. However, this important property right has eroded deeply during exile. Among refugee pastoralists, the average herd has decreased from more than seventy head of cattle to fewer than five animals. With impoverishment, most women no longer have effective control over the cattle once given to them. And with declining control of productive resources has come a concomitant loss of social status and power.

The nature of the host society and economy is a third important factor. Ways that the "external" political economy force resource rights to be dispersed are often overlooked.[22] Previous chapters examined the changing character of relationships among refugees after resettling in an economy where their sources of livelihood were conditioned by a dramatic increase in commodification. This process has specific ramifications for women. The process of refugee flight combined with resettlement in a commodity-based economy has severely undermined women's access to land and their ability to command labor and resources. As noted already, among subsistence cultivators in Eritrea, many women maintained a portion of the family agricultural plot under their control. The same is not true in Sudan, however. None of the women I interviewed controlled any agricultural land and therefore lacked the ability to dictate how the product was dispensed with. Each woman was asked whether she believed that life was better for women in Sudan and Eritrea. In the succinct words of one interviewee, "Life is better there because women own land, sheep, and perhaps even a few owned cows ...." In Sudan, men invariably control all the purse strings. In a study of woman's survival strategies in Sudanese refugee camps, one respondent spoke for many when she said: "I am a beggar even in my home, every morning I am asking him for money to feed our children."[23]

Impoverishment plays an important role in one overt form of social decomposition – divorce. While divorces remained very rare in Eritrea, they appear to be more common in Sudan. According to Baraka, the "disability of men to provide for daily needs" is the main reason for this change. Not surprisingly, household conflicts usually relate to the basic means of survival. "Misunderstandings arise over food and livelihoods," noted Arafa, but "Now a wife does not obey as much due to unsatisfactory life."

Divorces might be more common if women had stronger supportive networks or better prospects of earning their own livelihood. Becoming refugees involves the loss of home in a relational sense. Prior to flight, the "life world" of Eritrean women was deeply rooted in supportive networks that have eroded substantially during exile. Most of my respondents noted that women were closer in Eritrea. As Fatna M. put it, "Before [in Eritrea] women would plait their hair together and have coffee, chatting affectionately ... but [in Sudan] they are no longer as friendly, kind and affectionate." Arafa depicted female relations in starker terms: "Women there are more kind," but "here hearts hate each other."

Divorces also are rare because self-employment opportunities for refugee women are so limited in the informal sector. Job diversity is minimal at best. Basket making, thread spinning, and hair braiding provide token income. The more remunerative sources of income like prostitution and alcohol brewing bear the threat of imprisonment and fines. But this has not always been the case. In the 1970s, by which time most refugees had arrived in Sudan, the government of Sudan collected taxes from alcohol producers rather than prosecute them.[24] In 1984, President Nimeri first outlawed alcohol in an attempt to placate Muslim agitators and thereby lengthen his tenure as president of Sudan. Sudanese governments since then have moved increasingly toward a hard-line Islamic fundamentalism. In so doing, male police officers and secret service *men* have increasingly stronger grounds for taking action against refugee women who, invariably, are the likeliest candidates to resort to alcohol production and sales as a form of income generation. Eritrean women who come from the highland region, where Christianity rather than Islam dominates, are most susceptible to abusive treatment.

The politics of gender are played out even more starkly for female prostitutes who are "assumed by society and all local authorities to be the root cause of social problems, rather than the victims."[25] These women are subject to the personal interests of men in two different ways. Most obviously, women are treated as objects of sexual satisfaction. Due to their fear of clients' aggression, many women secure the protection of a quasi husband to act as a guard.[26] However, the price of such protection is to share the household income with that quasi husband.

Resource rights are clearly tied to decision-making power, which constitutes a key nexus point of authority and power within households. The process of leaving an old social context and entering another, as refugees do, can create new decision-making roles. The promise of such a chance is especially true for women who become heads of their household. Generally speaking, however, households headed by females are the exception among self-settled populations. Husbands remain the primary adults with whom adult women covertly or overtly negotiate, save for rare occasions when they interact with parents, in-laws, patriarchal figures, or siblings.[27]

To each of my female respondents, I posed the same question: What household decisions do you make? Somewhat rhetorically, Khadija M. replied, "What else do women have to decide except foodstuffs?" Kaltoum concurred: "The only decision women make is how much *dura* [sorghum] she should take to the mill and what kind of *mulah* [porridge] to cook." And she hastened to add, "if her husband asks her to change her mind, she will do so." Men and women rarely discuss decisions that involve income. And men may spend a substantial portion of household earnings on the market-based activities of coffee, tea, or domino betting. Men also decide about children's names and schooling. According to Asha, "It is the *man's* children, so he decides about schooling [author's emphasis]."

Age Matters

Not women or men, but children constitute the majority of virtually every refugee population. Approximately 47.7 percent of the Ethiopian and Eritrean refugees in Sudanese camps are children less than fifteen years of age.[28] The proportion is only slightly lower among unassisted households (45 percent in my sample of 131 households). Despite their numerical importance, refugee children have not constituted a significant area of inquiry among research conducted in the Horn of Africa.[29] While there is a general and serious dearth of information regarding exiled children, there is even less on how the process of rural transformation has affected the life experience of refugee children.

The "life world" of children is often redefined during asylum. Based upon extensive fieldwork at another rural site in central Sudan, Katz has documented how the processes of commodification, social differentiation, and agrarian change dissolve the unity of work and play and thereby deskill the next generation of the peasant population.[30] In keeping with Katz's findings, Khajija F. remembers happy memories of games and wandering far from home, but notes that now children play less, remain around the house, and often spend their spare time sleeping. One reason the locus point for children's identity is changing so rapidly is that many families are no longer a functional unit of production as they once were.

Children's responsibilities now focus on the home rather than in the field or the pastoral range. Typical premarriage responsibilities for girls include sweeping the house and courtyard, caring for younger children, fetching water, making porridge, and milking animals, as well as washing and ironing clothing. Boys, although they may help with (and be quite skilled at) such tasks, are more likely to be found outside the yard, tending animals and making trips to the store. As children mature, their respective degree of "spatial freedom" changes radically. As girls reach puberty, their freedom of movement diminishes, but activity space steadily enlarges with age among boys. Young Maria and Beni Amer men are one example. As long as the hosts are related as consanguineal kin, they often "float" from house to house to eat where they will and even to sleep elsewhere.

That the current generation of children has a different life perspective than their predecessors is evidenced in three prominent ways. One visual reminder appears on the faces of children. Among the Maria, for example, facial scarification was phased out in the mid-1980s. Children younger than twenty years old are thus unmarked. Another important indicator is associated with the place which individuals most readily identify as "home." Most older children, like twenty-four-year-old Easa, want to return to Eritrea and think of that as "my country." Meanwhile, however, Sulieman, his thirteen-year-old brother and his cohorts consider Sudan their home and thus want to stay in Sudan. A third key indicator are changes associated with marital ages. Among those refugees whose livelihood is based on subsistence cultivation, the marriage age is dropping. Key incentives have changed. Given the prevailing land squeeze in Sudan, fathers have less incentive to retain the agriculture labor that their daughters might offer. But the wedding age is going up among pastoralists. For lack of cattle to meet the traditional bride price of seven cows, men and women have been marrying later than ever before.

Conclusion

This chapter has investigated the core relationships within refugee households and how gender-based and age-based identities are loosened and restructured during exile. By its very nature, displacement poses a natural crisis of cultural norms and the potential transformation of gender relations.[31] Recall one of the motivating questions for this chapter: Has displacement loosened or strengthened pre-migration patriarchal social relations? The position of women varies across ethnic circumstances and economic conditions, but I conclude that subordination of women has been exacerbated rather than transformed in asylum.

While the picture is still partial and incomplete, this conclusion is based on the fact that the spatial and social domain of Eritrean women has shrunk and that refugee men now have more control over household resources, property, and decisions. But why? Some factors are associated with the processes of migration, rural transformation, and immiseration. During flight, refugee women lost ownership to many forms of property and many social guarantees to resources previously provided by kinship structure. Second, the shift into a commodity-based economy has severely undermined refugee women's access to land and their ability to command labor and resources. And third, the quality of life for the majority of people in Africa, whether refugees or not, has deteriorated throughout the 1980s and 1990s. Within this situation it is commonly acknowledged that the situation of women, rendered particularly vulnerable by their subordinate status, has worsened disproportionately.[32]

In newly independent Eritrea, much has been done to strengthen the status of women in society. Formed in 1979, the National Union of Eritrean Women (NUEW) is self-consciously feminist in its orientation. Legal measures provide women with guarantees to the rights of land ownership, to entry into the marriage of their choice, to divorce, and to retain custody of children. New laws protect women's rights within the family. But the status of exiled women is moving in the opposite direction. As Fatna K. expressed: "[The man] is the owner of the household."

Notes

1. S. Martin, *Refugee Women* (London, 1991), 4. For notable exceptions, however, see the following: P. Daley, "Gender, Displacement and Social Reproduction: Settling Burundi Refugees in Western Tanzania," *Journal of Refugee Studies* 4 (1991): 248–66; A. Spring, "Women and Men as Refugees: Differential Assimilation of Angolan Refugees in Zambia," in *Involuntary Migration and Resettlement*, ed. A. Hansen and T. Oliver-Smith (Boulder, 1982), 37–47.
2. I had hoped to survey an equivalent number of boys and girls. However, given the sensitive nature of gender relations in a Muslim society, it was especially difficult to interview younger girls. Hence, twelve interviews were conducted with boys and three with girls.
3. Information about women's lives was collected both purposely and incidentally while residing within the community and moving from place to place on foot to conduct interviews during 1987 and 1988. In 1993, I returned to Wad el Hileau to refine the scale of analysis. Every interviewee came from an unassisted household whose head I had previously interviewed. This allowed me to identify differing perspectives within the same household and to link data collected from women, youths and children to their respective household's migration history, ethnic affiliation and class position.
4. L. Pulsipher, "'He Won't Let She Stretch She Foot': Gender Relations in Traditional West Indian Houseyards," in *Full Circles: Geographies of Women Over the Life Course*, ed. C. Kaatz and J. Momsen (London, 1993), 121.
5. E. Berry, "Finding the Invisible Women: Intra-household Dynamics as a Challenge to Conventional Theories of the Household," A Review of *A Home Divided:*

Asylum and the Making of Home Terrain | 143

Women and Income in the Third World, ed. D. Dwyer and J. Bruce, *Women's Studies Forum* 13 (1990): 614–17.
6. D. Dwyer and J. Bruce, *A Home Divided: Women and Income in the Third World* (Stanford, 1988); L. Østergaard, *Gender and Development: A Practical Guide* (London, 1992); C. Katz and J. Monk, ed. *Full Circles: Geographies of Women Over the Life Course* (London, 1993); J. Momsen and V. Kinnard, ed. *Different Places, Different Voices: Gender and Development in Africa, Asia and Latin America* (London, 1993).
7. E. Berry, "Intra-household Dynamics: Indications of Women's Autonomy in the Third World," Unpublished paper presented at the meetings of the Association of Women in Development (Washington, DC, 1989).
8. Pulsipher, "'He Won't Let She.'"
9. J. Bourdier and T. Minh-Ha, *Drawn from African Dwellings* (Bloomington, 1997).
10. P. Williams, "Constituting Class and Gender: A Social History of the Home, 1700-1901" in *Migrants, Emigrants and Immigrants: A Social History of Migration*, ed. C. Pooley and I. Whyte (New York, 1991), 155.
11. Rotating cooking duties offers a certain efficiency for it lowers the cost of charcoal, and thus of food, for individual families.
12. This estimate is higher than the previous estimate of 7 percent for the village J. Wijbrandi, "Organized and Spontaneous Settlement," in *Enduring Crisis: Refugee Problems in Eastern Sudan*, ed. T. Kuhlman and H. Tieleman (Leiden, 1990), 55–83.
13. Wijbrandi, "Organized and Spontaneous Settlement," 82.
14. Waldron, "Blaming the Refugees"; G. Kibreab, *Refugees and Development in Africa: The Case of Eritrea* (Trenton, N.J., 1987); Bulcha, *Flight and Integration;* Daley, "Gender, Displacement."
15. Daley, "Gender, Displacement," 254.
16. Østergaard, *Gender and Development*, 5.
17. Katz and Monk, *Full Circles*, 265.
18. In 1984, Kaltoum did visit her mother in Eritrea when, according to her husband, "I gave her one month's leave."
19. Daley, "Gender, Displacement," 263.
20. A. Whitehead and H. Bloom, "Agriculture" in *Gender and Development: A Practical Guide*, ed. L. Østergaard (London, 1992), 41–56.
21. Ibid., 48.
22. J. Carney and M. Watts, "Manufacturing Dissent: Work, Gender and the Politics of Meaning in a Peasant Society," *Africa* 6 (1990): 207–41.
23. T. Demeke, Survival Strategies of Refugee Women: Case Study Eastern Sudan – Analysis from a Gender Perspective, MA Thesis (University of East Anglia, 1992), 30.
24. Ibid., 36.
25. Ibid., 40.
26. Ibid., 40.
27. Dwyer and Bruce, *A Home Divided*.
28. el Bashir, cited in el Nagar, "Children and War in the Horn of Africa," in *Beyond Conflict in the Horn: Prospects for Peace, Recovery and Development in Ethiopia, Somalia and the Sudan*, ed. Doornbos et. al. (London, 1992), 17.
29. el Nagar, "Children and War," 15.
30. C. Katz, "Sow What You Know: The Struggle for Social Reproduction in Rural Sudan," *Annals of the Association of American Geographers* 81 (1991): 488–514.
31. Displacement can lead to an intensification of the subordination of women in asylum or prove to be a liberating force. Daley, "Gender, Displacement," 34.
32. A. Mama, "The Need for Gender Analysis: A Comment on the Prospects for Peace, Recovery and Development in the Horn of Africa," in *Beyond Conflict in the Horn: The Prospects for Peace, Recovery and Development in Ethiopia. Somalia, Eritrea and Sudan*, ed. M. Doornbos et. al. (London, 1992), 74.

Refugees have been repatriating back to Eritrea since the war ended in 1991. More than one thousand families were given tents at this resettlement site near Ghinda.

8

Repatriation and the Search for Home

The day the war ends, I will return home ...

Eritrean refugee
Interview in Wad el Hileau

Too often it is taken for granted that the return of refugees to their country of origin is a "natural" and "problem-free" process.

John Rogge
Repatriation of Refugees: The Not-So-Simple "Optimum" Solution

Introduction

The 1990s have been proclaimed "the decade of repatriation." While legal, financial and logistical impediments to repatriation are important, too often the perspective of refugees themselves, is overlooked. This chapter examines refugees' motivation and logic for repatriation, recognizing that the decision usually involves a combination of motivations, intentions, perceptions, conditions, and expectations. The experiences of exiled Eritreans living in Wad el Hileau provides the basis for analysis. In doing so, the central focus of this book, the relationship between refugees and rural transformation, resurfaces. Not only does it play a prominent role in determining the prospects for repatriation, but it affects the process by which refugees reach a decision and influences the prospects of success upon reintegration in the homeland.

Notes for this section begin on page 160.

Going Home: The Moment and the Myth

In May of 1991, a series of rapid events in Ethiopia brought the Eritrean war to an abrupt end. In early May, then-President Haile Mengistu was forced to flee from Ethiopia by an oncoming offensive mounted by the Ethiopian People's Democratic Revolutionary Front (EPDRF). Menguistu's departure completely destabilized Ethiopian forces in Eritrea, and they began evacuating Asmara immediately. A bloody and chaotic retreat ensued and in a matter of days EPLF forces secured the entire country. On 24 May, Eritrea was declared independent. Twenty-four years of open conflict had forced more than one million Eritreans to seek refuge in other counties. At last it would seem that the refugee community in eastern Sudan, including those of Wad el Hileau, could finally return home.

Repatriation began slowly. During the remainder of 1991, ten thousand Eritreans repatriated of their own accord. Meanwhile, however, negotiations between UNHCR and Eritrea's provisional government for a large-scale repatriation became locked in a stalemate. Whereas the Eritrean side envisaged an outlay of $200 million (U.S.), UNHCR proposed only $69 million (U.S.), insisting that it could not promise more given its restricted mandate and donors' reluctance to increase their commitments amid multiple crises elsewhere. Eritrean officials refused to acquiesce for at least two strategic reasons.[1] First, they balked in the hope of securing a larger and firmer commitment from donors. Second, by delaying a full-scale operation, the provisional government could better prepare to receive a large influx. One respondent in Wad el Hileau summarized the passivity of the EPLF office: "They asked us when we wanted to go, but nothing more."

The longer the de facto government held out in the hope of convincing donors to provide more funding, the more momentum for repatriation was lost. In a direct request to donors for assistance, the Commission for Eritrean Refugee Affairs (CERA) emphasized that "... the [repatriation] endeavor will become a recipe for social disaster unless the minimum conditions which enable the returnees to restart a productive life are created."[2] UNHCR's initial plan for the Eritrean operation largely ignored the reconstruction component.[3] Repatriation negotiations finally succeeded only when UNHCR relinquished its authority to counterpart agencies – the UN Department of Humanitarian Affairs and the UN Development Program.

UNHCR's organized repatriation program finally began in late 1994. In the months of November and December, the UN helped some 8,000 refugees return to Eritrea, plus an additional 15,000 in the first five months of 1995.[4] Meanwhile, even more Eritreans repatriated without UN assistance; 33,000 in 1994, another 25,000 in 1995, and 11,000 more in 1996. Only a few thousand Eritreans have returned since then, despite a 1995 survey which indicated that a majority of those remaining in Sudan still wished to repatriate.[5] In sum, approximately 160,000 Eritreans have returned, but 320,000 more remain in Sudan. Seventeen UN settlements still house 100,000 refugees.[6] The remainder are unassisted refugees, including all but a few of those residing in Wad el Hileau.[7]

Clearly, the fundamental preconditions for voluntary repatriation – the cessation of military conflict coupled with political independence – were met, but they prove to be insufficient to prompt a large scale repatriation back to Eritrea. Although conditions for repatriation may not have been to their liking or choosing, exiled Eritreans had the option to return home without facing open warfare. The fact that so many chose not to return to Eritrea raises fundamental questions about their depth of motivation for return. The removal of pressures that once forced refugees to migrate has been insufficient to ensure their return. This suggests the distinct possibility that many refugees relied on a "myth of return" to help sustain them through hardships during exile.[8]

The strength of attraction and attachment to the homeland is one critical factor associated with the "myth of return." Incentives to repatriate often begin with the amount of "location-specific capital"; that is, the relative strength of those factors that "tie" a person to a particular place.[9] These include, for example, a person's familiarity with the physical environment, ties with the community, or family relationships. But location-specific factors depreciate with time; old friends may have died or become refugees themselves, homes and land have been destroyed or appropriated by others, and information about home areas has become obsolete. Thus, as the interval of absence lengthens, the propensity for refugees to repatriate home becomes weaker. Most Eritreans fled to Sudan more than fifteen years ago. Refugees may insist – as they often did in Wad el Hileau – that the day the war ended, they would return home. But the opportunity to actually migrate back is the true test both of their resolve and of their resources. The fact that the majority of Eritreans still remain in Sudan suggests the possibility that their actual attraction to the "promised land" has depreciated significantly. According to a survey published in 1996, nine out of every ten Eritreans in Sudan still want to repatriate eventually.[10] Whether they ever will actually return to Eritrea remains to be seen.

Going Home: The Decision-Makers

Changes in the locus of decision-making authority often accounts for the reluctance to return. As seen in previous chapters, Eritreans exiled in Sudan have been integrated into competitive relations of production based on agrarian capitalism rather than reciprocal relations of production which typified their former way of life in Eritrea. The bases for collective decision-making found in shared social activities and productive cooperation have been severely eroded, and the locus of decision-making has shifted from traditional leaders of kinship groups to individual heads of households. Only 27 percent of the unassisted respondents in Wad el Hileau suggested that their sheik would have any influence whatsoever over their decision to repatriate. In the words of one interviewee, "I have to decide what is best for me." Clearly, a crucial shift has occurred; community interests are now secondary to those of the household and the individual.[11]

It is important to note, however, that camp refugees are more likely to rely on leaders for repatriation decisions than are unassisted refugees. In Sudan, a marked expansion in authority figures has occurred in camps and settlements. One researcher, for example, reported an "amebic" proliferation in the number of small sheikdoms in the Qala en Nahal settlement.[12] His study found that during a twenty-year period the number of authority figures had grown from forty sheiks to more than 220 authority figures – a 550 percent increase. The growth can be attributed to several factors: (1) the significantly higher dependency ratios that typify camp populations (i.e., women, children, elderly, and the infirm); (2) the fact that camp refugees are buffered by physical space and financial assistance from outside influences; and, (3) an ossification of authority structures amid the highly structured regime of camp life.

The decision to repatriate is also linked to important intragenerational factors. Different generations within the refugee population are ambivalent toward repatriation. Older members of the Eritrean population frequently perceive that they are not wanted in Eritrea as much as younger generations are but younger members of the Eritrean population are hesitant to move too. In fact, the majority of the refugee population has never lived in Eritrea or were so young when they left that they have no recollection of "their" homeland. For these second- and third-generation refugees repatriation necessitates leaving "home" rather than returning to it, and they are generally hesitant to move. Their cited reasons include mandatory obligation in the national service (e.g., twelve to eighteen months), superior educational opportunities in Sudan, and, perhaps most importantly, the undesirability of returning to the way of life they associate with preflight Eritrea (i.e., pastoralism and subsistence agriculture).

Finally, gender plays a key role in repatriation decisions. Returnees from official camps include a much higher proportion of female-headed households compared to those from unassisted concentrations where intact families are more common. A large survey of nearly twenty thousand Eritreans who repatriated shortly after the cessation of conflict indicated that 39.5 percent of repatriating households were female-headed.[13] Among unassisted populations, however, it is almost always men who make the decision. When asked, 61 percent of the forty-five respondents in Wad el Hileau indicated that they would not consult their wives at all regarding the repatriation decision. The remaining 39 percent planned to tell their wives of their decision. Only one man suggested that his wife would have any substantive input. Refugee women understand quite plainly their decision-making status. One woman, Kalthoum, stated it in her own curt summary, "What say do I have? I am told to go or to stay."

Going Home: Perceptions and Conditions

The process of assessing the pros and cons of repatriation begins as refugees collect information about conditions at home. Like other migrants, most refugees find personal contacts with travelers – new arrivals, temporary visitors, and persons who have made a return visit – to be the most effective source of information. Ninety-six percent of my respondents had spoken directly with someone from their original village within two years of the war's end. In most instances, visitors conveyed very specific and personalized information about conditions in Eritrea. Eighty-nine percent of the sample could identify, for example, the present condition of their former agricultural land as either overgrown, cultivated by family members, confiscated, or damaged. According to a recent survey of exiled Eritreans living outside the Sudanese capital of Khartoum, more than half of the refugee families have sent a family member to visit Eritrea to assess conditions.[14] The most important information invariably relates to two key issues associated with Eritrea – democracy and development.

The Political Participation Factor
In Eritrea, both rumored and real political and religious factionalism between highlanders and lowlanders acts as a strong deterrent

against repatriation. Thirty-two percent of the unassisted respondents in Wad el Hileau suggested that political factionalism in Eritrea was the primary reason keeping them from going home. Interest in returning to Eritrea fell precipitously after the first flush of excitement at the war's end. In the UN camp adjacent to Wad el Hileau, refugees were asked to enroll for repatriation shortly after the cessation of conflict in Eritrea and again six months later. Between July 1991 and the following December, the number of lowlanders who indicated their willingness to repatriate fell from 3,975 registrants to 1,194.[15] Figure 8.1 compares the distribution of enrollees in January with those in July. Although the proportion of highlanders grew by 12 percent, the percentage of lowlanders (the Nara, Kunama, Beni Amer, and Maria) fell 70 percent.

There is a distinct sense among many refugees that the Eritrean victory was not their own. Their ambivalence illustrates two basic categories of refugees with differing attitudes toward repatriation.

First, there are those who hold a firm conviction that their opposition to events at home, and which caused them to seek asylum, is shared by the majority of their compatriots. Thus, they are likely to retain a strong

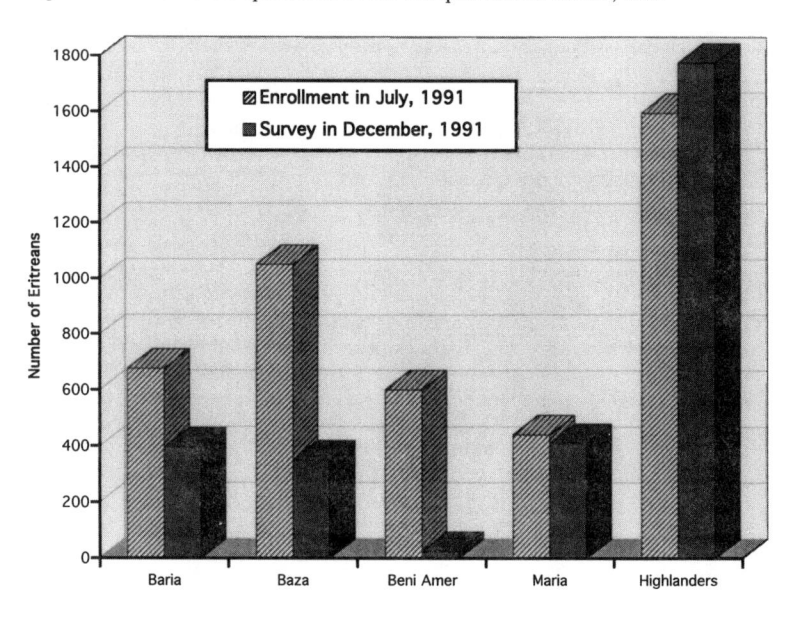

Figure 8.1 Interest in Repatriation at UN Camp at Wad El Hileau, 1991

Source: Adapted from tabled data obtained from the Sudanese Commission for Refugees, Local Office, Wad el Hileau, Sudan, February 1992

bond with their home areas – Kunz referred to such refugees as *majority identified refugees*... such refugees are clearly the ones most likely to want to repatriate when the cause of their exile is removed. It is also clear that many of Africa's refugees fall into this category. A second category is refugees who, on leaving their home areas, feel alienated from the rest of their homeland population, and probably also feel discriminated against. Such refugees may be referred to as *events related refugees;* they are less likely to have a strong desire to return home, especially if there have not been any fundamental changes to the social or political systems which alienated them on the one hand, or if they have become economically and/or socially integrated in their country of asylum on the other hand ...[16]

Unassisted respondents were asked to prioritize six ethnic groups from the lowlands of Eritrea, ordering them from the one they believed would repatriate first to the one that might be last. Kunama and Nara were clearly front runners, followed by the Maria, Beni Amer, Bargo, and finally Hausa. The marked differential among these six different ethnic communities reflects to a large extent the degree to which each community identifies with Eritrea. The fact that Naran refugees are more apt to repatriate than any other lowland group can be traced directly to the participation of members of that community in the first band of guerrilla fighters led by Idris Awate in the early 1960s. Border locations often become a base for "refugee warrior communities."[17] In 1988, more than 175 men and their families were on the EPLF payroll in Wad el Hileau; sixty-five enlistees were Nara, fifty were Kunama, and sixty-five more from the highlands of Eritrea. Predictably, these so-called "majority identified refugees" are most apt to repatriate.

Conspicuously absent from the EPLF payroll were members of three other ethnic groups – the Beni Amer, Maria, and Bargo. The prospects for their repatriation are directly linked to the context in which members of each one left Eritrea. Generally speaking, the Beni Amer, Maria, and Bargo fled violent conflict that was not directly targeted against them, but which spilled over into their region. Hence, these constitute what Kunz categorizes as "events related refugees" who are unlikely to have a strong desire to return home, especially if they have become integrated in the country of asylum. Both the Beni Amer and Maria do, in fact, have a long history of association with Sudan linked to transborder pastoral migration. Moreover, motivated in large part by the desire to gain access to subsidized quotas of sugar or grain, the Maria, Beni Amer, and Bargo asserted and won their right to Sudanese "citizenship" in a localized, informal manner at Wad el Hileau during the mid-1980s. Their efforts to identify with the host community is therefore an important factor associated with their reluctance to repatriate.

The implications of understanding repatriation in terms of majority identified refugees versus events identified ones are manifold. First, events identified refugees are more apt to remain in exile for several years because of apprehension about security.[18] Second, the experience of the earliest returnees becomes a critical test case for other event identified refugees who might consider following them back to the homeland. UNHCR's official planning mission for the Eritrean repatriation rightly noted that "the successful repatriation of the first groups will determine the success of the whole operation."[19] Third, the repatriation process has become segmented between majority identified and events identified refugees; that is, the repatriation of highlanders took place before that of lowlanders (see Table 8.1). Lowlanders remain skeptical about their position in the political future of Eritrea.

Table 8.1 Eritrean Lowlanders and Highlanders in Sudanese Refugee Camps, 1991[a]

Settlement	Lowlanders	Highlanders
Um Saguata	39,700	300
Kashm el Girba	7,500	500
Kilo 26	11,400	1,000
Um Garqur	4,950	50
Karkora	9,500	500
Abuda	4,000	1,200
Um Ali	2,650	350
Um Rakoba	2,000	13,000
Tawawa	3,000	21,000
Um Gulja	500	8,000
Hawata	2,000	2,000
Mafaza	2,100	2,000
Abu Rakham	1,000	4,000
Wad Awad	1,300	700
Teneba	3,000	2,000
El Suki	3,500	3,000
Wad el Hileau	3,000	6,500
South Tokar Dis	17,000	3,000
Shagarab	26,000	20,000
Fau	8,000	10,000
Hilet Hakuma	1,000	9,000
Total	**153,100**	**91,700**

[a] Data estimated from 1987 through 1988
Source: Adapted from UNHCR literature on Sudan

The Economic Development Factor

Refugees also take into account the magnitude of destruction and the state of the home economy. Before repatriating, refugees make their own assessment of the impact that war has had on the specific region into which they might move. Twenty-six percent of those interviewed in Wad el Hileau indicated that economic factors (i.e., lack of services, transportation infrastructure, and available jobs) were the primary reasons keeping them from going home. Eighty percent of those surveyed in a larger 1996 study said that devastation and underdevelopment in Eritrea were major impediments to their return home.[20]

The environmental toll is an even greater concern than the destruction of the infrastructure. Military campaigns of the 1960s, 1970s, and 1980s were designed to render the land sterile. They included napalm contamination, the destruction of irrigation canals and wells, the denudation of the landscape of live trees, and extensive land-mining operations in agricultural fields. The indirect environmental cost of the war was the virtual suspension of all development activity such as reforestation, well digging, and terrace construction to control soil erosion.[21] Establishing a healthy, self-reliant economy, and providing essential social services and utilities for as many as three million people amid the massive toll on the environment is neither easy nor quick. And importantly, refugees understand that fact. Ninety-five percent of the sample taken in Wad el Hileau indicated their desire to resettle in Eritrea at the same location from which they fled, but refugees have serious questions as to whether the specific location from which they fled will have sufficient natural resources – grain, building materials, and livestock fodder – to sustain them. Many refer to their homeland as "empty" and to many inhabitants as "disabled" (i.e., economically impoverished).

Meanwhile, rapid population increase has taken place. The Eritrean population, which was estimated at about 1.65 million when conflict began in 1961, more than doubled by 1991. The impact of destroy-and-desolate campaigns carried out by the Ethiopian military during the war, coupled with rapid population growth, has created a severe shortage of arable land. During the war the peasantry in many regions was forced to overexploit and under maintain its environment.[22] Only with the end of the war did Eritreans have the "space" to manage the fragile ecosystem in keeping with the country's zealous commitment to self-reliant development.

The prevailing precipitation pattern is a key factor in strengthening Eritrea's food security. Since 1967, the Sahel has experienced twenty-five years of below-average rainfall. Reliable rainfall data are not available for Eritrea, but recent rainfall data in adjacent Sudan suggests that the average annual precipitation has generally declined. The constriction of the rainy season as well as its variability has serious consequences for refugees who choose to return home. Pastoralists and small-scale cultivators are in the most precarious position.[23] Drought already has taken its toll on each of these livelihoods. During the 1980s, crop production is estimated to have declined by 40 percent, and the number of livestock fell by 50 percent.[24] Additional losses continued under low rainfall conditions during the first two agricultural seasons of the 1990s. The 1992 season, however, experienced the best rains in fifteen years, and the total harvest quadrupled that of the previous season.[25] Nonetheless, imports had to cover half of the country's grain needs.

Common property resources like wood, water, grazing rights, and agricultural land are common "flash points" of contention between returnees and their compatriots who remained during the war. There are no formal systems of land measurement or registration in the western lowlands. Instead, agricultural land – once deemed "pubic domain" during Italian colonialism – is collectively owned by respective ethnic communities. Respondents in Wad el Hileau are confident that conflicting claims over land ownership can be resolved by way of social and cultural networks within those communities. Sixty-eight percent of the respondents in Wad el Hileau anticipate no difficulty reclaiming their land, twenty-one percent anticipate a dispute, and eleven percent are uncertain. But conflicts over resource management are still likely in view of a weakened authority structure. As another researcher notes, "… it will be more difficult than before to manage common property resources collectively … because individual decisions have replaced collective decision-making regarding production and resource allocation."[26]

The Risk Aversion Factor

Classic migration theory posits "pull" factors associated with the potential destination in the homeland and "push" factors with the present place of residence. The same may be true for refugees who have the choice of repatriation. Hence, this section focuses on the dynamics of repatriation associated with different ways in which refugee households have been integrated within the host economy.

In Sudan, the reluctance to repatriate relates to the position of refugees at both ends of the socioeconomic ladder. For wealthier refugees, the knowledge that they risk losing accumulated wealth or economic status acts as a strong deterrent against repatriation.[27] Field observations in eastern Sudan indicate that refugee merchants are keenly aware that they will forfeit a hard-earned position among traders in Sudan by repatriating, and then, they may face the prospect of having too small a clientele to sustain a new enterprise in

Eritrea. Their decision not to repatriate poses a central problem associated with repatriation. Although they were forced to flee from their country of nationality for reasons of fear, these refugees are choosing not to return for reasons of economic prosperity.

Most refugees, however, face the repatriation decision at a time in which they are more impoverished than ever before. Although those holding the lowest position in the social hierarchy are usually thought of as most apt to migrate, the poorest segment of the refugee community in Sudan may chose to remain. Twenty-six percent of the respondents in Wad el Hileau suggested that the simple lack of financial resources to pay for transport was the primary factor keeping them from going home. Mohammed Idris Awate offers one illustration of this phenomenon.

> Mohammed is a focused person with eyes of intensity that suggest someone who has seen hard times. And indeed he has witnessed much war and work. Short and stocky, this Nara man brought terse answers and a straight-forward bent to our conversations. Mohammed was born in 1952 in O'Garo, the fourth child of ten. His eldest brother, Hamid, is a central figure in the Eritrean conflict, for it was he who first took up arms against the Ethiopian forces in the western lowlands of Eritrea. While exonerated as a hero among Eritreans, Hamid Idris Awate was known as an armed bandit to Ethiopian authorities who repeatedly came to Mohammed requesting that he help them arrest his brother. The family moved to Guluje, a small village near the Sudanese border, to remove themselves from harassment. This meant that Mohammed had no opportunity to begin formal schooling.
>
> In 1961, young Mohammed – then age nine – joined his brother's fledging guerrilla band. This was the start of twenty years of service in the liberation struggle. While fighting with his brother Hamid, then with the ELF, and later with the EPLF, Mohammed fought in the battles of Tessenei, Om Hager, and Guluje in the lowlands as well as elsewhere in the highlands. His EPLF experience meant that he learned Tigrinia and Arabic.
>
> In 1978, Mohammed married. Their first child was born in 1981. Serving in the EPLF without pay, the practical necessities of supporting a family forced him to leave the army. At the same time the Ethiopian forces intensified their activity in the western lowlands – killing indiscriminately and setting fires. Given his famous namesake (Awate), Mohammed was particularly wary of a reprisal directed against him, so he and his family, mother, and five other families left for Sudan. Their late arrival in Wad el Hileau, necessitated settling on the outskirts of the village. Because agricultural land was no longer available, he resorted to agricultural wage labor. The entire family's subsistence remains linked to agricultural schemes – weeding, harvesting sesame, harvesting *dura*, then cleaning underbrush during the dry season. This necessitates being gone for as long as a month at a time.
>
> Beginning in 1990, Mohammed shifted to a new dry season occupation – hauling water. In a typical day, he makes six trips to the river with

a donkey cart (i.e., two barrels mounted on a pipe frame). A day's total earnings are £480 (Sudanese). Fodder for the donkey fodder takes £80 (Sudanese) and the owner of the cart and donkey gets another £200. He "works every day unless I am sick." Attempting to augment his income, in 1992 he cultivated a small plot of land previously owned by his sister who died the year before. Without money to hire a tractor, he cultivated the five *feddans* by hand. But his labor was not rewarded as the plot yielded nothing.

Mohammed has not returned to Eritrea since he left in 1981, principally because he has not had the means to do so. This same problem remains true. When asked about repatriation, he responds rhetorically, "What makes me stay here?" Locked in a "trap of necessities," he is without the means to finance his own repatriation. Thus, his plans to return to Eritrea remain unclear. When? "As God wills." With no reason to stay, but no means to go, Mohammed reminisces about the good old days in Eritrea. He refers to life there as "*aduna bakir*" (pleasant in every way). He compares the fragmented and torn nature of life in Sudan to that of Eritrea where "life hung together"; that is, livestock, culture, and farming worked together in a collective fashion. Even so, he acknowledges that life is Eritrea is no longer the same. As much as he could use financial help from relatives still living in Eritrea, he admits "they don't have enough for themselves, let alone me."

One can readily understand why the Arabic derivative for *lajeene* (refugees) means "down-trodden".[28] Seventy-seven percent of the Eritrean households I interviewed in Wad el Hileau during 1987/88 were located in a marginalized position within the local economy. The 1992 and 1993 survey coupled together with data gathered in 1987/88 indicates that most refugees in Wad el Hileau (and there is good reason to believe throughout the entire eastern region) are poorer than they have been at any time before. As noted in Chapter 6, the cattle herds of pastoralists based in Wad el Hileau, which had dropped from an average size of seventy-five head per household upon entry to Sudan to fifteen by 1988, had fallen still further to an average of five as of 1993. Meanwhile, small-scale cultivators are working less and poorer land due to the massive expansion of mechanized agriculture during the last two and one-half decades. Given severe constraints on the amount of land available, cultivators have, as seen in Chapter 5, abandoned virtually all fallow practices in order to obtain a subsistence. The quality of the soil in the area is declining, and the incidence of witchweed, which decimates sorghum yields, is increasing.

The impoverished status of most refugees has made them far more sensitive to the crisis potential associated with repatriation than to the opportunities it might offer. One-third of unassisted respondents in Wad el Hileau indicated that they would prefer to repatriate independently in order to avoid the social stigma associated with being camp refugees the crowded conditions during transport, and in order to retain the freedom to choose when to repatriate. The remaining two-thirds preferred an official program. During a study published in 1996, about 85 percent of the respondents indicated that assistance levels in Eritrea would be a major determinant in their decision about whether to go home.[29]

The dominant preference for a UN-sponsored program illustrates how vulnerable and fearful of risk most refugees become. Their reluctance to return is linked to more than the questions of food and transport. Apart from the lack of foodstuffs to help them through the transition back to Eritrea, what marginalized refugees fear is the possibility of social breakdown and destitution associated with the irreversibility of the repatriation decision. Thus, the vulnerability produced by long-term poverty in Sudanese society helped to make very unlikely a large-scale, "spontaneous" repatriation among unassisted refugees.

Risk aversion is also manifested by a repatriation strategy that most households prefer; when asked, most heads of unassisted households indicated that they wanted to go to Eritrea first, then return to Sudan and bring the rest of the family several months thereafter. Eighty-five percent of all interviewees preferred this "split family" tactic. They justify it on the basis of their need to register land, rebuild homes, and establish trade linkages before the whole family returns. This deployment tactic is not surprising given the protracted length of time that refugees have been away from Eritrea, the massive amount of destruction that has occurred since they left, and the risk-avoidance tactics that poor people must adopt. Unfortunately, the deployment of household members on either side of the border is not consistent with UNHCR's protocol for repatriation exercises, which requires that households return as a complete unit. UNHCR consultants were concerned that Eritrean households would engage in cross-border movements or split their families into locations on either side of the border in order to gain entitlements in Sudan as well as Eritrea.[30] Advocacy for phasing out assistance to Eritreans in Sudan is intended, in some measure, to keep refugees from adopting this approach.

Going Home: The Expectations for Return

The majority of the respondents in Wad el Hileau (63 percent) predict that life will be easier in Eritrea, but many are referring to the nonmaterial advantages afforded by return. One respondent noted that "at home you are free to behave in all senses," while another stressed that in Sudan "you are always a guest." Eighty-eight percent of the respondents believe they will be welcomed back by the current inhabitants, but host communities are not as willing to accommodate returnees as repatriating refugees often expect.[31] Major cultural and social transformations in exile complicate attempts to return to traditional agrarian societies or to promote cooperative activities to work the land, rebuild homes, and reestablish basic services.[32]

Ninety-one percent of my respondents believe that upon return they will go back to "the ways of *nafir*" (group work parties). Free exchanges of labor in group work parties were the quintessential expression of the social interdependence and reciprocity that characterized preflight economies in the lowland region. Although respondents readily acknowledge that *nafir* is dying out in Sudan, they stress that it is still a "habit" for those who remained in Eritrea during the war and that a revival of such customary relationships can be expected in Eritrea because only a limited amount of money is circulating throughout rural areas.

At the same time, however, returnees have very different expectations from those they had when they left. Livelihoods and lifestyles have both changed. One study, based upon a sample of 380 households that returned during the first nine months of 1990, reported a drop from 85 percent to 65 percent in the proportion of households engaged in agricultural activities.[33] In Sudan, most Eritreans have shifted to a form of agriculture that is far more dependent upon mechanization, wage labor, and large capital inputs. For interviewed households in Wad el Hileau, thirteen *feddans* was the average size holding before flight. When the same respondents were asked how many *feddans* they would require upon return, they indicated an average of thirty *feddans*. So, too, the vast majority of refugee peasants have relied on tractors for cultivation in Sudan, whereas more than 90 percent of subsistence farmers in Eritrea rely on draught animal power.[34] Hence, the reintegration program will need to take into account the impact of rural transformation during exile.

The process of reintegration also will be especially difficult for those who have lived in large refugee camps. Returnees have a greater desire to settle in urban locations because their extended stays in camps and settlements have included the amenities of urban life – ready access to schools, clinics, running water, and flour mills.

Employment poses yet another challenge to returnees, especially given the fact that returnees must compete with one hundred thousand former soldiers for jobs. Undoubtedly, agricultural wage labor in Sudan will remain an important alternative for many returnees.

Fifty-four percent of the respondents in Wad el Hileau anticipated travel back to Sudan after repatriation. Many of the first to return are allocating their labor on both sides of the border. Male members return to Sudan during the peak of the agricultural season and entrust subsistence plots in Eritrea to the rest of the household. Under Eritrea's first investment code, the clearing of large-scale "agricultural estates" akin to those of Sudan has begun.[35] But this clearing will take time, and the area under expansion is limited to the Om Hager region. Additional migration can be expected among pastoralists, who now know the eastern region of Sudan and are wary of losing more livestock if they shift their herds back to western Eritrea. Markets and educational opportunities will draw former refugees back as well. Thus, maintaining an "open door" policy, whereby people can move freely back and forth across the border, is important to the success of the reintegration process in Eritrea. At the moment, however, military hostilities along the border have made travel risky and Sudanese authorities at the border have posed an additional obstacle to repatriation by imposing taxes on the possessions of some Eritreans who return home.[36]

Conclusion

This chapter has focused on the socioeconomic dimension of repatriation by way of a central hypothesis; that the different ways in which unassisted refugees are integrated into the host economy play an important role in determining the possibility, pace, and scale of their repatriation. Among exiles in Sudan the commodification of social relationships has eroded the bases for productive cooperation that once existed between households. Potential returnees were confident that "dormant" social and cultural networks would help them resolve conflicting land claims in Eritrea, and rebuild their homes. Most permanent returnees have reported no problems reclaiming land in Eritrea yet many current refugees express concern about land availability.[37] Nonetheless, it remains to be seen if cooperative work parties actually will be a central component of agrarian life and society. If cooperative efforts do emerge, will they be rooted in social relationships, in "survival" imperatives, or in political associations? Undoubtedly, the answer may be all three. The residual legacy of social relationships is a basis on which to build, but there is also the imperative of subsisting in a fragile ecosystem and an "ethic" of collective solidarity forged by the EPLF during thirty years of conflict. Meanwhile, the transformation of subsistence agriculture is clearly a central factor in short-term and long-term success of returning households as well as to the entire country. The terms of trade for agricultural products and access to land, credit, fertilizer, improved seed, and farm machinery are all fundamental issues. Their importance lies in the fact that they are the very preconditions that encourage refugees to stay in agricultural occupations; to generate capital locally and thereby stimulate recovery and growth in rural areas; and to remain "on the land" when inevitable crises of climate and food resources occur. In sum, then, an understanding of the relationship between refugees and rural transformation can provide a means by which to better anticipate responses to repatriation opportunities as well as to better assist those who choose to return.

Notes

1. These two justifications did not satisfy Eritreans for several reasons: 1) the United Nations' direct hand in precipitating the Eritrean war by enacting federation with Ethiopia rather than granting Eritrea its independence in 1950; 2) the expenditure of more than $150 million (U.S.) to repatriate 50,000 Ethiopian soldiers back to their country after the war ended in Eritrea; 3) the higher per capita allocation of funds by UNHCR to other repatriations (Namibians, South Africans, and Cambodians) as compared to the Eritreans. For further study of strategic factors see the following: L. Zeager and J. Bascom, "Refugee Repatriation in a Changing World Order: A Game Theoretic Analysis," *Journal of Conflict Resolution* 40 (1996): 460–85.
2. CERA, Appeal to Donor Governments, Commission for Eritrean Refugees Affairs, Provisional Government of Eritrea (1992): 2.
3. However, the UNHCR took a mostly passive stance with respect to reconstruction based on the long-standing precedent that UNHCR functions as an intermediary to facilitate contact between states in respect to voluntary repatriation but leaves countries of origin to create in their own territory the conditions which will persuade refugees that they can return without fear, i.e., economic and social conditions as well as legal protection.
4. V. Hamilton, *1995 World Refugee Survey* (Washington, 1996), 70.
5. Ibid., 97.
6. E. Weisburg, Faxed message from UNHCR (Washington, 1997).
7. In early 1992 and then again in early 1993 I returned to Wad el Hileau to conduct repatriation interviews with the heads of thirty-five households from my original sample of more than two hundred gathered in 1987/88. Although all but one respondent believed that it was physically "safe" to return to Eritrea, only sixteen households of nearly one thousand in Wad el Hileau did so during the first nine months after the cessation of conflict. Moreover, there was no evidence among respondents, or the community at large, that additional households are making any preparations to leave (i.e., selling their home, belongings, and agricultural

land, or deconstructing their house to salvage building materials).
8. Dahya, cited in J. Sorenson, "Opposition, Exile and Identity: The Eritrean Case," *Journal of Refugee Studies* 3 (1990): 309.
9. J. DaVanzo, "Microeconomic Approaches to Studying Migration Decisions," in *Migration Decision Making: Multidisciplinary Approaches to Microlevel Studies in Developed and Developing Countries*, ed. G. De Jong and R. Gardner (New York, 1981), 116.
10. Hamilton, *1997 World Refugee Survey*, 98.
11. UNHCR's planning mission for repatriation acknowledged the dissolution of the "household" in its recommendations: "An issue that is likely to occur frequently at point of registration is the presentation of requests for the separate processing of individuals ... registrars cannot be expected to engage in social analysis at the registration table and will need simple, readily applicable criteria with which to handle such requests routinely. Is age alone sufficient to qualify one as an independent householder? Is marriage? What about widows, widowers and divorced persons?" T. Ali, Sudan Planning Mission for Voluntary Repatriation to Eritrea: Resignation, Assistance Entitlement, and Population Processing, Programme and Technical Support Section Mission Report (Geneva, 1991): 35.
12. G. Kibreab, Prospects for Re-Establishment of the Returning Eritrean Refugees, Symposium for the Horn of Africa on the Social and Economic Aspects of Mass Voluntary Return Movements of Refugees, Addis Abada, Ethiopia, September 15–17, United Nations Research Unit for Social Development (UNRISD) (1992).
13. Commission for Eritrean Refugee Affairs, Current Status of the Repatriation Programme and the Way Forward, conference paper (29 April 1992).
14. Hamilton, *1997 World Refugee Survey*, 98.
15. J. Bascom, "The Dynamics of Refugee Repatriation: The Case of Eritreans in Eastern Sudan" in *Population Migration and the Changing World Order*, ed. W. Gould and A. Findlay (London, 1994), 239.
16. J. Rogge, "Repatriation of Refugees: A Not-So-Simple 'Optimum' Solution," in *When Refugees Go Home*, ed. T. Allen and H. Morsink (Trenton, N.J., 1994), 32.
17. W. Wood, "Long Time Coming: The Repatriation of Afghan Refugees," *Annals of the Association of American Geographers* 79 (1989): 345–69.
18. J. Akol, "Southern Sudanese Refugees: Their Repatriation and Resettlement After the Addis Ababa Agreement," in *Refugees: A Third World Dilemma*, ed. J. Rogge (Totowa, 1987), 143–58.
19. UNHCR, Social Services Mission, 21 October–2 November, 1991, Community-Based Approach for Repatriation to Eritrea, Programme and Technical Support Section, PTSS Mission Report 91/32, (Geneva, 1991).
20. Hamilton, *1997 World Refugee Survey*, 70.
21. S. Jones, "Environment and Development in Eritrea," *Africa Today*, 2nd Quarter (1991): 55–60.
22. K. Mengisteab, "Rehabilitation of Degraded Land in Eritrea's Agricultural Policy: An Exploratory Study," in *Emergent Eritrea: Challenges of Economic Development*, ed. G. Tesfagiorgis (Washington, 1992), 110–17.
23. Agriculture is the mainstay of the Eritrean economy. Four-fifths of the total Eritrean population earn their living from the land. According to a survey of two-thirds of Eritrea's one hundred and eight-two districts, carried out in late 1987 with the cooperation of the Eritrean Peoples Liberation Front (EPLF), 61 percent of the rural population are settled agriculturists, 31 percent are agropastoralists, and the remaining 8 percent are pastoralists. Agriculture and Rural Development Unit report cited in Pateman, *Eritrea: Even the Stones are Burning* (Trenton, 1990), 179.
24. Agricultural Commission, 92.

25. Agricultural Commission, 92.
26. G. Kibreab, "Left in Limbo: Prospects for Re-Establishment of the Returning Eritrean Refugees and Responses of the International Donor Community," in *When Refugees Go Home,* ed. T. Allen and H. Morsink (London, 1994), 53–64.
27. J. Rogge and J. Akol, "Repatriation: Its Role in Resolving Africa's Refugee Dilemma," *International Migration Review* 23 (1989): 184–200.
28. Rogge, "Repatriation of Refugees," 8.
29. Hamilton, *1997 World Refugee Survey,* 98.
30. Ali, Sudan Planning Mission.
31. Tapscott and Mulongeni, cited in Simon and Preston, "Return to the Promised Land: The Repatriation and Resettlement of Namibian Refugees," in *Geography and Refugees, Patterns and Processes of Change,* ed. R. Black and V. Robinson (London, 1993), 46–63.
32. Rogge, "Repatriation of Refugees," 8.
33. E. Habte-Selassie, "Eritrean Refugees in the Sudan: A Preliminary Analysis of Voluntary Repatriation," in *Beyond Conflict in the Horn: Prospects for Peace, Recovery, and Development in Ethiopia, Somalia and the Sudan,* ed. M. Doornbos, L. Cliffe, A. Ahmed, and J. Markakis (London, 1992), 23–31.
34. T. Gebremedhin, "Agricultural Development in Eritrea: Economic and Policy Analysis," in *Emergent Eritrea: Challenges of Economic Development,* ed. G. Tesfagiorgis (Washington, 1992), 102.
35. Issaias Afewerki, chairman of the provisional government of Eritrea, declared that "Hotels, industries and agricultural estates are on sale. Anyone can buy them. We need money to rebuild our economy." Cited in F. Misser, "Eritrea Seeks to Attract Foreign Investment," *African Business,* 1992, 47. Eligible investments in agriculture are exempt from income tax for two years if they are under $300,000 and for five years if they are over $1 million U.S. Whether sufficient investment in mechanized agriculture will occur to stimulate a sizable demand for agricultural wage laborers remains to be seen. Southwestern Eritrea is the prime location for such ventures. Ideally, these mechanized, rain-fed schemes will increase agricultural productivity and employment opportunities in an environmentally sound manner. Eritrea can ill afford the kind of wholesale degradation that has characterized the spread of mechanized agriculture in eastern Sudan.
36. Hamilton, *1997 World Refugee Survey,* 97.
37. Ibid., 70.

9

Concluding Reflections

> For us, the poor, there is no action, / But only to wait and to witness.
>
> T. S. Eliot
> *Murder in the Cathedral*
>
> By the time the fool has learned the game, the players have dispersed.
>
> *African Proverb*

We now turn to the implications of the analysis presented in the preceding chapters. This concluding chapter has three sections. The first one summarizes the findings presented in this study. The second portion suggests the implications of those findings for future studies of refugees. And the third section suggests their applications for refugee policy.

Part I: Primary Findings

While this book aims to help redress the dearth of empirical data about unassisted refugees, its primary contribution to the growing refugee literature is that of relating refugees to the larger context of rural transformation. We have focused on East Africa, a region of the world that has perhaps the most extensive refugee experience. During the last forty years, more than 6.5 million people have been uprooted and sought asylum in the countries of Eritrea, Ethiopia, Djibouti, Kenya, Somalia, Sudan, Uganda, and Tanzania. Of these host countries, only Tanzania has made provision for granting permanent residency and citizenship to refugees, and even then, only a few have accepted it. Third-country resettlement off the African con-

Notes for this section begin on page 176.

tinent is an opportunity enjoyed by only one African refugee in every ten thousand.[1] Current trends are for more refugees than in the past to return home of their own accord despite conflict conditions, but the vast majority remain in the country of asylum. Figure 9.1 shows the widening gap between the total number of African refugees that remain in exile and the total number that repatriate home.

Given the fact that most refugees remain in the country of first asylum, they are forced to negotiate livelihoods from the opportunities and constraints posed by that economy. These vary from country to country, subregion to subregion, and from one point in time to another. Chapter 2 surveyed the border settings throughout East Africa where refugee populations have migrated with a specific focus on, and appreciation for, the process of rural transformation. We attempted to illustrate some connections between refugee migrations and rural transformations, and we looked beyond "the refugee horizon" in order to link the larger political economy and its changes to refugee influxes and integration.

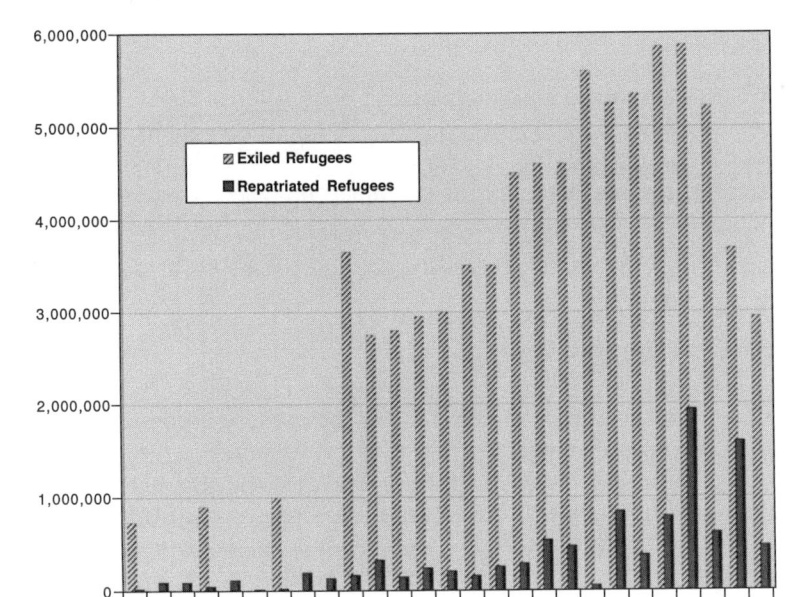

Figure 9.1 Repatriated African Refugees vs. Newly Exiled African Refugees, 1971–1997

Source: Adapted from Rogge, J. and Akol, J. "Repatriation: Its role in Resolving Africa's Refugee Dilemma," *International Migration Review,* 23, 1989, and V. Hamilton (ed), *World Refugee Survey,* Washington, DC, 1990–1997

To chart at a more specific level the relationship between refugees and rural transformation required a more refined approach at the level of real world relationships between human beings. This necessitated the choice of an appropriate and specific location in which to intensify the analysis by investigating specific social relations of production and exchange that mediate the integration of refugees with their hosts. We turned to the border region between Eritrea and Sudan, where our basic approach was to explore the changing dynamics of structure, process, and power that weave rural transformation together with refugee flight, settlement, integration, and repatriation. This field area constitutes one of the largest and most prolonged refugee crises in East Africa. Despite the fact that asylum began in early 1967, several hundred thousand Eritreans still remain in Sudan. Their thirty years of asylum provides sufficient time-depth for a longitudinal study.

The next step in our analysis was to compare the nature of the preflight social formation in Eritrea with the post-flight formation in Sudan. Chapters 3 and 4 illustrated the magnitude of social and economic change associated with refugees' migration across the border. Eritreans' flight to Sudan entailed a movement between two radically different social formations. Refugees from the Eritrean lowlands came from kin-driven production; their social structure still retains the "imprint" of that precapitalist economy, but their sources of livelihood are now conditioned by a wholly different system of production. Commodified labor relations have replaced reciprocal ones. The two "traditional" forms of production, pastoralism and small-scale cultivation, are breaking down. On one hand, the process of social differentiation is intensifying as a result of *mushrooah* expansion coupled with mechanization and the commodification of agricultural land, labor, and inputs. On the other hand, *mushrooahs* are also encroaching on rangeland, intensifying commodification of grazing rights, and destroying pastoralism as a form of production. As commodity relations take hold, both forms of production are being redefined by the logic and reproductive needs of peripheral capitalism, a larger production system into which rural refugees are now being integrated.

Previous researchers have not explored fully the way refugees compete for physical, social, and financial resources. Chapters 5 and 6 delineated the social relations of production that mediate the integration process for refugees, be they pastoralists or small-scale cultivators. In so doing, we identified mechanisms of appropriation and impoverishment that structure the rural economy into which Eritreans were forced to move. A direct relationship exists between the point in time at which refugees came to Sudan and their subsequent position in the agrarian class structure (i.e., landless, marginalized, subsistent, and accumulative). Land scarcity has forced most refugees to join the ranks of the agricultural labor force. For refugee farmers at the upper end of the social hierarchy, cash crop mortgages place a "lid" on their ability to accumulate capital, and at the same time refugees are hastening the emergence of a rural elite within the Sudanese host community. Claimant classes rely on "primary" relations of exploitation as well as "secondary" ones. *Mushrooah* operators appropriate surplus directly from a ready-made and relatively cheap labor force, largely comprised of refugees, while merchants appropriate surplus indirectly in the form of interest rates buried in the mortgage terms established for cash crops. The expansion of their appropriative activities has intensified class stratification within the refugee community and pressed refugee women and children into new roles and responsibilities.

Chapter 6 documented the commodification of pastoral production and the primary mechanisms that have debilitated refugee households that depend upon livestock as a way of life. Pastoralists are fast becoming the net losers in the politics of land use as rangeland is expropriated and production costs rise.

Chapter 7 moved down in scale to the "terrain" within refugee homes. External pressures are reshaping the allocation of labor among refugee children, women, and men as well as altering age- and gender-related roles, rights, and responsibilities during exile. Subordination of women has been exacerbated rather than transformed in exile. The spatial and social domain of refugee women has shrunk, and men have more control than ever over household resources.

Chapter 8 addressed the relationship between rural transformation and repatriation. It demonstrated that the larger political economy plays a direct role in refugees' decisionmaking with respect to repatriation as well as their expectations upon return. The impoverished status of most refugees makes them much more sensitive to the crisis potential associated with repatriation than to the opportunities it might offer. What marginalized refugees fear is the possibility of social breakdown and destitution associated with the irreversibility of the repatriation decision. The vulnerability produced by long-term poverty renders a large-scale, "spontaneous" repatriation among unassisted refugees very unlikely.

In summary, rural transformation can radically change the social landscape across which refugees move. Key forms of social interdependence and reciprocity buffer fewer and fewer refugees from the loss of "home" and subsequent impoverishment. Instead, the survival strategies of rural refugees, especially unassisted ones, are increasingly defined by the social relations of production and exchange in a cash economy. Hence, the results of this study are applicable to refugee contexts elsewhere in East Africa as well as in other developing countries throughout Africa, Asia, Latin America, and the Middle East.

Part II: Implications

Many of the specific findings reached in this study challenge broader assumptions posited in the refugee literature or in other fields of study. Accordingly, this section underscores the importance of context to refugee studies, challenges the myth of "spontaneous self-settlement," argues for a clearer awareness of social differentiation within refugee populations, and illustrates different ways in which this study can inform African peasant studies.

The Impress of Context

Refugee populations in developing countries did not become the focus of a sizable body of scholarly research until the last two decades.[2] Focusing on the distinctive nature of involuntary migration is a natural consequence of making it the subject of study. Not surprisingly, the literature reveals two continuing trends – assignment of exceptional status to involuntary migration, and abstraction of refugee groups from the larger context in which they exist.[3] If the relationship of uprooted populations to the host community and the regional economy is ignored, then such work is rightly criticized as a "refugee-centric."[4] Although studies of interactions between refugees and their host populations or their structured position within host societies and economies have been too few, the refugee experience is now being "opened up" to insights from other literature.[5] This study has sought to relate refugees to the literatures on social theory, peasant societies, and agrarian change.

Some authors imply that the sheer complexity of the refugee phenomenon precludes theoretical abstraction.[6] However, salient features of the political economy in asylum areas can be analyzed to make sense of the "survival strategies" that refugee households employ as well as to elucidate the interaction between incoming refugees and their hosts. By explicating the position of refugees in the social relations of production, one can, for example, better understand why some refugees become markedly better off during exile while others remain destitute. Using a perspective that is more fully cognizant of the transformation of peasant and pastoral economies has provided a basis from which to explain the logic of survival strategies adopted by refugees (including land management practices and labor allocation to assess the differential impact of refugees on the host community), to explore the restructuring of roles and functions within the household labor force during exile, and to predict different responses by refugees to repatriation opportunities. Important issues for further investigation include the political ecology of environmental degradation associated with large refugee influxes, and the material roots of social tension between refugees and the host community.

To resummarize, refugee movements are increasingly conditioned by identifiable social, economic, and class forces that intersect within the household or individual. For that reason refugee settings can be most effectively studied within the broader context of processes operative in most agrarian societies. The present study analyzed refugee integration at the level of political economic relations and sought to demonstrate the value of viewing refugee settlement as "a process unfolding within the context" of larger social processes at work in East Africa.[7]

The Myth of "Spontaneous Self-Settlement"

The prevailing misunderstanding of refugee settlement as a "spontaneous" process among unassisted refugees is a consequence of two main factors. The first one is the imbalance favoring research in refugee camps. Research attention often accompanies funding to refugees in official camps and resettlement schemes, and camp refugees are a captive audience who are not as able to escape the interest of investigators. Hence, unassisted refugees are often overlooked despite the fact that they represent, as of early 1997, more than half of East Africa's two million refugees. The second contributing factor is the consequence of not conceptualizing the larger social processes in host societies. The demise of *nafir* and lesser forms of social reciprocity illustrate the importance of class relations and social transformation during exile.[8] Class relations are becoming more and more critical, while the utility of ethnicity and kinship as variables of explanation is decreasing in value as the control of land and labor passes from refugees' control into the hands of their hosts.

The term "spontaneous settlement" originated in the refugee literature with documented cases like the welcome of neighboring Guinea-Bissauans by Senegalese who shared everything with the refugees including lodging, tools, seeds, and food stocks.[9] By the late

1970s, however, the term became more a benign label to dismiss the problem of refugees by supporting the idea that it is better to not interfere with the "natural" course of events.[10] More recent research calls into question the whole concept of "spontaneous self-settlement." That expression may have typified the ease with which rural refugees moved between precapitalist economies in the past by relying on ethnic and kinship relationships to expedite the process of resettlement.[11] But many refugee movements now occur between substantially different social formations. Thus, the concept of "spontaneous" integration has been rightly challenged as a misnomer, and perhaps, it should be reevaluated as a euphemism and dismissed from the refugee literature altogether.[12]

This line of reasoning also places the term "self-settlement" in question. Although the term is used to distinguish between refugees who are in official camps from those who are not, there are two basic problems with its use. First, the term "self-settlement" tends to attribute to unassisted refugees more autonomy than this study has documented. Second, it fails to describe the complex adjustments that unassisted refugees make in the resettlement process. Refugees do not move into a social or economic vacuum.[13] Unlike camp refugees, unassisted refugees must contend with constraints and opportunities offered by the preexisting social relations of production and power in the host economy. In this sense, refugees never "self-settle." Although refugee researchers are not apt to dispense with the term "self-settlement" as distinct from "camp-settling," they should not allow the term to obscure the way in which structural forces shape and condition the process of refugee resettlement.

The Importance of Differentiation

This study has demonstrated the need to clearly apprehend differentiation in various forms. Ethnic, political, age, gender, and class differentiation all exist among uprooted populations, and they invariably impact each stage of the refugee experience. The contemporary media and its proclivity for visual images give the impression that refugees are mass "flows."[14] But this study has challenged the perception of refugees as a homogeneous social entity and documented the widening class differentiation amid rural transformation.

Researchers are beginning to recognize diversity among refugee populations.[15] But more efforts are needed to identify structures, mechanisms and processes that create forms of differentiation. Of special concern are the qualitative differences that exist within refugee homes. The household is generally viewed as the essential unit of analysis, despite a large body of literature outside refugee studies that raises serious questions about how the household is best defined, studied, and assisted. This study has sought to show the importance of obtaining analyses of refugee resettlement that are disaggregated by gender and age. Insightful work on the question of identity can be found in the recent refugee literature on eastern European refugees, but the same scrutiny is needed for refugee settlement areas in agrarian settings.

The Lessons for Peasant Economies

Refugees studies like this one can make a special contribution to peasant studies because the kind of crisis conditions that surround involuntary migrants can amplify dynamics that might otherwise remain "muted." Involuntary migrations provide, for example, a unique testing ground for theories of societal resilience, coping and adaptation, emergent groups, social solidarity, conflict and empowerment, and minority groups.[16] Displacement and resettlement can also throw into high relief public policy questions such as state-local relations.

The present study can be used to inform African peasant economies in several ways. First, it underscores the fragility of social obligations and expectations grounded in a "traditional" economy. The argument that rural communities have a capacity to resist capitalist penetration by reinventing or retreating into a subsistence way of life was a popular one in the literature of the 1980s.[17] Moreover, it was asserted that economies based on reciprocity played a major role in the integration process for African refugees. However, the evidence presented in this study suggests the opposite. Informal, traditional relationships disintegrate quickly in the face of mechanization, land scarcity, altered labor relations, and other components of rural transformation. As commodity relations replace reciprocity, social obligations lose their central roles in production and become restricted to far less important, redistributive functions.

Second, the process of refugee resettlement magnifies the relationships that underlie rural economies, but which tend to be less visible under "normal" conditions. Because survival is at stake, refugees must accept, rather than choose, the opportunities (or niches) available within the prevailing relationships of production and of exchange. As a result, their experience often brings to the surface appropriative mechanisms that lead to immiseration (e.g., *sheil* and *t'ackul wa gwoom*).

Third, this study illustrates that a large population influx can accelerate the pace of rural transformation. Population movements occur in many forms, each of which can change the pace of social transformation in agrarian societies. In addition to refugees, there are, for example, more than four million internal displacees in East Africa. Large influxes also occur in rural areas as a result of population resettlement programs like that of western Ethiopia or development projects like the New Halfa project in Sudan. As such scenarios become more common, the relationship of large population influxes to agrarian change deserves more research attention because they may, in fact, keep the transformation process from stalling.

Fourth, this study underscores the fact that refugees can play a key role in restructuring agricultural labor markets. Because prevailing wage rates are so low in countries like Sudan, many members of the domestic community that were once available for agricultural work are now pursuing alternative sources of employment in urban centers or other countries. Refugee populations can represent a substantial supply of replacement labor. If their movement – out of a given region or into certain occupations – is limited, then refugees are apt to resort to agricultural wage labor as a means of livelihood. In the case of Sudan, for example, refugee labor has become "tied" or "fettered" to the eastern region by stringent travel restrictions imposed on refugees. Refugees are barred from government employment by restrictive definitions of nationality and, on occasion, from trading licenses and charcoal permits.[18] The powerful effect of these measures is reflected by the fact that *mushrooah* operators have retracted incentives used formerly to attract wage laborers from elsewhere in Sudan. While agricultural wages have not increased in real terms the last twenty-five years the labor force in eastern Sudan has been restratified on the basis of "Sudanese" versus "foreigners." [19]

Part III: Applications

Refugee policy considerations in the 1990s have become more critical than ever. Coupled with dramatic growth in the size, distribution, and complexity of refugee populations is the fact that most host societies are today confronted with related and steadily worsening problems. Often, these problems – stagnant or declining economies, rapidly growing populations, environmental degradation, increased competition for jobs and land, rising crime levels, and increased social tensions – are exacerbated by strict constraints on the amount of public expenditure devoted to wages and social welfare under structural adjustment programs.[20] In East Africa, the average GNP per capita has fallen in real terms from $320 (U.S.) in 1980 to less than $280 (U.S.) in 1995. Population growth is nearly 2.8 percent per annum (a regional doubling rate of twenty-five years). Environmental degradation has reached crisis proportions, particularly in Ethiopia and Somalia. Kenya is rapidly acquiring a reputation as a haven for violent crime, and social tensions are on the rise throughout the region. To comply with stringent conditions posed by structural adjustment programs, expenditures for public welfare are at an all-time low in Sudan, Tanzania, and Uganda. These endemic problems make policy choices with respect to refugees even more important.

The Basic Poverty of Refugee Policy

The state plays a more decisive role in defining the everyday conditions of refugees than is often recognized. Its operation in resettlement areas can take different forms (e.g., state capital in the form of rural development programs, state control in the form of marketing boards, and surplus extraction in the form of permits and taxes). In the case of Sudan, the state gives a decided advantage to *mushrooah* schemes by facilitating cheap access to rainfed land and subsidizing the cost of agricultural inputs. Although it is difficult to substantiate the amount, a very sizable portion of the sorghum and sesame grown and harvested in Sudan is smuggled out of the country for sale in non-Sudanese markets.[21] *Mushrooah* operators accumulate surplus at the expense of the national economy, thereby perpetuating underdevelopment in Sudan.

Why does the state maintain this favorable posture toward *mushrooah* expansion? Because the state is, in fact, a microcosm of condensed class relations whose interests shape development policies.[22] Policy shifts represent a new articulation of the changed composition of the dominant class rather than a fundamental change in class interests. As agrarian classes vie for resources, refugees compete at a disadvantage. They are denied access to the central means of production by the government-approved appropriation of land for *mushrooahs*. Pastoralism is rapidly retreating as a form of production, and peasant agriculture remains "petrified" because the state is not helping peasants to expand their production.[23]

The ability of the state to protect and assist dominant classes is a major impediment to whatever aid humanitarian agencies hope to deliver to refugees. Camp refugees are buffered perhaps from the surrounding political and economic environment, but the state plays a central role in the integration process by defining the structural features of the economy into which they are absorbed. Refugee agencies may be able to ameliorate refugee problems, but the social locations that refugees occupy lie largely beyond their reach. This fact underscores the basic poverty or limits of refugee policy and the importance of understanding the context within which donors and relief agencies operate. A clear understanding of the dominant classes that vie for control of the state is essential to the formulation of more effective types of refugee relief and assistance.

Smart Aid in Environments of Decay

There is a direct link between an increased understanding of a specific context and improvement in designing and managing aid allocated to displaced peoples. Authors like Sen underscore how frequently policies are conceived of in narrow technical or economic terms, and thereby fail to attack the root of the problem embedded within social and political structures.[24] Understanding mechanisms of immiseration that act as leverage points between agrarian classes may lead to some palliative changes in refugee assistance programs. (For example, credit programs might offset production losses associated with *sheil*.) But that refugees and host populations are forced to compete for physical, social, and financial resources suggests the need to shift the focus of assistance from refugee relief to integrative development programs.

For too long, refugees were overlooked in studies of rural and regional development. This stems from a long-standing distinction between development assistance and relief assistance, a dichotomization that was first challenged at the first International Conference on Assistance for Refugees in Africa (ICARA I).[25] Faced with rising "refugee overloads," the Second International Conference on Assistance to Refugees in Africa (ICARA II) introduced the concept of project funding for "refugee-affected regions". Infrastructure projects were designed and funded to assist both refugees and their host community.[26] Additional support for "refugee-affected areas" is now available from UNDP and from the EEC under LOME IV.[27] In 1993, 8 percent of UNHCR's US $284 million dollar budget for Africa was designated for non-camp settings.[28]

An integrative focus on refugees and regional development is apropos given the protracted nature of refugee crises. Without the opportunity to repatriate, the percentage of refugees within the national population has reached as high as 25 percent in Somalia, 14 percent in Djibouti, and 5 percent in Sudan.[29] In some rural areas, the proportion of refugees has exceeded that of the indigenous population. In Yei River District, southern Sudan, for example, Ugandan refugees once outnumbered Sudanese by a 3:1 ratio.[30] Similar "refugee overloads" currently exist in eastern Zaire, western Tanzania, northwestern Somalia, and northern Kenya. In light of the fact that many host countries are also beset by severe economic problems such as soaring inflation, rising foreign debt burdens, and decreasing agricultural production, the hospitality of host countries in Africa is beginning to wear thin. In the words of an official in Goma, the Zairian town to which Rwandans fled, "The refugee population overwhelmed Zairian resources, destroyed our environment, introduced uncontrolled inflation into our market and abused our hospitality. We want them out of here soon."[31]

Yet another set of implications surround the question of refugee participation in planning and programming. Harrell-Bond has long championed the need to give refugees an "authentic voice" in the assistance they receive.[32] She advocated that UNHCR provide self-settling refugees with "creative, fine-pointed forms of assistance" so that they could receive aid without sacrificing their ability to control where they want to live.[33] Although some question how much assistance actually reaches self-settled refugees, the need to put refugees in camps in order for them to be counted and qualify for assistance is finally being obviated.[34] UNHCR has begun to provide assistance to refugees outside the confines of formal camps and settlements. But a second related issue is how to provide the kind of assistance that will augment and empower refugees' own choices surrounding repatriation. Although UNHCR, in principle, provides refugees with the necessary information regarding conditions in their country of origin to ensure their repatriation is voluntary, refugees often want to appraise conditions for themselves. The UNHCR assisted prospective returnees to Mozambique in making visits to appraise the range of opportunities.[35] Allowing refugees to help determine what kind of assistance they most need for their reintegration is a third way to raise the level of participation. Involving refugees in that process accomplishes two important tasks: it strengthens policy and programs, and it enables refugees to rebuild their morale, identity, and sense of responsibility for the future.

Conclusion: Regaining Place

The last three decades reveal an unfolding progression in the development of the refugee literature. The early literature of the 1970s focused on the process and dynamics of flight. In the 1980s, as the magnitude of the refugee crisis grew in East Africa (and elsewhere), the focus of attention shifted to resettlement. Repatriation has become the "lead" theme of the 1990s. What began as a focus on causality and flight from the sending country is now culminating in a shift in focus back to the country of origination. Of added impetus is UNHCR's growing concern and involvement with internally displaced persons. Since 1991, while the number of wars between sovereign states has dropped to a negligible level, the number of internal wars has grown to as many as thirty-five.[36] Thus, conflicts are increasingly within states rather than between them. This qualitative change in the dominant character of conflict reinforces the need for added concern with originating countries. In its search for new solutions, UNHCR has expanded its commitment to help create economic conditions that will induce people to repatriate and keep them there. The central fact is that if repatriation is not linked to the rehabilitation of productive capacity, a vicious circle of renewed disintegration and displacement is likely to emerge.[37]

Border studies are another critical area of analysis. The growing scale and complexity of involuntary migration has made it more and more difficult to sustain the fairly rigid distinction that humanitarian organizations have traditionally made between refugees, returnees, internally displaced people, and the resident population. In border areas of Ethiopia and Somalia, for example, it is possible to find people from all four groups living alongside each other in indistinguishable circumstances.[38]

The recent interventions in Somalia and Rwanda have created yet another impetus for shifting the focus of concern back to the circumstances that impel people to leave their homelands in the first place. These painful sagas of involvement have made the international community increasingly aware of the need to expedite conflict resolution in the source country so that refugees can return to take vigorous action (including emergency response to crises and the provision of international protection on site), to eradicate the causes of flight before refugees flee, and to initiate more proactive intervention to prevent the development of conditions that might impel people to migrate.[39] UNHCR's new approach is one that is far more proactive than the reactive orientation of the past as well as sensitive to host communities – not solely refugee-specific. In so doing, it is more in touch with the full circle of refugee experience.

Similarly, newer perspectives in the refugee literature are fusing basic dichotomies whose elements were often placed in opposition to one another – refugees versus hosts, voluntary versus involuntary, and micro-scale versus macro-scale levels of analysis. This study is in keeping with that trend. In an attempt to move beyond what Chambers termed a "refugee-centric" perspective that overlooks the impact of refugees on their hosts, we have grappled with the process of rural transformation using concepts from the literature on social theory, political economy, and peasant economy.[40] In an attempt to move beyond an exclusionist perspective on refugees, we have sought to place their flight, resettlement, and repatriation back into the context of agrarian societies. And we have also addressed the third dichotomy. In an attempt to refuse the micro-scale and macro-scale levels, we have focused on the tension and interplay between choice and context. This study has sought to explain the principle ways by which rural refugees negotiate their subsistence from the "opportunity structures" afforded by the host society and economy. All facets of the refugee experience – migration, resettlement, repatriation, and reintegration – represent an ongoing process of choices made and played out in a changing context. Indeed, it is this interplay between choice and context, agency and structure, that is the central dynamic at work in the refugee experience.

Notes

1. The United States, Canada, and Australia are the only countries with planned levels for an annual intake of African refugees (3,000, 1,000, and 250 respectively). Less than 35,000 Africans have been resettled in the West during the last decade compared to the over one million Indochinese. Rogge, "Repatriation of Refugees," 9.
2. During the 1960s and 1970s, African refugees were largely overlooked in the development literature. Geographers, for example, studied African rural-urban migration but paid scant attention to the problems surrounding the forced movement of refugees. J. Rogge, "A Geography of Refugees: Some Illustrations from Africa," *Professional Geographer* 29 (1977): 186. Remarkably few studies were written on refugee flight and resettlement in Africa before 1980. By the late 1970s, however, neither policymakers nor academicians could ignore the refugee dilemma any longer. In the face of recurrent social and political instability, the number of Africans with refugee status had exceeded three million people. In 1979, the First International Conference on Assistance to Refugees in Africa (ICARA I) was held in Arusha, Tanzania. The field of refugee studies has come of age since then.
3. R. Black, "Refugees and Displaced Persons."
4. Chambers, "Hidden Losers?"
5. Black, "Refugees and Displaced Persons," 293–4.
6. Wijbrandi, "Organized and Spontaneous Settlement."
7. Samatar, "Pastoral Transformation," 3.
8. Some authors argue that class approaches are the most fruitful way to study ethnicity in all social formations, be it a moral economy or a capitalist one. E. Bonacich, "Class Approaches to Ethnicity and Race," *The Insurgent Sociologist* 10 (1982): 9.
9. Zartman, "Portuguese Guinean Refugees," 151.
10. Chambers, "Rural Refugees."
11. Zartman, "Portuguese Guinean Refugees."; Hansen, "Once the Running Stops."; Hansen, "Refugee Dynamics."

12. Bulcha, *Flight and Integration*, 24.
13. J. Bascom, "Social Differentiation among Eritrean Refugees in Eastern Sudan: The Case of Wad El Hileau," *Journal of Refugee Studies* 2 (1991), 403.
14. Rogge, "Repatriation of Refugees," 14–49.
15. el Shazali, "Eritreans in Kassala"; Bulcha, *Flight and Integration*.
16. A. Hansen and T. Oliver-Smith, *Involuntary Migration and Resettlement: The Problems and Responses of Dislocated People* (Boulder, Colo., 1982).
17. G. Hyden, *Beyond Ujamaa in Tanzania: Underdevelopment and an Uncaptured Peasantry* (Berkeley, 1980); G. Hyden, *No Shortcuts to Progress*; R. Bates, *Essays on the Political Economy of Rural Africa* (Cambridge, 1983).
18. O'Brien, "Agriculture Labor Force," 32.
19. ILO, *Incoming-Activities for Refugees in the Sudan, A Study Carried Out Within the Framework of the ILO/UNHCR Project on Income-Generating Activities for Refugees in Eastern and Central Sudan* (Geneva, 1982): 11.
20. UNHCR, "UNHCR Financial Needs in 1994," *Refugees* 96 (1995): 5, 37.
21. The amount of sorghum smuggled out of Sudan each year is very difficult to estimate. Ahmed reported that 32.3 percent of the 1961/62 harvest was delivered to Sudanese markets, 54.7 percent was delivered after the 1962/63 season, and only 29.0 percent was delivered after the 1963/64 season. T. Ahmed, "The Cultivation of Hunger: Towards the Political Economy of Agricultural Development in the Sudan, 1956–1964," Ph.D. diss. (University of Toronto, 1982), 248. More recently, the government has repeatedly had to ban exports despite the massive expansion of area under cultivation as *mushrooah* schemes.
22. Ahmed, "The Cultivation of Hunger," 16.
23. el Shazali, "Peripheral Urbanism," 84.
24. A. Sen, *On Ethics and Economics* (Oxford, 1984).
25. A frequently quoted policy recommendation from ICARA I states, "The Conference stresses that the programme covering rural refugees should be planned and implemented within the context of national, sub-national and regional endeavors." L. Ericksonn, G. Melander, and P. Nobel, *An Analysing Account of the Conference on African Refugee Problems – Arusha, May 1979* (Uppsala, 1981).
26. UN, Declaration and Program of Action of the Second International Conference on Assistance to Refugees in Africa, A/Con. 125/L.1, July 10 (Geneva, 1984).
27. J. McGregor and S. Aikman, "Avoiding Camps," *Refugee Participation Network* 10 (1991): 4.
28. The $22.4 million (U.S.) spent on "local settlement" compares to $166.4 million for refugees in camps and settlements, $71.4 million for voluntary repatriation programs, $14.5 million for administration, $9.1 million for emergency assistance operations, and $0.8 million for third country resettlement programs. UNHCR, *The State of the World's Refugees 1993: The Challenge of Protection* (New York, 1993).
29. CIMADE, INODEP, and MINK, *Africa's Refugee Crisis: What's to be Done?* (London, 1986), 89.
30. Harrell-Bond, *Imposing Aid*.
31. UNHCR, "Financial Needs," 5, 37.
32. B. Harrell-Bond, "Repatriation: Under What Conditions is It the Most Desirable Solution for Refugees? An Agenda for Research," *African Studies Review* 32 (1989): 41–69.
33. Chambers, "Rural Refugees"; B. Neldner, "Settlement of Rural Refugees," *Disasters* 3 (1979): 393–402; Hansen, "Self-Settled Rural Refugees"; Harrell-Bond, *Imposing Aid*.
34. McGregor and Aikman, "Avoiding Camps," 4.
35. R. Preston, Report to an Inter-Agency Mission on Education for Mozambican Refugees in Malawi and Zimbabwe, UNDP (1991).

36. UNHCR, "Financial Needs," 108.
37. UNHCR, *The State of the World's Refugees 1993: The Challenge of Protection* (New York, 1993).
38. UNHCR, "Financial Needs," 37.
39. UNHCR, *State of the World's Refugees*.
40. Chambers, "Hidden Losers?"

Bibliography

Abdulrahim, K. (1988) Interview with Veterinarian at Gedaref Veterinary Office, 10 July 1988.
Abia, H. (1986) *Strategy for Development of Rainfed Agriculture*, Khartoum: University of Khartoum Press.
Affan, K. (1984) *Toward an Appraisal of Tractorisation Experience in Rainlands of Sudan*, DSRC Monograph Series, No. 19. Khartoum: University of Khartoum Press.
African Studies Branch. (1961) "Problems of Taxation" in Gould, P. (ed.) *Africa: Continent of Change*, pp. 153–59. Belmont, Calif.: Wadsworth Publishing.
Agricultural Commission (the), EPLF. (1992) "Problems, Prospective Policies and Programs for Agricultural Development in Eritrea" in Tesfagiorgis, G. (ed.) *Emergent Eritrea: Challenges of Economic Development*, pp. 91–100. Washington, DC: Provisional Government of Eritrea and Eritreans for Peace and Democracy in North America.
Ahmad, U. (1986) "Self-Settled Refugees in Gedaref (Eastern Sudan)." Report for United Nations High Commissioner for Refugees, Khartoum.
Ahmed, T. (1982) "The Cultivation of Hunger: Towards the Political Economy of Agricultural Development in the Sudan, 1956–1964," Ph.D. diss., University of Toronto.
Ajil, A. (1988) Interview with the Sheik of Wad el Hileau, 21 January 1988.
Ake, C. (1981) *A Political Economy of Africa*. Essex, U.K.: Longman.
Akol, J. (1987) "Southern Sudanese Refugees: Their Repatriation and Resettlement After the Addis Ababa Agreement" in Rogge, J. (ed.) *Refugees: A Third World Dilemma*, pp. 143–58. Totowa, N.J.: Rowman and Littlefield.
Ali, T. (1991) "Sudan Planning Mission for Voluntary Repatriation to Eritrea: Registration, Assistance Entitlement, and Population Processing – 21 October–5 November 1991," Programme and Technical Support Section Mission Report 91/35. Geneva: UNHCR.
Amin, S. (1972) "Underdevelopment and Dependence in Black Africa," *Journal of Modern African Studies*, 10:503–24.

_____ (1976) *Unequal Development: An Essay on the Social Formation of Peripheral Capitalism.* Paris: Monthly Review Press.

Archetii, E. and Stolen, K. (1975) *Explotacion Familiar y Acumulacion de Capital en Camp Argentino.* Buenos Aries: Siglo XXI.

Athreya, V., Böklin, G., Djurfeldt, G., and Lindberg, S. (1987) "Identification of Agrarian Classes: A Methodological Essay with Empirical Material from South India," *Journal of Peasant Studies*, 14:148–90.

Ati, H. (1988) "The Process of Famine: Causes and Consequences in Sudan," *Development and Change*, 19:267–300.

el Awad, A. (1988) Interview with Collection and Loan Officer for the Agricultural Bank of Sudan, Gedaref Office, 7 July 1988.

Babiker, F. (1984) *The Sudanese Bourgeoisie – Vanguard of Development?* London: Zed Books.

Babiker, M. (1984) "The Peasantry and the 'Differentiation Question' in 'Peripheral' Capitalist Social Formations: Towards a Resolution of the Debate," Manuscript of presentation to the Seminar on Capital, State and Transformation in the Sudan, School of Development Studies, University of East Anglia (16–18 July 1984).

Bach, R. and Schraml, L. (1984) "Migration, Crisis and Theoretical Conflict," *International Migration Review*, 16:320–41.

el Bagir, I., Dey, J., Gadir, A., Barnett, T., Ghosh, J., and Wagner, A. (1984) *Labor Markets in the Sudan, A Study Carried Out Within the Framework of the ILO/UNHCR Project on Income-Generating Activities for Refugees in Eastern and Central Sudan.* Geneva: ILO.

Barker, J. (1989) *Rural Communities Under Stress: Peasant Farmers and the State in Africa.* Cambridge: Cambridge University Press.

Bascom, J. (1990) "Food, Wages and Profits: Mechanized Schemes and the Sudanese State," *Economic Geography*, 66:140–55.

_____ (1990) "Social Differentiation among Eritrean Refugees in Eastern Sudan: The Case of Wad El Hileau," *Journal of Refugee Studies*, 2:403–18.

_____ (1990) "Border Pastoralism in Eastern Sudan," *The Geographical Review*, 80:401–15.

_____ (1993) "The Peasant Economy of Refugee Resettlement in Eastern Sudan," *Annals of the Association of American Geographers*, 83:320–46.

_____ (1994) "The Dynamics of Refugee Repatriation: The Case of Eritreans in Eastern Sudan" in Gould, W. and Findlay, A. (eds.) *Population Migration and the Changing World Order*, pp. 225–48. London: John Wiley & Sons.

_____ (1996) "Reconstituting Households and Reconstructing Home Areas: The Case of Returning Eritreans" in Allen, T. (ed.) *In Search of Cool Ground: War, Flight, and Homecoming in Northeast Africa*, pp. 66–79. London: James Currey.

_____ "Refugee Settlements in Southern Sudan: Using Multivariate Analysis to Assess Household Well-being," (Unpublished manuscript under review).

Bassett, T. (1988) "The Political Ecology of Peasant-Herder Conflicts in the Northern Ivory Coast," *Annals of the Association of American Geographers,* 78:453-72.

____ (1993) "Introduction: The Land Question and Agricultural Transformation in Sub-Saharan Africa" in Bassett, T. and Crummey, D. (eds.) *Land in African Agrarian Systems,* pp. 3-34. Madison: University of Wisconsin Press.

Bates, R. (1983) *Essays on the Political Economy of Rural Africa.* Cambridge: Cambridge University Press.

Bernstein, H. (1977) "Notes on States and Peasantry," *Review of African Political Economy,* 21:44-62.

____ (1979) "Concepts for the Analysis of Contemporary Peasantries," *Journal of Peasant Studies,* 6:421-43.

____ (1981) "Notes on States and Peasantry," *Review of African Political Economy,* 21:44-62.

____ (1992) "Agrarian Structures and Change: Sub-Saharan Africa" in Bernstein, H., Crow, B., and Johnson, H. (eds.) *Rural Livelihoods: Crises and Responses,* pp. 65-84. Oxford: Oxford University Press.

Berry, E. (1989) Intra-household Dynamics: Indications of Women's Autonomy in the Third World. Paper presented at the Association for Women in Development, Washington, D.C., November 1989.

____ (1990) "Finding the Invisible Women: Intra-household Dynamics as a Challenge to Conventional Theories of the Household," a Review of *A Home Divided: Women and Income in the Third World,* Dwyer, D., and Bruce, J. (eds.) *Women's Studies Forum,* 13:614-17.

Berry, J. (1988) "Acculturation and Psychological Adaptation: A Conceptual Overview" in *Ethnic Psychology: Research and Practice with Immigrants, Refugees, Native Peoples, Ethnic Groups and Sojourners,* Selected papers from a North American regional conference of the International Association of Cross-Cultural Psychology held in Kingston, Onto., 16-21 August 1987, pp. 41-52. Amsterdam: Swets and Zeitlinger, 1988.

Berry, S. (1988) "Concentration Without Privatization? Some Consequences of Changing Patterns of Rural Land Control" in Downs, E. and Reyna, S. (eds.) *Land and Society in Contemporary Africa,* pp. 53-75. Hanover and London: University of New Hampshire.

Betts, T. (1980) *Spontaneous Settlement of Rural Refugees in Africa.* London: Euro Action - ACORD.

Black, R. (1991) "Refugees and Displaced Persons: Geographical Perspectives and Research Directions," *Progress in Human Geography,* 15:281-98.

Bonacich, E. (1982) "Class Approaches to Ethnicity and Race," *The Insurgent Sociologist,* 10:9-23.

Bourdier, J. and Minh-Ha, T. (1997) *Drawn from African Dwellings.* Bloomington: University of Indiana Press.

British Administration Report. (1947) Annual Administrative Report - 1947, Khartoum.

Bulcha, M. (1988) *Flight and Integration: Causes of Mass Exodus from Ethiopia and Problems of Integration in the Sudan.* Uppsala: Scandinavian Institute of African Studies.

Bun, C. (1991) "Refugee Camps as Human Artifacts: An Essay on Vietnamese Refugees in Southeast Asian Camps," Hitchcock, L. *Journal of Refugee Studies*, 4:284–90.

Carney, J. and Watts, M. (1990) "Manufacturing Dissent: Work, Gender and the Politics of Meaning in a Peasant Society," *Africa*, 6:207–41.

Castell, M. (1975) "Immigrant Workers and Class Struggles in Advanced Capitalism: The Western European Experience," *Politics and Society*, 5:33–66.

Chambers, R. (1979) "Rural Refugees in Africa: What the Eye Does Not See," *Disasters*, 5:381–92.

_____ (1982) "Rural Refugees in Africa: Past Experiences, Future Pointers," *Disasters*, 6:21–30.

_____ (1986) "Hidden Losers? The Impact of Rural Refugee Programs on Poorer Hosts," *International Migration Review*, 20:245–63.

Chayanov, A. (1986) *The Theory of Peasant Economy* (first published in 1926). Madison: University of Wisconsin Press.

Chordi, V. (1988) "South Kassala Agricultural Project – Water Component," Technical Support Service, Mission Report, Geneva: UNHCR.

Christensen, H. (1982) *Survival Strategies For and By Camp Refugees.* Geneva: UN Research Institute for Social Development.

Christodoulou, D. (1990) *The Unpromised Land: Agrarian Reform and Conflict Worldwide.* London: Zed Press.

CIMADE, INODEP, and MINK. (1986) *Africa's Refugee Crisis: What's to be Done?* Trans. Michael John. London: Zed Press.

Cloke, P., Philo, C. and Sadler, D. (1993) *Approaching Human Geography: An Introduction to Contemporary Theoretical Debates.* London: Paul Chapman.

Commission for Eritrean Refugee Affairs (CERA). (1992) Appeal to Donor Governments, Commission for Eritrean Refugees Affairs, Provisional Government of Eritrea, 22 March 1992.

Commission for Eritrean Refugee Affairs (CERA). (1992a) "Current status of the Repatriation Programme and the Way Forward," Conference paper, presented 29 April 1992. Mimeographed.

Commission for Eritrean Refugee Affairs (CERA). (1993) Repatriation and Reintegration Project, Project Document by the Provisional Government of Eritrea (22 March 1993).

Connor, K. (1989) "Factors in the Residential Choices of Self-Settled Refugees in Peshawar, Pakistan," *International Migration Review*, 23:904–32.

Crow, B. and Thorpe, M. et al. (1988) *Survival and Change in the Third World.* Oxford: Oxford University Press.

Cuny, F. and Stein, B. (1989) "Prospects for and Promotion of Spontaneous Repatriation" in Loescher, G. and Monahan, L. (eds.) *Refugees and International Relations*, pp. 293–312. Oxford: Oxford University Press

Curtin, P., Feierman, S., Thompson, L., and Vansina, J. (1978) *African History*. Boston: Little, Brown.
Da Vanzo, J. (1981) "Microeconomic Approaches to Studying Migration Decisions," in De Jong, G. and Gardner, R. (eds.) *Migration Decision Making: Multidisciplinary Approaches to Microlevel Studies in Developed and Developing Countries*, pp. 90–130. New York: Pergamon Press.
Daley, P. (1991) "Gender, Displacement and Social Reproduction: Settling Burundi Refugees in Western Tanzania," *Journal of Refugee Studies*, 4:248–66.
____ (1993) "From the Kipande to the Kibali: The Incorporation of Labour Migrants and Refugees in Western Tanzania 1900 to 1987," in Black, R. and Robinson, V. (eds.) *Geography and Refugees: Patterns and Processes of Change*, pp. 17–32. London: Belhaven Press.
Davidson, B., Cliffe, L. and Selassie, B. (eds.) (1980) *Behind the War in Eritrea*. Nottingham: Spokesman.
De Briey, P. (1961) "The Productivity of African Labour," in Gould, P. (ed.) *Africa: Continent of Change*, pp. 138–53. Belmont, Calif.: Wadsworth Publishing.
De Janvry, A. and Deere, C. (1979) "A Conceptual Framework for the Empirical Analysis of Peasants," *American Journal of Agribusiness Economics*, 61:601–11.
Demeke, T. (1992) Survival Strategies of Refugee Women: Case Study Eastern Sudan – Analysis from a Gender Perspective. MA Thesis, University of East Anglia.
Doornbos, P. (1984) "Trade in Two Border Towns: Beida and Foro Boranga (Darfur Province)" in Manger, L. (ed.) *Trade and Traders in the Sudan*, pp. 139-88. Bergen: University of Bergen.
Downs, R. and Reyna, S. (1988) *Land and Society in Contemporary Africa*. Hanover, N.H.: University Press of New England.
Drumthra, J. (1994) Conversation, U.S. Committee for Refugees, Washington, D.C., March, 1994.
Duda, G. and Schönmier, H. (1983) *Psychological Aspects of the Refugee Situation in the Sudan*. Saarbrucken, Fed. Rep. of Ger.: University of the SAAR.
Duffield, M. (1983) "Change Among West African Settlers in Northern Sudan," *Review of African Political Economy*, 26:45–59.
Dwyer, D. and Bruce, J. (1988) *A Home Divided: Women and Income in the Third World*. Stanford: Stanford University Press.
Eriksson, L., Melander, G., and Nobel, P. (1981) *An Analysing Account of the Conference on African Refugee Problems – Arusha, May 1979*. Uppsala: Scandinavian Institute of African Studies.
Firebrace, J. (1985) *Never Kneel Down: Drought, Development and Liberation in Eritrea*. Trenton, N.J.: Red Sea Press.
Foreign Office Research Department Memorandum. RRX(a)/37/ii, Document WO230/168 xc3613, Colonial Records Office, Kew Gardens, London.

Four Power Commission of Investigation for the Former Italian Colonies – Volume I. Report on Eritrea, FO 1015 23 XC 3882, 50, Colonial Records Office, Kew Gardens, London.

Gebremedhin, T. (1992) "Agricultural Development in Eritrea: Economic and Policy Analysis" in Tesfagiorgis, G. (ed.) *Emergent Eritrea: Challenges of Economic Development*, pp. 101-9. Washington, D.C.: The Provisional Government of Eritrea and Eritreans for Peace and Democracy in North America.

Giddens, A. (1985) *The Constitution of Society*. Cambridge: Polity Press.

Gordenker, L. (1983) "Refugees in Developing Countries and Transnational Organization," *The Annals of the American Academy of Political and Social Science*, 467:62-77.

Gorman, R. (1985) "Private Voluntary Organizations in Refugee Relief," in Ferris, E. (ed.) *Refugees in World Politics*, pp. 82-103. New York: Praeger.

Greenfield, R. (1980) *The OAU and Africa's Refugees: Assistance to Refugees – Alternative Viewpoints*. London: Minority Rights Group.

_____ (1980b) "Pre-Colonial and Colonial History," in Davidson, B., Cliffe, L. and Selassie, B. (eds.) *Behind the War in Eritrea*, ed. B. Davidson, L. Cliffe, and B. Selassie, pp. 16-31, Nottingham: Spokesman.

Greenway, D. (1987) "Prospects for the Resettlement of Afghan Refugees in Pakistan: A Cultural-Geographical Assessment" in Rogge, J. (ed.) *Refugees: A Third World Dilemma*, pp. 193-99. Totowa, N.J.: Rowman and Littlefield.

Habte-Selassie, E. (1992) "Eritrean Refugees in the Sudan: A Preliminary Analysis of Voluntary Repatriation" in Doornbos, M., Cliffe, L., Ahmed, A., and Markakis, J. (eds.) *Beyond Conflict in the Horn: Prospects for Peace, Recovery and Development in Ethiopia, Somalia and the Sudan*, pp. 23-32. London: James Currey.

_____ (1992a) "Reintegration of Returnees: Challenges in Post Liberation Eritrea." Paper prepared for Symposium for the Horn of Africa on the Social and Economic Aspects of Mass Voluntary Return Movements of Refugees, Addis Ababa, Ethiopia, 14–18 September. Mimeographed.

Hakovirta, H. (1993) "The Global Refugee Problem: A Model and its Application," *International Political Science Review*, 14:35-57.

Hamilton, V. (ed.) *1994 World Refugee Survey*. Washington, D.C.: U.S. Committee for Refugees.

_____ *1996 World Refugee Survey*. Washington, D.C.: U.S. Committee for Refugees.

_____ *1997 World Refugee Survey*. Washington, D.C.: U.S. Committee for Refugees.

Hance, W. (1964) *The Geography of Modern Africa*, New York, Columbia University Press.

Hansen, A. (1979) "Once the Running Stops: Assimilation of Angolan Refugees into Zambian Border Villages," *Disasters*, 3:369-74.

_____ (1981) "Refugee Dynamics: Angolans in Zambia 1966-72," *International Migration Review*, 1:175-94.

_____ (1982) "Self-Settled Rural Refugees in Africa: The Case of Angolans in Zambian Villages," in Hanson, A. and Oliver-Smith, T. (eds.) *Involuntary Migration and Resettlement: The Problems and Responses of Dislocated People*, pp. 13–36. Boulder, Colo.: Westview Press.

_____ (1990) Refugee Self-Sufficiency Versus Settlement on Government Schemes: The Long-Term Consequences for Security, Integration, and Economic Development of Angolan Refugees (1966–1989) in Zambia, United Nations Research Institute for Social Development Discussion Paper No. 17. Geneva: United Nations.

_____ (1993) "African Refugees: Defining and Defending Their Human Rights" in Cohen, R., Hyden, G., and Nagen, W. *Human Rights and Governance in Africa*, pp. 226–66. Gainesville: University of Florida Press.

Harrell-Bond, B. (1985) "Humanitarianism in a Straitjacket," *African Affairs*, 86:3–14.

_____ (1986) *Imposing Aid: Emergency Assistance to Refugees*. London: Oxford University Press.

_____ (1989) "Repatriation: Under What Conditions Is It the Most Desirable Solution for Refugees? An Agenda for Research," *African Studies Review*, 32:41–69.

Harriss, B. (1984) "Analysing the Rural Economy – A Practical Guide," Discussion Paper No. 164, School of Development Studies, University of East Anglia.

Hathaway, J. (1991) "Reconceiving Refugee Law as Human Rights Protection," *Journal of Refugee Studies*, 4:113–31.

Hendrikson Associierte Consultant (HAC). (1984) Refugees in the Eastern Region of Sudan, Consulting Report.

Holborn, L. (1975) *Refugees: A Problem of Our Time*. Metuchen, N.J.: The Scarecrow Press.

Hoodfar, H. (1988) "Household Budgeting and Financial Management in a Lower-Income Cairo Neighborhood" in Dwyer, D. and Bruce, J. *A Home Divided: Women and Income in the Third World*, pp. 120–42. Stanford: Stanford University Press.

Hyden, G. (1980) *Beyond Ujamaa in Tanzania: Underdevelopment and an Uncaptured Peasantry*. Berkeley: University of California Press.

_____ (1983) *No Shortcuts to Progress: African Development Management in Perspective*. Berkeley: University of California Press.

Ib Nauf, M. (1988) Interview with the Eastern Region Officer for the Mechanized Farming Corporation – Khartoum, 16 April 1988.

ILO (1982) *Incoming-Activities for Refugees in the Sudan*. Geneva.

Johnson, T. (1979) "Eritrean Refugees in Sudan," *Disasters*, 3:417–22.

Johnson, T. and Johnson, M. (1981) "Eritrea: The National Question and the Logic of Protracted Struggle," *African Affairs*, 80:181–95.

Jones, S. (1991) "Environment and Development in Eritrea," *Africa Today*, 38:55–60.

Kallay, F. (1958) "A New Home for Italian Refugees from Venezia Giulia," *Annals of the Association of American Geographers*, 48:274.

Karadawi, A. (1983) "Constraints on Assistance to Refugees: Some Observations from the Sudan," *World Development*, 11:537–47.
_____ (1987) "The Problem of Urban Refugees in Sudan," in Rogge, J. (ed.) *Refugees: A Third World Dilemma*, pp. 115–29. Totowa, NJ: Rowman and Littlefield.
_____ (1995) *Refugee Policy in the Sudan, 1967–1984*, Ph.D. diss., University of Oxford.
Katz, C. (1991) "Sow What You Know: The Struggle for Social Reproduction in Rural Sudan," *Annals of the Association of American Geographers*, 81:488–514.
Katz, C. and Monk, J. (1993) *Full Circles: Geographies of Women Over the Life Course*. London: Routledge.
Keely, C. (1981) *Global Refugee Policy: The Case for a Development-Oriented Strategy*. New York: Population Council.
Keller, S. (1975) *Uprooting and Social Change: The Role of Refugees in Development*. New Delhi: Manohar Books.
Kibreab, G. (1985) *African Refugees: Reflections on the African Refugee Problem*. Trenton, N.J.: Africa World Press.
_____ (1987) *Refugees and Development in Africa: The Case of Eritrea*. Trenton, N.J.: Red Sea Press.
_____ (1990) "Host Governments and Refugee Perspectives on Settlement and Repatriation in Africa," Paper for the Conference on Development Strategies on Forced Migration in the Third World, Institute of Social Studies, The Hague, August.
_____ (1991) The State of the Art Review of Refugee Studies in Africa, Uppsala Papers in Economic History, Research Report No. 26. Uppsala.
_____ (1994) "Left in Limbo: Prospects for Re-Establishment of the Returning Eritrean Refugees and Responses of the International Donor Community" in Allen, T. and Morsink, H. (eds.) *When Refugees Go Home*, pp. 53-64. London: James Currey.
Killion, T. (1992) "Refugees and Environmental Change on the Sudano-Ethiopian Frontier: The History of Wad el Hileau Refugee Camp, 1967–1987," draft of presentation to the 6th Conference on Northeast African Studies, Michigan State University, East Lansing, April.
Kitching, G. (1980) *Class and Economic Change in Kenya*. New Haven, Conn.: Yale University Press.
Kliot, N. (1990) "Borderlands As 'Refugeeland' – Political Geographical Considerations," Presentation at the 1990 meetings of the Association of American Geographers, Toronto, 19–22 April.
Koskinies, J., Mickels, G., and Westman, H. (1987) "Mechanization of Agriculture in the Refugee Settlement Areas in Eastern Sudan: Evaluation and Project Perspective," Evaluation/Project Preparation Mission 1:6/14.6, FINNIDA.
Kuhlman, T. (1991) "The Economic Integration of Refugees in Developing Countries: A Research Model," *Journal of Refugee Studies*, 4:1–20.

Kunz, E. (1973) "The Refugee in Flight: Kinetic Models and Forms of Displacement," *International Migration Review*, 7:125-46.
____ (1981) "Exile and Resettlement: Refugee Theory," *International Migration Review*, 15:42-51.
Le Breton, G. (1995) "Stoves, Trees, and Refugees: The Fuelwood Crisis Consortium in Zimbabwe," *Refugee Participation Network*, 18:9-12.
Legum, C. and Firebrace, J. (1983) *Eritrea and Tigray*, Report No. 5, London: Minority Rights Group.
Little, P. (1985) "Absentee Herd Owners and Part-Time Pastoralists: The Political Economy of Resource Use in Northern Kenya," *Human Ecology*, 13:131-51.
Llambí, L. (1988) "Small Modern Farmers: Neither Peasants or Fully-Fledged Capitalists?" *Journal of Peasant Studies*, 15:350-72.
Loescher, G. and Monahan, L. (eds.) (1989) *Refugees and International Relations*. Oxford: Oxford University Press.
Longrigg, S. (1974) *A Short History of Eritrea*. (Originally published in 1945 by Clarendon Press) Westport, Conn.: Greenwood Press.
Luciuk, L. (1990) "A Landscape of Despair: Comments on the Geography of the Contemporary Afghan Refugee Experience," presentation at the 1990 meetings of the Association of American Geographers, Toronto, 19-22 April.
Mama, A. (1992) "The Need for Gender Analysis: A Comment on the Prospects for Peace, Recovery and Development in the Horn of Africa" in Doornbos, M., Cliffe, L., Ahmed, A., and Markakis, J. (eds.) *Beyond Conflict in the Horn: The Prospects for Peace, Recovery and Development in Ethiopia, Somalia, Eritrea and Sudan*, pp. 72-8. London: James Currey.
Mamdani, M. (1987) "Extreme But Not Exceptional: Toward an Analysis of the Agrarian Question in Uganda," *Journal of Peasant Studies*, 14:190-222.
____. (1993) "Class Formation and Rural Livelihoods: A Ugandan Case Study" in Bernstein, H., Crow, B., and Johnson, H. (eds.) *Rural Livelihoods: Crisis and Responses*, pp. 195-216. Oxford: Oxford University Press.
Martin, S. (1991) *Refugee Women*. London: Zed Press.
Marshall, C. and Rossman, G. (1989) *Designing Qualitative Research*. London: Sage Publications.
Marx, E. (1990) "The Social World of Refugees: A Conceptual Framework," *Journal of Refugee Studies*, 3:189-203.
Massey, D. (1984) *Spatial Divisions of Labor: Social Structures and the Geography of Production*, New York: Metheun.
Mazur, R. (1989) "The Political Economy of Refugee Creation in Southern Africa: Micro and Macro Issues in Sociological Perspective," *Journal of Refugee Studies*, 2:441-67.
McDowell, D. (ed.) (1996) *Understanding Impoverishment: The Consequences of Development-Induced Displacement*. Providence, R.I.: Berghahn Books.
McGregor, J. and Aikman, S. (1991) "Avoiding Camps," *Refugee Participation Network*, 10:3-4.

Mechanized Farming Corporation. (1981) Report – Gedaref.
_____ (1989) Report – Gedaref.
el Medani, S. (1986) "Rainfed Mechanized Farming in Southern Gedaref" in Zahlan, A. (ed.) *The Agricultural Sector of Sudan: Policy and Systems Studies*. London: Ithaca Press.
Meillassoux, C. (1975) *Maidens, Meal and Money: Capitalism and the Domestic Community*. Cambridge: Cambridge University Press.
_____ (1983) "The Economic Bases for Demographic Reproduction: From the Domestic Mode of Production to Wage Earning," *Journal of Peasant Studies*, 11:51–66.
Mengisteab, K. (1992) "Rehabilitation of Degraded Land in Eritrea's Agricultural Policy: An Exploratory Study" in Tesfagiorgis, G. (ed.) *Emergent Eritrea: Challenges of Economic Development*, pp. 110–17, Washington, D.C.: Provisional Government of Eritrea and Eritreans for Peace and Democracy in North America.
Mickels, G., and Yousif, H. (1987) "The Problems for Mechanization of Agriculture in Refugee Settlement Areas of Eastern Sudan: A Study of Context and Beneficiaries," Report for FINNIDA.
Miles, M. (1994) *Qualitative Data Analysis: A Sourcebook of New Methods*. London: Sage Publications.
Misser, F. (1992) "Eritrea Seeks to Attract Foreign Investment," *African Business*, 47.
Momsen, J. and Kinnard, V. (1993) *Different Places, Different Voices: Gender and Development in Africa, Asia and Latin America*. London: Routledge.
Mustafa, A. (1986) "Livestock Farming Systems" in Zahlan, A. (ed.) *The Agricultural Sector of Sudan: Policy and Systems Studies*, pp. 215–38. London: Ithaca Press.
el Nagar, S. (1992) "Children and War in the Horn of Africa" in Doornbos, M. et. al. (eds.) *Beyond Conflict in the Horn: Prospects for Peace, Recovery and Development in Ethiopia, Somalia and the Sudan*, pp. 15–21. London: James Currey.
Natural Features of Eritrea. WO 230/168 xc3613, Colonial Records Office, Kew Gardens, London.
Neldner, B. (1979) "Settlement of Rural Refugees," *Disasters*, 3:393–402.
O'Brien, J. (1977) "How Traditional is 'Traditional' Agriculture?" ESRC Bulletin, No. 62, Khartoum.
_____ (1980) Agriculture, Labor and Development in Sudan, Ph.D. diss., University of Connecticut.
_____ (1983) "The Formation of the Agriculture Labor Force in Sudan," *Review of African Political Economy*, 26:15–33.
_____ (1986) "Understanding the Crisis in Sudan," *Canadian Journal of African Studies*, 20:275–79.
_____ (1986b) "Sowing the Seeds of Famine: The Political Economy of Food Deficits in Sudan," in Lawrence, P. (ed.) *World Recession and the Food Crisis in Africa*, pp. 193–200. Boulder, Colo.: Westview.
Oliver, R. and Gervase, M. (1963) *History of East Africa*. Oxford: Oxford University Press.

Oliver-Smith, A. (1991) "Involuntary Resettlement, Resistance and Empowerment," *Journal of Refugee Studies*, 4:132–49.

Østergaard, L. (1992) *Gender and Development: A Practical Guide*. London: Routledge.

Pankehurst, S. (1952) *Eritrea on the Eve*. Essex, U.K.: Wolford Green.

Pateman, R. (1990) *Eritrea: Even the Stones are Burning*. Trenton, N.J.: Red Sea Press.

Patnaik, U. (1976) "Class Differentiation Within the Peasantry: An Approach to the Analysis of Indian Agriculture," *Economic and Political Weekly*, 11:82–101.

Pendergast, J. (1990) *The Struggle for Sudan's Soul: Political and Agrarian Roots of War and Famine*. Washington, D.C.: Center of Concern.

Porter, P. (1987) "Of Wholes and Fragments: Reflections on the Economy of Affection, Capitalism and the Human Cost of Development," *Geografiska Annaler*, 69:1–14.

Pred A. (1982) "Social Reproduction and the Time-Geography of Everyday Life" in Gould, P. and Olsonn, G. (eds.) *A Search for Common Ground*, pp. 157–86. London: Pion.

Preston, R. (1991) Report to an Inter-Agency Mission on Education for Mozambican Refugees in Malawi and Zimbabwe, UNDP.

Pretty, J. (1989) RRA Notes – Proceedings of RRA Review Workshop, Number 7, Sussex: International Institute for Environment and Development.

Prothero, R. (1965) *Migrants and Malaria*, London, Longman.

Pulsipher, L. (1993) "'He Won't Let She Stretch She Foot': Gender Relations in Traditional West Indian Houseyards" in Kaatz, C., and Momsen, J. (eds.) *Full Circles: Geographies of Women Over the Life Course*, pp. 107–21. London: Routledge.

Radai, A. (1950) Letter from Ali Radai, Secretary-General of the Moslem League of the Western Province of Eritrea, FO 371 80996 XC3882, Letter dated 18 August 1950 sent on 14 August, 1950 by E. W. Mulcahy/dge, 1950.

Rahmato, D. (1987) Famine and Survival Strategy: A Case Study from Northeast Ethiopia, Food and Famine Monograph Series, No. 1, Institute of Development Research, Addis Ababa University.

Ranger, T. (1994) "Studying Repatriation As Part of African Social History" in Allen, T., and Morsink, H. (eds.) *When Refugees Go Home*, pp. 279–94. Trenton, N.J.: Africa World Press.

_____ (1996) "Concluding Reflections on Cross-Mandates" in Allen, T. (ed.) *In Search of Cool Ground: War, Flight, and Homecoming in Northeast Africa*, pp. 318–29. London: James Currey.

Reyna, S. (1988) "Concentration Without Privatization? Some Consequences of Changing Patterns of Rural Land Control" in Downs, E. and Reyna, S. (eds.) *Land and Society in Contemporary Africa*, pp. 53–75. Hanover and London: University of New Hampshire.

Richmond, A. (1988) "Sociological Theories of International Migration: The Case of Refugees," *Current Sociology*, 36:7–25.

_____ (1993) "Reactive Migration: Sociological Perspectives on Refugee Movements," *Journal of Refugee Studies,* 6:7-25.
Robinson, V. (1990) "Into the Next Millennium: An Agenda for Refugee Studies. A Report of the 1st Annual Meeting of the International Advisory Panel, January 1990," *Journal of Refugee Studies,* 3:3-15.
Roe, M. (1987) "Central American Refugees in the United States: Psychosocial Adaptation," *Refugee Issues,* 3:21-30.
Rogge, J. (1977) "A Geography of Refugees: Some Illustrations from Africa," *Professional Geographer,* 29:186-89.
_____ (1981) "Africa's Resettlement Strategies," *International Migration Review,* 15:195-212.
_____ (1985) *Too Many, Too Long: Sudan's Twenty-Year Refugee Dilemma.* Totowa, N.J.: Rowman and Littlefield.
_____ (1987) "When is Self-Sufficiency Achieved: The Case of Rural Settlements in Sudan" in Rogge, J. (ed.) *Refugees: A Third World Dilemma,* pp. 86-97. Totowa, NJ: Rowman and Littlefield.
_____ (1994) "Repatriation of Refugees: A Not-So-Simple 'Optimum' Solution" in Allen, T. and Morsink, H. (eds.) *When Refugees Go Home,* pp. 14-49. Trenton, N.J.: Africa World Press.
Rogge, J. and Akol, J. (1989) "Repatriation: Its Role in Resolving Africa's Refugee Dilemma," *International Migration Review,* 23:184-200.
Roth, M. (1993) "Somalia Land Policies and Tenure Impacts: The Case of the Lower Shabelle" in Bassett, T. and Crummey, D. (eds.) *Land in African Agrarian Systems,* pp. 298-326. Madison: University of Wisconsin Press.
Samatar, A. (1988) "The Political Economy of Pastoral Transformation: The Case of Somalia." Manuscript.
_____ (1989) *The State and Rural Transformation in Northern Somalia, 1884-1986.* Madison: University of Wisconsin Press.
_____ (1992) "Social Decay and Public Institutions: The Road to Reconstruction in Somalia" in Doornbos, M. et. al. (eds.) *Beyond Conflict in the Horn: Prospects for Peace, Recovery and Development in Ethiopia, Somalia and the Sudan,* pp. 213-16. London: James Currey.
Samatar, A., Salisbury, L., and Bascom, J. (1988) "The Political Economy of Livestock Marketing in Somalia," *African Economic History,* 17:81-97.
el Sammani, M. (1976) Fieldnotes from consulting assignment for Huntington Associates, Entry 1, 5 January 1976, pg. 9.
el Sammani, M. and Martin, A. (1976) "Settlement Project for Ethiopian Refugees from Eritrea in East Central Sudan," Preliminary report for UNHCR, Huntington Technical Services.
Sarre, P., Phillips, D., and Skellington, R. (1989) *Ethnic Minority Housing: Explanations and Policies.* Aldershot, U.K.: Avebury.
Save the Children. (1987) Independent Census Conducted for Wad el Hileau by Save the Children, U.S.A. – Gedaref office.
Sayer, A. (1984) *Method in Social Science: A Realist Approach.* London: Hutchinson.

Scott, J. (1976) *The Moral Economy of the Peasant: Rebellion and Subsistence in Southeast Asia*. New Haven, Conn.: Yale University Press.

Sen, A. (1984) *On Ethics and Economics*. Oxford: Basil Blackwell.

Shaaeldin, E. (1984) *The Evolution and Transformation of the Sudanese Economy Up to 1950*, DSRC Monograph Series, No. 20, Khartoum: University of Khartoum Press.

Shack, W. (1974) *The Central Ethiopians: Amhara, Tigrinia, and Related Peoples, Ethnographic Survey of Africa*, Northeastern Africa, Part IV. London: International African Institute.

Shannon, D. (1988) "Report of the Institutional Specialist," Pre-Appraisal Mission, South Kassala Agricultural Project, by Templeton Shannon Associates for the World Bank.

el Shazali, S. (1980) *Beyond Underdevelopment: Structural Constraints on the Development of Productive Forces Among the Jok Gor, the Sudan*, African Savannah Studies, Bergen Occasional Papers in Social Anthropology, No. 22, Bergen, Nor.: Universal Printer.

_____ (1985) "Peripheral Urbanism and the Sudan: Explorations in the Political Economy of the Wage Labor Market in Greater Khartoum, 1900–1984," Ph.D. diss., University of Hull, U.K..

_____ (1987) "Eritreans in Kassala," (draft of final report), Joint Research Project of the Development Studies and Research Centre, University of Khartoum and the Free University of Amsterdam, Centre for Development Cooperation Services.

Simon, D. and Preston, R. (1993) "Return to the Promised Land: The Repatriation and Resettlement of Namibian Refugees," in Black, R. and Robinson, V. (eds.) *Geography and Refugees: Patterns and Processes of Change*, pp. 46-63. London: Belhaven Press.

Simpson, I., and Simpson, M. (1978) "Alternative Strategies for Agricultural Development in the Central Rainlands of the Sudan with Special Reference to Damazin Area," Rural Development Studies No. 3, University of Leeds.

Smock, D. (1982) "Eritrean Refugees in Sudan," *Journal of Modern African Studies*, 20:451–65.

Sorenson, J. (1990) "Opposition, Exile and Identity: The Eritrean Case," *Journal of Refugee Studies*, 3:298–319.

Southern Kassala Agricultural Development Project (SKAP). (1992) Land Use Survey Report, Masdar (UK) Ltd. and S A Consultants Ltd., February 1992.

Spring, A. (1982) "Women and Men As Refugees: Differential Assimilation of Angolan Refugees in Zambia," in Hansen, A. and Oliver-Smith, T. (eds.) *Involuntary Migration and Resettlement*, pp. 37–47. Boulder, Colo.: Westview Press.

Standing, G. (1981) "Migration and Modes of Exploitation: Social Origins of Immobility and Mobility," *The Journal of Peasant Studies*, 8:173–211.

Stavrianos, A. (1981) *Global Rift: The Third World Comes of Age*. New York: William Morrow.

Stein, B. (1986) "Durable Solutions for Developing Country Refugees," *International Migration Review*, 20:264–82.

───── (1992) "Policy Challenges Regarding Repatriation in the 1990s: Is 1992 the Year for Voluntary Repatriation?" Paper commissioned by the Program on International and U.S. Refugee Policy. Boston, Mass.: Fletcher School of Law and Diplomacy, Tufts University.

───── (1994) "Ad Hoc Assistance to Return Movements and Long-Term Development Programmes" in Allen, T. and Morsink, H. (eds.) *When Refugees Go Home*, pp. 50–70. Trenton, N.J.: Africa World Press.

Stein, B. and Clark, L. (1990) "Refugee Integration and Older Refugee Settlements in Africa," Paper presented at the 1990 meeting of the American Anthropological Association, New Orleans, November.

Styan D. (1996) "Eritrea 1993 – The End of the Beginning" in Allen, T. (ed.) *In Search of Cool Ground: War, Flight, and Homecoming in Northeast Africa*, pp. 80–95. London: James Currey.

Todaro, M. (1976) *Internal Migration in Developing Countries: A Review of Theory, Evidence, Methodology and Research Priorities*. Geneva: ILO.

Tothill, J. (1948) *Agriculture in Sudan*, London: Oxford University Press.

Trevaskis, G. (1960) *Eritrea: A Colony in Transition: 1941–1952*. London: Oxford University Press.

Tunley, H. (1948) "Revenue from Land and Crops" in Tothill, J. (ed.) *Agriculture in Sudan*, pp. 198–209. London: Oxford University Press.

UN. (1984) Declaration and Program of Action of the Second International Conference on Assistance to Refugees in Africa, A/Con. 125/L.1, 10 July, Geneva.

UNHCR. (1988) April 1988 Briefing Notes, Khartoum: UNHCR.

───── (1991) Social Services Mission, 21 October–2 November, 1991, Community-Based Approach for Repatriation to Eritrea, Programme and Technical Support Section, PTSS Mission Report 91/32. Geneva.

───── (1993) *The State of the World's Refugees 1993: The Challenge of Protection*. New York: Penguin.

───── (1993a) "General and Special Programmes: Their Relationship," Paper presented at the 25th meeting of the Sub-Committee on Administrative and Financial Matters, Document Number EC/1993/SC.2/CRP.11.

───── (1993a) UNHCR Activities Financed by Voluntary Funds: Report for 1992–1993 and Proposed Programmes and Budget for 1994. Part I. Africa, A.AC.96/808 (Part I).

───── (1995) "UNHCR Financial Needs in 1994," *Refugees*, 96:5.

Waldron, S. (1987) "Blaming the Refugees," *Refugee Issues*, 3:1–19.

───── (1983) "Some Refugee Background Characteristics: Preliminary Results from the Qoriooley Camps," *Northeast African Studies*, 4:17–24.

Warner, D. (1994) "Voluntary Repatriation and the Meaning of Return to Home: A Critique of Liberal Mathematics," presentation at the 1994 meeting of the International Refugees Advisory Panel, Oxford, January. Mimeographed.

Watts, M. (1983) *Silent Violence: Food, Famine, and Peasantry in Northern Nigeria.* Berkeley: University of California Press.

_____ "Survey 11 – Powers of Production – Geographers Among the Peasants," *Environmental Planning D,* 5:215–30.

Weeks, C. (1978) *Africa's Refugees: The Uprooted and Homeless.* New York: Church World Service.

Weisburg, E. (1997) Faxed message from UNHCR–Washington, March.

Whitehead, A, and Bloom, H. (1992) "Agriculture" in Østergaard, L. (ed.) *Gender and Development: A Practical Guide,* pp. 41–56. London: Routledge.

Wijbrandi, J. (1990) "Organized and Spontaneous Settlement" in Kuhlman, T. and Tieleman, H. (eds.) *Enduring Crisis: Refugee Problems in Eastern Sudan,* pp. 55–83. Leiden, The Netherlands: African Studies Centre.

Williams, P. (1991) "Constituting Class and Gender: A Social History of the Home, 1700–1901" in Pooley, C. and Whyte, I. (eds.) *Migrants, Emigrants, and Immigrants: A Social History of Migration,* pp. 154–203. New York: Routledge.

Wilson, D. and Huff, D. (1994) *Marginalized Places and Populations: A Structurationist Agenda.* Westport, Conn.: Praeger.

Wolf, E. (1966) *Peasants.* Englewood Cliffs, N.J.: Prentice-Hall.

Wood, C. (1984) "Equilibrium and Historical-Structural Perspectives on Migration," *International Migration Review,* 16:298–319.

Wood, W. (1989) "Long Time Coming: The Repatriation of Afghan Refugees," *Annals of the Association of American Geographers,* 79:345–69.

World Bank. (1983) "Sudan Pricing Policies and Structural Balances," Volume III: Agriculture in Sudan, Report No. 4528a-SU.

_____ (1988) "South Kassala Agriculture Project, Staff Appraisal Report," 11 September 1988.

Wubneh, M. (1988) *Ethiopia: Transition and Development in the Horn of Africa.* Boulder, Colo.: Westview Press.

Zack-Williams, A. (1982) "Merchant Capital and Underdevelopment in Sierra Leone," *Review of African Political Economy,* 28:74–82.

Zaki, E., Hassan, I., and Settar, A. (1986) "Strategy for Development of Rainfed Agriculture," (main report and annexes I-IV, Khartoum: Khartoum University Press.

Zartman, I. (1970) "Portuguese Guinean Refugees in Senegal," in el Ayouty, E. and Brooks, H. (eds.) *Refugees South of the Sahara: An African Dilemma,* pp. 143–161. Westport, Conn.: Negro University Press.

Zolberg, A., Suhrke, A., and Aguayo, S. (1991) *Escape from Violence: Conflict and the Refugee Crisis in the Developing World.* Oxford: Oxford University Press.

Census of Wad el Hileau

Ethnic Group	Number of Familes	Average Household Size	Total Number[a]	Percentage of Population
Lowland Eritrean Refugees				
Beni Amer	140	7.7	1076	11.3
Kunama	62	5.8	360	3.8
Maria	120	7.8	936	9.8
Nara	99	5.6	554	5.8
Highland Eritrean Refugees				
Aswa'orta	10	6.9	69	0.7
Belain	7	7.0	49	0.5
Ethiopian Refugees				
Amhara	45	3.4	153	1.6
Jabarta	35	6.2	217	2.3
Tigrean	40	2.1	84	0.8
Wollgeyiet	25	5.6	140	1.5
West Africans Displaced from Eritrea				
Bargo	112	8.5	918	9.6
Hausa	131	12.4	1624	17.0
Sudanese Nationals				
Beni Amer	70	7.7	539	5.7
Humran	–	–	425	4.5
Ja'aliin	–	–	472	5.0
West Africans as Residents in Sudan				
Bargo	112	8.5	952	10.0
Fulani	–	–	170	1.8
Hausa	64	12.4	794	8.3
Totals			9534	100.0

[a] Estimates for the number of individuals per group were derived by multiplying the average household size (obtained from the sample population) by the number of households each sheik reported.

Source: Interviews with village sheiks conducted by author and Hamid Ahmed el Amin October 1987 through December 1987

Glossary

ardeb	weight unit: 1 ardeb = 2 sacks = 183 kg of sorghum or 147.5 kg of sesame
bildat	farming hinterland adjacent to village comprised of small-holdings
cashif	a pledge "list" distributed among villagers
combo	work camp built for storing supplies and housing laborers on *mushrooahs*
cowad	camping site for herders with a common firepit
dalal	a middleman who is paid for his brokerage role in livestock sales
damin	a middleman who guarantees the ownership of a sale animal for the buyer
damour	Sudanese cotton cloth
dar	portion of land under the traditional authority of an *omda* (or *nazir*)
dahawa	a common unit of time for wage labor (7:00–10:00 am)
dukhn	millet
dunbeleb	grass on the Butana plain preferred by cattle (*Sehima Ischamoides*)
dura	sorghum (*Sorghum Vulgare*)
fatuur	breakfast meal
feddan	1.04 acres or 0.42 hectares
feter'ita	red-grained sorghum (drought resistant)
gelli'ita	a mud-baked surface on which to beat dura
ghaada	afternoon meal
ghaffier	guard
gueroorah	credit line opened with merchants
gussab	*dura* stalks and grass

guwaal	labor contract made between *mushrooah* operators and wage laborers
hafir	water reservoir
harig	shifting cultivation
hawasha	land unit, tenancy; generally associated with 10 *feddan* unit
hilla	pile or stack of sesame in a field
jallabe	herder who is hired to drive cattle to the livestock market
jebel	rocky outcrop, or inselberg
kalla	vacant, unused area
kandunka	short-handled digging hoe used for cultivation
kantar	100 lb or 45 kg
kedayab	weeding
khafif	rainy season (June through August)
kharija khattit	unsurveyed schemes
khor	seasonal river or stream
kitr	*acacia melifera*
£S	Sudanese pound; 1 £S equals 100 piasters or U.S. $4.45 (as of July 1988)
la'jeene	refugees
marrissa	sorghum beer
murah	the "perfect" one hundred head of cattle
mushrooah	large mechanized schemes 2 km x 2 km (914 *feddans*)
mezrha	small farms which vary in size from 1–100 tractor hours (5–500 *feddans*)
nafir	traditional reciprocal labor arrangement in group work parties
omda	traditional leader of pastoralist groups (*nazir*)
qayih	lower caste of the Mariya (primarily livestock herders)
reyhee	livestock herder (either owns or is hired to watch the animals)
ropta	a common unit of measurement used during sesame harvest; a handful cut
sabbabis	petty livestock traders
se'if	hot, dry season (March through June)
seluka	instrument used to poke a hole in the ground for each seed when sowing
sheil	cash crop mortgages

sheik	village head (or head of a particular ethnic group)
shiftas	thieves or bandits
shit'a	cool, dry season (December through February)
sikken	cutting knife or sickle used for harvesting grain
sim-sim	sesame (*Sesum Indicum*)
sona al jefaaf	"the year of the emergency" drought year of 1984/85
souq	market
striga	witchweed (*Striga Hermonthetica*)
subik-sagim	transhumance; to "come" with cattle in the dry season and "go" after rains
suwa'ag	driver (tractor or truck)
sweeba	storage container for grain built from natural materials
t'akul wa gwoom	to "eat and move", as applied to renters who move from plot to plot each year
tajiir itmalii	wholesale merchant
tajiir gatai	retail merchant
teras	small ridges of soil preventing runoff in fields
torea	two-handed digging hoe
tukul	a grass-thatched hut (round and mud-walled)
umbaz	sesame seed cakes used for cattle fodder
ustamfiir	call on people for help (the noun form is *nafir*)
wadi	riverbed
wakeel	manager or foreman for *mushrooah* operator
wusta	a commercial middleman, although formerly applied to ceremonial functions
werko	payment to local militia for livestock protection in Ethiopia
woluuf	supply of tea, coffee, and sugar carried by cattle herders
yoomiiya	common unit of time for wage labor (7.5 hours) that includes a meal
zakat	tithe under Islamic law, now used for tax purposes
zaribah	livestock pen
zeer	water container

Index

A
Afewerki, I., 162n35
agrarian change, 3, 26–31, 77–86, 94–101, 165–6
Agricultural Bank of Sudan, 54, 56, 60, 81–82
Ali, A. M., 124
Awate, M. I., 155–6

B
Bargo, 75, 131, 151
Beni Amer, 45, 70, 111–3, 124, 126n9, 151
Berry, S., 28
border studies, 164, 175
Boserup, E., 136

C
cash crop mortgages, 100–1, 173
cattle, 113–5, 116, 120–4
CERA (Commission for Eritrean Refugee Affairs), 146
Chambers, R., 5
class analysis, 60, 92–94, 106, 107, 107n1, 107n2, 108n3
colonialism
    East Africa, 17–22
    Eritrea, 40–48, 63n36, 113
    Sudan, 52–54
Colson, E., 28
commodification
    grazing rights, 117–8, 165
    farm inputs, 95–96
    land and labor, 94–95, 106, 138, 165
COR (Sudanese Office of the Commissioner for Refugees), 49, 63n42

D
decision-making, 139, 148–9, 154–7
divorce, 138–9
drought, 123

E
East Africa, 15–22, 26–27, 28, 29, 32–33, 163, 174
"economies of affection", 24–25
environmental degradation, 32–33, 57–58, 80–81, 105–6, 153–4, 172
EPLF (Eritrean Peoples Liberation Front), 46–47, 74, 146, 159
Eritrea
    highlands, 42, 149–52
    history, 40–48,
    western lowlands, 41, 42–43, 44, 70–72, 149–52
Ethiopia, xviiin6, 44, 45–48, 88n20, 118–20, 146

F
flight, 45–48, 114, 130

G
gender, 8–9, 134–5, 149
geographers, 3, 11n5
Gezira, 53

H

Habab, I. F., 114–5, 117–8
Hangoos, A. H., 83–84
Hansen, A., 25
Harrell-Bond, B., 9, 25
Hausa, 75, 103, 105, 131, 151
Hoben, R., 30
Humran, 87n1, 103–4, 105
hunger rents, 98–100
Hyden, G., 24–25

I

ICARA (International Conference on Assistance to African Refugees), 173, 177n25
IMF (International Monetary Fund), 61
interviews, xiv–xvi, 142n3, 160n7
Islam, 44–45, 133, 136

J

Ja'aliin, 87n1
Jallaba, 103, 105, 109n15

K

Katz, C., 140
Kenya, 17, 18, 20, 21
kinship, 15, 20, 42, 86, 108n8, 137, 168–9
Kunama, 75, 100, 132, 135–7, 151
Kunz, E., 4, 151

L

labor migration, 20–21
land tenure, 97–98
livestock market, 120–3, 125

M

Madi, 20
Mahdi, 51
Mamdani, M., 30
Maria, 46, 70, 111–3, 114–5, 126n3, 126n9, 141, 151
Mengistu, H., 47, 146
merchants, 101–5, 108n14, 126
MFC (Mechanized Farming Corporation), 56, 64n58, 80, 88n25

mushrooah, 29, 54–60, 79–86, 88n25, 88–89n41, 117–8, 125–6, 165
"myth of return", 147

N

nafir, 79, 94, 108n7, 158
Nara, 46, 74, 100, 151, 155–6
native tribute, 41
Nigerians, 70, 87n8
NUEW (National Union of Eritrean Women), 142

P

pastoralism, 111–26
patriarchy, 133–4
peasant studies, 3, 9, 23–24, 94–95, 170–1
precipitation, 51, 83, 106, 153–4
purdah, 134–5

R

Ranger, T., 33
refugee
  definition, 36n58
  literature, 2–5, 176n2
  policy, 172–4
  status, 3–4, 36n58
  theory, 2–7, 130–1, 167–8, 174–6
"refugee-centric", 5, 167, 175
refugees
  assisted, 26, 172, 174
  children, 131, 140–1, 142n2, 148
  households, 9, 99–100, 129–32, 140
  integration, 9, 10, 78, 158
  labor, 60, 79–86, 92–98, 135–7, 171
  participation, 174
  poverty, 77, 154–7
  "self-settled", 23, 25, 168–9, 174
  unassisted, 74–75, 99, 132, 156–7, 169, 174
  women, 133–140, 149
regional development, 173–4
Regulation of Asylum Act, 48
repatriation
  decisions, 148–9, 154–7
  Eritrea, 145–8
  expectations, 157–9
  perceptions and conditions, 149–56

spontaneous, 152
voluntary, 32
research methodology, xiv–xvi
resettlement, 48–51, 74, 91–107, 163, 170–1
resource rights, 137–40
Richmond, A., 4
rural transformation, 15–31, 125–6, 164–6

S

Selassie, H., 41, 45, 62n28
sesame, 57, 59, 78, 80–86, 89n43
al Shafir, O. A., 95–96, 101, 105
social differentiation, 8, 92–94, 165, 169–70
social relations of production, 7–8, 15, 20, 42, 86, 92–101, 107, 108n8, 135–7
soils, 58
Somalia, 18, 29, 33
sorghum, 57, 59, 78, 80–86, 177n21
state, 80–82, 172–4
structuration, 5–6, 10
Sudan, 17, 18, 20, 21, 29, 51–61

T

Tanzania, 31
taxes, 17–8, 21, 52

U

Uganda, 18, 20, 28, 29, 30
UNHCR (United Nations High Commissioner for Refugees), 23, 49, 72, 73, 146, 157, 161n11, 174–5
United States, 45, 62n28, 176n1
UN Refugee Convention, 36n58, 48

W

Wad el Hileau, 69–79, 101–5, 117, 131–2, 135, 146–7, 149–51
wage labor, 79–86, 97–98, 135–7
World Bank, 56

Z

Zambia, 25
Zartman, I., 25
Zolberg, A., 6, 10